720.9
BRA

KU-367-361

HISTORICAL
ARCHITECTURE

by the same author

★

THE STORY OF ENGLISH ARCHITECTURE

AN INTRODUCTION TO ENGLISH MEDIEVAL
ARCHITECTURE
(Faber and Faber)

THE ENGLISH CASTLE
THE STORY OF THE ENGLISH HOUSE
(Batsford)

THE CENTURIES LOOK DOWN
(Richards Press)

OLD LONDON BUILDINGS
(Convoy Publications)

A triumphal arch of Imperial Rome frames the temple portico
(Sbeitla)

HISTORICAL ARCHITECTURE

*The Development
of Structure and Design*

by

HUGH BRAUN
F.S.A., F.R.I.B.A.

STIRLING
DISTRICT
LIBRARY

FABER AND FABER LIMITED
24 Russell Square
London

794178 A

720.9
BRA

First published in mcmliii
by Faber and Faber Limited
24 Russell Square London W.C.1
Printed in Great Britain by
R. MacLehose and Company Limited
The University Press Glasgow
All rights reserved

FOREWORD

This book is an attempt by an architect to outline the history of his craft as he sees it. The statements expressed in it are his own, based upon his examination of many buildings ranging down the centuries and scattered all across the Old World. The story wanders where the tale takes it—beyond the pleasant countries of Romance and the limits of the Grand Tour—past the black wreck of Bosra to the lonely mound of Tepe Gawra gazing towards the Kurdish mountains where, perhaps, it all began.

If there is a thesis underlying his tale, it is perhaps the belief that the mighty Empires of Byzantium and Islam between them forged the architecture of Europe and that only towards the end of the story did it begin to deck itself out in the faded trappings of the Classics.

H. B.

CONTENTS

ILLUSTRATIONS

PLATES
Holder of copyright indicated by italics

ILLUSTRATIONS

ILLUSTRATIONS

ILLUSTRATIONS

LINE DRAWINGS IN TEXT
drawn by J. S. Goodall, R.I., from photographs.

INTRODUCTION

The architect is the designer of buildings: great and small, monumental and domestic. 'Building', wrote Sir Henry Wotton early in the 17th century, 'hath three Conditions: Commoditie, Firmeness, and Delight'. The first of these is the craft of planning; the second concerns the mechanics of construction. It is, however, from the third and least important aspect that buildings make themselves aware to the populace at large. Thus it is that architecture—in reality a very exacting science—is always classed as an art; it nevertheless remains an art which it is impossible to study at all without due regard being given to the canvas upon which it is applied.

Of the many books published during the last century or so on the subject of architectural history only a few have been written by architects, the majority having been compiled by amateurs interested in the buildings as *objets d'art* rather than as products of the creative ability of builders. Through lack of training or experience in the practical aspect of their subject many historians of architecture have allowed themselves to be lured away from the truth under the spell of the ornamentation of the buildings whose planning and construction they should have been studying. For variations in the design of mouldings or the form of a capital—very much the concern of the amateur of art—play an insignificant part in the history of architectural design. There are also other historians who will treat buildings—the Parthenon for example—as memorials of some particular historical or cultural epoch, which is of course tantamount to ignoring them entirely as the creations of architects.

Amongst those who conduct original researches into the history of old buildings are the archaeologists who excavate the foundations of vanished structures, measure them, and produce plans of the result. A plan is only a part of the documentary system by which an architect conveys his ideas to a builder; it is meaningless without its complementary drawings and when supplied by itself conveys—even to the trained and experienced architect—but little of the three-dimensional form of the structure. Plans are but patterns traced upon the ground. To represent a building by a plan is like producing a footprint instead of a portrait—the reader of this book will therefore seek in vain these faithful companions of most architectural histories.

The assembling of the illustrations for this book has proved an exceedingly difficult task. As most of the research upon which the histories of architecture are based was undertaken more than fifty years ago, the majority of the professional photographs of the more celebrated buildings are antiquated and unacceptable by modern standards. A considerable number of excellent photographs taken by amateurs are available but the subjects are limited by reason of the fact that students naturally prefer to seek their architectural sources in countries offering an amiable climate and adequate tourist facilities—thus the Byzantine world, for example, is practically unphotographed.

I should particularly like to record my appreciation of the assistance given me by the Courtauld Institute of Art, by Senor Montero de Madraza of the Ministerio de Asuntos Exteriores in Madrid, and for the loan of several of Mr. D. R. Buxton's photographs of Russian churches, procured by him with considerable difficulty and appearing in his 'Russian Mediaeval Architecture'.

Chapter I

FIRST PRINCIPLES

Inspiration, triumphant over apprehension, urged the daring masons of mediaeval Beauvais towards the beckoning clouds through which the exultant steel-and-concrete engineers of Manhattan have at last penetrated.

More than sixty centuries ago, in the dawn of architecture, the Sumerian hillman left his sheltered home and, wandering down into the vast empty plain, wondered how he should set about building himself a house.

For architecture is building. So much has been written concerning the aesthetic development of what is certainly an art that there is always the danger of overlooking the fundamentals underlying what is also a science, the science of building construction. It is such discoveries as the invention of masonry or the calculation of the abutments of an arch so that it will not fall down which are the great moments in architecture. The ornamentation of the wall or the shape of the arch is of secondary importance. Styles and fashions are but superficial— often ephemeral—but the inventor of the dome could have watched its passage down the ages, through Byzantium to the Baroque. Only great civilizations have produced architects; it was builders, helped on occasion by engineers, who laboured through the centuries to weave the often patchwork fabric of architecture.

Without builders there can be no architecture. Architects can design and engineers devise, but it is the builder who has in the end to carry out the work. Often he has had to employ his own practical, hereditary, skill in order to solve a problem thrust upon him by an ambitious designer. The builder's task is to satisfy his customer. Presented with the latter's requirements, he has to consider how he can best produce the desired accommodation with the materials at his disposal. For the skill of the craftsman is of no avail if there is no material upon which it may be utilized; it is indeed for just this reason that the nature of the materials available has always exercised the most fundamental influence upon the architecture of a region. Carrying this precept to its logical conclusion, it will be realized that the building style of a country is directly related to the natural characteristics of the country itself, its geographical situation and geological composition.

Let us consider home-finding in its elementary stages. Primitive lairs in trees do not come within the scope of the architectural student; the discovery of fire and its use to eject wild animals from caves is however of greater importance as it introduced primaeval man to the comforts accruing from having a roof over one's head. Excavation, although not technically a form of construction, is nevertheless an operation often necessary in architecture, as in levelling a site or terracing. Artificial caverns are fairly common; Syria, Palestine, and North Africa exhibit whole troglodyte towns of which the most famous is Petra with its amazing façades hewn from the cliff-face. The littoral of the eastern Mediterranean is honeycombed with rock-cut tombs, many of considerable architectural interest.

A cave-dwelling race which outgrew its available cave-space would have to set about the construction of shelters to accommodate the surplus population. This is where real building begins. The easiest material to employ for this purpose is pieces of rubble stone gathered from the surface of the ground and piled as skilfully as possible into windbreaks. Overhanging portions of cliff-face might be utilized to help with roofing-in the shelter. Although a wall on the weather side is better than nothing, it is really the roof which is the most desirable feature of a true home; a roof of rubble stone, however, would be far beyond the constructional ability of primitive men.

In regions possessing trees, the branches of these could be wrenched or cut away and piled against a cliff-face to form both wall and roof. Thus we find timber being introduced as a building material. Wrought or squared timber is a later improvement, with the invention of joinery as a development of the use of this very important architectural substance.

Stone is of course the building material par excellence. Even rubble stone, properly laid, can produce reliable walling suitable for a building of architectural importance. An early method of laying rubble was to set the stone in courses with each stone on its edge and leaning against that next to it. The stones in each course leant the opposite way from those in the course on either side, so that a herring-bone pattern was formed like that in cloth; the interlocking effect produced by this method resulted in a far stronger wall than would be achieved by laying the stones flat as in masonry walling.

Most of the great buildings of the world have been constructed in wrought stone or masonry. The origin and development of this fascinating craft is still shrouded in mystery and even to-day is still a matter for romantic speculation. The mason undoubtedly played a vital part in the economy of the ancient world. A man of authority, the essential nature of his craft and the apparently uncanny knowledge which he displayed in its execution, may have surrounded him with an aura of mystery such as cannot in these enlightened days be appreciated. Masonry presumably began when someone knocked a projecting snag from an ill-shaped piece of rubble in order to make the stone fit its place more conveniently. As tools improved, stones might be shortened, trimmed, and eventually squared, until a wall of coursed square stones could be constructed. Masonry would pro-gress more rapidly in regions possessing soft freestone than in those where the rock was harder.

The first stone walls would have been thin ones carrying no great weight. With the development of monumental building, however, thicker walls would be required. An ordinary wall has two faces which show; the stonework between these does not. It therefore became the practice to concentrate the work of the masons upon these two faces, leaving the stones unwrought where they came within the wall. This is the true practice of masonry: the setting out of the wall to its required thickness and the erection of two fair faces of perfectly wrought stone upon either side. Ancient walls were often hollow within; later on, the pieces dressed from the stone were thrown, together with mortar, into the core of the wall.

In districts where it was available, mud was an important building material. Walls of rubble stone could be waterproofed by plastering them with mud. The framework of timber huts could be covered with a network of wattling or woven reed and this could be covered with mud. The use of mud to waterproof rubble walling may have suggested its use as a mortar in which to set the stones when they were laid, a function which was afterwards usurped by a mortar made of burnt limestone slaked with water and mixed with sand. A mud pack applied to a thatch of any sort produces a very strong material, difficult to break up; thus a mixture of mud and chopped straw forms a primitive concrete.

The custom of mixing stone chips with lime mortar and placing them in the core of walls led to the discovery that the removal of the facing stones left a mass of hard concrete occupying the centre of the wall; it was thus possible to build quite thin skins of facework, or even temporary faces, to a wall and then cast its interior in pre-mixed concrete. The use of burnt cement-stone instead of limestone and, later, the fabrication of artificial cement, led to the discovery of the tough concrete employed to-day.

In regions where mud was used, experiments were soon being made with artificial rubble stones made out of mud reinforced with chopped straw and left to harden in the sun before being used. Later these bricks were made in moulds which gave them standard sizes; later still the moulds were struck with a straight-edge so that every face of the brick was flat and regular. Where the district could provide adequate fuel, bricks were fired in kilns instead of being laid in the sun to harden.

Artificial building materials such as brick and concrete are due to the development of building under the aegis of some civilizing influence; even the working of stone and timber are dependent upon good tools and the skill with which to employ them. The primitive materials, upon which architecture is founded, are rough timber and rubble stone; let us therefore see how from these two origins architectural style developed.

The purpose of building is, primarily, to produce a roof. A lodge of boughs, leaning against a cliff-face, is an obvious way of achieving this purpose. On open sites, the provision of a pair of lean-to roofs meeting upon a ridge-pole, actually achieves a passable house. This style of building, which produces a triangular section, may be called the furcated style, as the developed structure consists of a series of pairs of rafters, each pair forming an inverted fork. There are two main kinds of building timber. Hard-wood trees such as oak produce curved timber suited to furcated construction, as rafters can be laid concave side inwards so as to increase the headroom within the triangular prism formed by the building. It is to this fact that we owe the Gothic architecture of western Europe; the soft-wood forests of the North know it not. It is important to note that timber buildings adhere to a rectangular plan and are enlarged by elongation.

In regions having no timber at all, the problem of providing a roof is a serious one. Rubble stone, however, can be made to serve if it is laid in courses so that each of these overlaps the one above. A straight wall built in this way will, however, soon topple over; it is thus preferable to set out a circular hut and lay each course so that its stones are wedged together like a series of horizontal arches. A roughly conical hut is thus formed which, after the discovery of the arch, took the form of a true dome. It should be noted that the plan remains circular—as this figure is impossible of enlargement it may have been through striving to solve the problem thus presented that the race of Byzantine engineers were encouraged to produce their glorious designs.

Countries having neither timber nor stone were hard put to it for house-building; yet it so happens that the two great early civilizations, the Egyptian and the Sumerian, were faced with this problem from the outset. In the two types of roof described above, it will be noted that each is sloped or pitched so as to throw off rain; Egypt and Sumer being practically rainless, the inhabitants could afford to build roofs which were flat. A flat roof by itself does not make a house; it must be raised above the ground upon walls; thus the wall as part of a house was a structural problem to be faced by these early stone-less, timber-less peoples. Perhaps only they could have found a solution for their three rivers provided them with the material, mud, which they needed.

Thereafter, all architectural buildings employ the wall as an essential factor in the construction. While the great Mesopotamian civilizations continued to employ brick, the Egyptians transported stone from the cliffs fringing their narrow valley, so that their mighty buildings stand to-day while those of their Sumerian brethren have for the most part returned to the dust whence they sprang. Those countries lacking either stone or mud brick were inevitably late in developing their architecture. In northern Europe, walls were eventually built in blockwork, with straight tree-trunks laid like stone courses. After the development of joinery, it was possible to erect walls of timber framing; the hard woods of western Europe were best suited to this form of construction.

The beam laid horizontally across the wall-tops is an important factor in architectural building. In the days of the early civilizations it was a tree-trunk, rough and unwrought; later it became squared-up. When 'pitched' or sloping roofs were raised upon walls, it tied the tops of these together so that the roof timbers, deprived of the anchorage once afforded them by the ground, should not thrust at the walls and overturn them. Still later, when buildings rose in height, it served to support the flooring of upper stories. One of the first functions of the beam must have been to support the walling above the opening of a door or window. The ancients, however, always desperately short of timber, devised a different method of bridging the opening. A man held his bent forearm against one side of the gap whilst another man laid some bricks, set on edge, along it until a curved line of these had been laid across from side to side. The man took his arm away, the bricks stayed in place, and an arch had been constructed. In later days, a framed wooden centering took the place of the bent arm.

Early arches could only be employed for bridging quite small gaps. An imposing entrance being a desirable feature of any important building, some means had to be found of covering a wide opening. The beam was the only solution. After its length had been increased until it began to sag with the weight of the wall above, a timber prop was inserted beneath its centre. As this obstructed the entrance, however, the opening was enlarged still further until two props could be inserted beneath the beam. This is the origin of the portico.

The wooden post, at first a palm-trunk, was later translated into the architectural language of stone-building lands as a pillar of wrought stone, eventually becoming the column formed of large drums raised one upon the other; smaller columns were even turned in a lathe as if it had been of wood. It will be noted that the column was the first structural device to intrude upon the plan as an obstruction as well as a convenience; special attention being therefore paid to its appearance, it becomes the first architectural feature.

We have now examined the fundamentals of building, some of the principal materials available, and the elementary principles followed in their use. The all-important roofing problem has been discussed and some consideration given to the various methods of constructing the walling upon which the roofs of all monumental buildings are supported. The structural inventions of the beam, the arch, and the pillar have been introduced. Let us now investigate the use to which these building devices were employed in the design of buildings.

Of all classes of building, the ordinary private house is the most important. No civilization could exist without houses; it was as a result of experimenting upon house design that each architectural style was inaugurated and developed for use in larger structures. In ancient and mediaeval times, the house was not merely a residence—indeed, the residential portion might well occupy but a small proportion of the area of the building, especially if there were riding, transport, or farm animals to be accommodated within it. In the days before banks, the whole of the owner's movable property would have to be stored in his home; some mercantile or industrial trade might also be carried on there. In early days, it was no suite of apartments that the householder and his family occupied; one or two rooms might serve to accommodate the whole of them, and possibly even some indoor servants as well.

In all civilizations, private houses vary in size from the hovel to the mansion of an aristocrat. The largest type of house is the palace of the ruler. In ancient times, the plan of the living quarters of a palace is often much the same as that of any other house, save that the rooms are larger and the whole scale of the planning system augmented so as to give dignity to the seat of government. Occasionally there are extra rooms for public purposes; accommodation is usually provided for extra staff, officials, servants and guards. As in the case of the private house, the palace has to have store rooms for the personal property of the ruler; often the whole of the public treasury has to be securely housed within the confines of the palace. It will thus be seen that the factor which is noticeable in palace plans is that of the area which it covers.

Houses and palaces are buildings designed for practical purposes. Religious edifices, however, fulfil no useful function; they are designed solely to produce an effect upon the worshipper who, for all practical purposes, could equally well say his prayers in the open air. Early temples are usually merely copies of the dwelling-house of the day, with the shrine of the god occupying the most private chamber of the householder. Size is not essentially a factor in temple plans as it is, of necessity, in the case of governmental buildings. Structural difficulties might preclude the provision of large apartments for housing massed congregations; a multiplicity of useless rooms would have been an embarrassment. Yet it was essential to bestow upon a religious building an architectural dignity which would make it stand out above all merely practical structures. Throughout the ages, therefore, it has always been the aim of the designers of religious edifices to raise the height of their structures above the normal. From the first, the temple was never a practical building. It had to possess a special quality of its own: an unreal atmosphere which set it apart as the dwelling place of gods, not men. It had to seem to approach the abode of the gods more closely than those about it; thus we see that *height* is the factor which sets its stamp upon the religious building.

The temple is the first building in which the emphasis is laid, not upon practical requirements, but upon the desire to obtain a monumental appearance. It is in this search for the monumental that building becomes architecture; the factor of height is therefore the primary architectural factor in the design of monumental structures. A building can cover a vast area but yet be no larger than is dictated by practical requirements; once it begins to rise higher than is actually necessary it becomes monumental.

In ancient days there were many vast buildings of no architectural importance. The governments of great cities needed huge storehouses in which to accumulate food supplies and munitions of war. It is only when we see the wealth of a nation being spent upon such entirely useless monuments as *ziggurats* or pyramids that we realize that we are looking upon the work of a civilization which subscribed to the principles underlying religious and aesthetic culture.

1. The *ziggurat* of Ur

2. A gate-temple at Ur

3. Eighteenth-Dynasty monumental site-planning at Thebes

From the beginnings of mankind, anyone who owned something might be envied by another who would try to take it from him. Thus most early settlements had to be protected in some way from the depredations of raiders. This is the origin of fortification, which in its humblest structural form is simply a wall. The wall of enceinte, as apart from the wall of a building, is thus an important architectural structure. Another military building—later, owing to its possessing the monumental factor of height, utilized for religious purposes—is the tower of refuge—the combination of tower and wall of enceinte produced many magnificent architectural compositions.

The enclosed courtyard, fundamental feature of most early houses of any importance, was also found in many temples. The restrictions imposed upon the span of roofed apartments by primitive structural means did not obtain in the case of courts open to the sky; there was thus no limit to the size of these. A courtyard enclosed by buildings could of course be no larger than was governed by the extent of those buildings. A courtyard enclosed merely by a wall would however suffer no such restrictions; the great court enclosed by a wall of enceinte thus became an important feature in religious, and therefore monumental, design. A great court of this class entirely enclosing a religious area is known as a *temenos*.

We have already considered the monumental factor, height, which governs the design of buildings. We have now discovered a monumental feature, the great court, which—in itself quite useless—appears in the monumental planning of a group or complex of buildings. The temenos itself is merely a glorified fence; empty but surrounded by fine buildings, the great court becomes a monumental area.

Thus an area, as well as a building, can become an architectural achievement. It suggests the considered arrangement of buildings with relation to it, and to each other, in place of a mere haphazard placing of these wherever a convenient empty space exists. A rectangular area of monumental proportions might have have some such feature as the entrance to an important building placed in the centre of one of its sides, thus creating an axis. The size of a great court being limited by the amount of unrestricted level space procurable, enlargements of the monumental area might have to be achieved by adding other courts; as the art of architectural planning developed, these courts would wherever possible be added upon the main axis of the whole lay-out.

Symmetry is not necessarily a feature of good architecture. It serves, however, as a simple means of regimenting the plan of a building towards monumental perfection, especially when applied to a vista, whether this should be across an area or within a building.

The external appearance of a building need not always be a concern of its designer. It is the interior which matters—buildings are not erected just to be looked at. The majority of urban structures are almost entirely surrounded by other buildings; even the entrance front of an important religious or civic building may form part of the frontage of a narrow street. It is only when the main front of a building is situated at the edge of an open area that the need for a considered 'elevation' becomes apparent; to carry this still further it will be seen that a completely isolated building might well have all its elevations consciously designed. Even the form of the cubic mass of such a structure should in reality be aesthetically considered. But neither in respect of this nor in connection with any elevational aspect of the building need symmetry be utilized, though in point of fact this primitive device has always played an important part in the history of elevational architecture.

While it is undoubtedly in the planning and subsequent erection of his buildings that the architect primarily demonstrates his skill, it is nevertheless by virtue of their elevational aspect that he is known to the world at large. In addition to the main proportions of the building and its component parts the designer can utilize various forms of ornamentation. One of the simplest of these is punctuation, generally achieved by the regimentation of essential architectural features such as window openings or the columns of a portico. Even 'blind' façades may be punctuated by introducing projecting bands or strips of masonry for the purpose.

The ultimate resort of the architect is to enlist the assistance of the pure artist who will mould, carve, or colour such portions of the structure as may offer suitable subjects upon which he may exercise his own particular craft. Such ornamentation is however beyond the sphere of architecture, which is connected primarily with planning, building construction, and the ordering of the architectural details of elevations only; applied ornament is but a veneer, often uncontrolled by the architect and even on occasion introduced to mask the cunning details of his construction. It is beneath all such superficial matter that the true architectural student must peer if the truth is to be revealed.

Throughout the history of architecture the builder—be he carpenter, bricklayer, or mason—has of necessity been a skilled tradesman. Equipped with the tools of his craft, including of course adequate measuring and levelling devices, he could be relied upon to carry out the spirit of his instructions and apply his own special skill to the task of translating these into concrete products of his own particular building technique.

The architect, on the other hand, was an amateur. Though able by virtue of his particular talent to visualize the general form of the structure contemplated he seldom had the technical knowledge of the tradesman. Nor had he any means of conveying—other than in the course of ordinary conversation—the sense of his ideas to the latter. He could not prepare accurate drawings from which a builder could work; when it came to setting out the structure upon the site neither he nor anyone else had any efficient measuring apparatus.

It is not too much to imagine the conference between architect and mason on the occasion of the initiation of a building project as being a matter of pacing about, patient explanation, and keen discussion accompanied by gestures indicating position, extent, height, form and so forth—before even the site pegs could be driven in. Certainly buildings were set out on the ground itself and not, as nowadays, transferred thither from paper.

The architect of today is the heir of more than fifty centuries of experience. He may telephone an army of specialists to his aid; his staff of draughtsmen are equipped with the latest devices for preparing detailed drawings by means of which he may convey his thoughts to a builder similarly endowed with the advantages of modern constructional systems. An ever-increasing list of novel materials is at hand to help the designer through the morass of difficulties inseparable from the complexities of modern building requirements. With urgency sounding in the hum of the traffic beyond his office window he tries to create fine buildings and at the same time maintain his craft upon a steady course while clients, contractors, sub-contractors, specialists, and in these days a host of disinterested but conscientious officials, are tugging it this way and that.

How often he must wish that the centuries might lead him back with them until the noise and bustle of our modern age should fade into oblivion. How pleasant to walk upon a bare building site with a mason and a few labourers—to scratch the outlines of an embryo cathedral with a stick upon the earth, returning a few months later to see if anything had been started yet. Then, formal admonitions dutifully bestowed, to retire once more to lead the life of a distinguished architect of other days.

Chapter II

THE DAWN
IN MESOPOTAMIA

In those misty days when the primitive huntsman crept from his ancient forests and began to tame wild animals to his purpose, it was yet too early for him to think of architecture. But as he wandered down the centuries after his grazing flocks he one day stumbled upon the secret of how to tame the land itself. He marked himself out a humble plot and settled beside it to tend his growing crop. A vagrant no longer, he could now make himself a home that would not have to be forever taken down and dragged away to pastures new.

Perhaps his newly-acquired field lay on some gentle plain, fertile and well-provided with small trees and reeds from which he could make himself a hut. In this case it might be that he would be content with such a home. Perhaps his lot fell in some wild hill-country where he would have to clear his land of trees before he could till it. When he had dragged away the trees and was beginning to clear away the lumps of rock which interfered with his rough ploughing he might find that the soil, once held together by tree-roots, was beginning to wash away downhill under the pressure of the rain. It would probably soon occur to him to make a line of salvaged rocks at the foot of his field to try to hold up the threatened soil. As the denudations continued he would have to add to the height of his wall of rocks to meet the soil piling up behind it; it is thus in the neighbourhood of ancient terrace-cultivations that we find the beginnings of permanent architecture.

The beginnings of architecture have yet to be sought. Modern research points to the region about what is now Kurdistan as that in which sophisticated building technique first appeared. Here there is plenty of rubble stone available for walling while poplar trees could provide beams, posts and rafters. It is now clear that before the end of the fourth millennium B.C. the inhabitants of this region were constructing two-storied houses and had discovered not only the principle of the arch but could use it to turn vaults over ground-floor apartments. They had also attained such a degree of culture that they were actually punctuating the elevations of their buildings with blind arcading. Yet we have as yet discovered no traces of monumental building in these areas and no inscriptions are left to give us any indication as to the civilization which produced this extremely advanced architectural style.

Thus the originators of architectural building appear to have been that race which we call the Indo-Europeans. It was when these vigorous hillmen began to wander down from their mountains to settle beside the lower reaches of the Euphrates that we find the beginnings of the first great civilization. Much research has yet to be pursued before we can state with any degree of certainty the period at which the Indo-Europeans of what is now Iran began to oust from the plain of Shinar its primaeval inhabitants; it seems, however, that the invaders first appear in Mesopotamia somewhere during the fifth millennium. Gradually settling down to a comfortable existence in the extensive plain, which they began to render more fertile by systematic irrigation, the newcomers had by the beginning of the third millennium inaugurated that impressive civilization which we know as the Sumerian.

When the early Sumerians first began to make mud bricks for building their houses, they at once gave away the secret of the origin of their race by the fashion after which they shaped their products. Obviously ignorant of the form which a proper building-brick should follow, they made theirs by simply pressing a pat of mud into a shallow box, whence it emerged looking more like a model of a piece of rubble stone than a proper brick. Sometimes they even built their walls of such bricks laid herringbone. Even after the firing of bricks was understood, the Sumerians still held to the 'plano-convex' form. Eventually, however, the properly-fashioned brick with all six sides flattened became universal; the most common type was about eighteen inches square and two inches thick. The custom of stamping such bricks with the name of the ruling king has been of great assistance in dating the buildings in which they appear.

The first building to rise in Sumer would have presumably been nothing more than an ordinary house: a rectangle of mud-brick walls roofed with mud-plastered matting supported upon rafters made of poplar-poles. The simplest plan would be a square; a rectangle, however, would present no problems, as the shortest dimension, or span, would remain the same.

The rectangular room forms the basis of all primitive houses of this type of construction. There is only one architectural feature, the entrance doorway. All rooms housing a family tend to develop two ends of which one is the more private; the entrance doorway would be at the opposite end, so as to increase still further the privacy which might be enjoyed at the 'upper' end. Still more privacy is attained if the entrance be sited, not in the end wall, but at the 'lower' end of one of the longer walls, which then becomes the 'front wall' of the house.

This rectangular room with the doorway at the 'lower' end of the 'front' wall, besides providing the normal arrangement for houses, also formed the nucleus of the early temple-plan. The primitive temple was intended to represent the house of a god; thus in early shrines the plan is that of a house, with the statue of the divine occupant taking the place of the couch of the human householder. The most usual device is to provide a niche designed like a blind doorway; framed by this feature, the god appears to be emerging from the celestial regions for the purpose of receiving the supplications of his worshipper.

In order to appreciate the stark simplicity of ancient domestic planning arrangements, it is necessary to divorce one's mind entirely from conditions as they exist to-day. For hundreds of centuries, a man's idea of a home for his family was simply what we should describe to-day as a room. Within the compass of its four walls would be accommodated the whole of his family—perhaps three or four generations of it—as well as such domestic animals as dogs, poultry, or even the family donkey. Internal divisions might be provided in some cases by means of hanging mats, but there would be no subdivision into rooms as we know them to-day.

If a man's estate flourished so that his possessions increased, he might consider the expansion of his house into what might be described as a 'great house'. He might have male slaves to accommodate and goods to store; he might like to provide a separate stable for the donkey. In ancient domestic architecture, a great house is an assemblage of what we should call to-day rooms (though such in their day might well have been regarded as houses). An additional room added to the nucleus as an 'ell' might be balanced by another at its opposite end; the enclosure of the internal area thus achieved by a fourth room would produce what we know to have been the universal form of the Sumerian great house, that is to say an assemblage of narrow rooms surrounding a small yard.

The owner of such a magnificent house would have been an important personage at the close of the fourth millennium when the Sumerian cities were rising along the lower reaches of the Euphrates and its attendant canals. These cities, each densely populated and becoming rich and powerful, were surrounded by strong walls of brickwork which enabled them to maintain their independence as city-states despite the fact that often a bare ten miles separated one from another. Most powerful of all, however, was the great city of Ur, seat of the early Sumerian kings.

The new civilization was attracting other races to the plain of Shinar. Upstream from Sumer, where the Euphrates approaches the Tigris near where Baghdad stands to-day, the city of Agade was being colonized by Semitic tribesmen who had subdued some of the neighbouring city-states and founded the rival kingdom of Akkad. About 2500 B.C., the great king Sargon of Akkad attacked and overwhelmed the Sumerian kingdom, seated himself upon the throne of Ur and proclaimed the unification of Sumer and Akkad. After some two centuries of Akkadian rule, however, a line of Sumerian kings was once again established; under this, the third dynasty of Ur, the Sumerian empire reached its zenith.

The great house of the day was becoming a more comfortable and imposing residence. The single room of the householder had received an addition in the form of another, wider, apartment which was ranged alongside it with a doorway connecting the two. This new room now became the private house of the owner; the outer apartment

4. Looking across the hypostyle hall of the temple at Karnak

5. The portal of the Egyptian temple is flanked by pylons
(Philae)

6. A small Ptolemaic temple at Edfu

7. Lions guard the gateway to the Hittite capital
(Boghaz Keui)

becoming an ante-chamber or reception room, similar to the 'mandara' of a modern Arab house. In the centre of the courtyard wall of the latter an imposing portal advertised the dignity of the master of the house. The courtyard before this portal was entered from the outside world through an entrance lobby sited in one of the angles facing the portal of the reception room.

The siting of two rooms alongside each other eventually produced a building unit consisting of an approximately cubical structure having the span of its roof-timbers halved by the insertion of a cross wall dividing the interior into two. It is this type of building which appears everywhere in early Mesopotamian domestic architecture as the principal feature in domestic plans.

The pair of rooms forming the actual residential portion of the Sumerian house forms the nucleus of the architectural planning of the era. In the royal palace, the reception room with its portal becomes the throne room; behind this, the large inner room of the private house is replaced by a group of small rooms surrounding an inner court, often long and narrow in form. The main courtyard of the palace is surrounded by offices, staff quarters, and store-rooms.

In the large temple of the great days of the Sumerian empire, the reception room of the house plan is sometimes the sanctuary; generally, however, there are an inner and an outer apartment, or even three of these in succession, always arranged side by side with the axis of the temple passing through them towards the niche containing the statue of the god. This device of setting rooms upon, but at right angles to, a main axis is typical of Sumerian planning and is due to their building technique of erecting large cubical blocks divided by one or two cross walls to help the rafters in their task of carrying a heavy mud-packed roof.

The confined area enclosed by the walls of Sumerian cities forced the planners of large buildings to keep these as compact as possible. It was in the designing of large blocks, each containing an elaborate assemblage of separate building complexes, that the Sumerian architects demonstrated their skill. The temples were the largest structures. Owing to the limitations of the planning forms available, a large temple had to consist of repetitions of these. Thus the visitor, passing through a monumental gateway set in a massive wall, would find himself in a spacious courtyard facing another gateway leading into a large apartment similar to the throne room of the king's palace or royal house. Passing through this he would find himself within the inner court of the palace of the god, at the end of which another imposing portal would indicate the entrance to the sanctuary itself or its antechamber. In some large temples there were actually three repetitions of the courtyard-reception-room system. Nevertheless their competence as planners enabled the Sumerian architects to gather together their maze of courts and apartments and order these into a rectangular shape which could be enclosed by a massive external wall, raised high above the temple roofs so as to introduce the monumental factor of height and cause the temple to tower over the surrounding buildings. Even though little remains to-day to give us an impression of the elevational appearance of the Sumerian temples it is clear from the plans alone that their architects of forty centuries ago were confident and experienced designers of very large monumental structures.

That there was no shortage of building potential is evidenced by a class of structure which only the Sumerians produced: the huge artificial hill known as the *ziggurat*. These extraordinary achievements supply the principal manifestations of the importance of the height factor in religious architecture. Their purpose is unknown; some believe they may be connected with the science of astronomy which was certainly well-known to the Sumerians and may have expanded by them into a form of astrology useful for purposes of religion. The moon-god Nannar certainly played an important part in the life of Ur, where the ziggurat appears to be connected with his cult. None other of the world's greatest civilizations produced any architectural achievements to compare with the terraced hills of brick-work, ascended by seemingly never-ending staircases and surmounted by those mysterious shrines which gazed out over the land of Sumer. Four thousand years have swept over these mighty monuments. The tempests of the ages have striven to reduce the humble materials of which they were formed until all should have returned to the desolate plain from whence they sprang. But over the land of Sumer the lonely ziggurats still mourn, imperishable cenotaphs of a great civilization of other days (Plate 1).

When one considers the competence displayed in the planning

achievements of the Sumerian architects, one may speculate as to what they might have produced had they not been limited to such humble materials. The heavy mud roofs, supported upon pliant poplar-poles, limited them to narrow rooms of which the most magnificent could not be wider than fifteen feet or so. Mud-brick is at the best an unreliable material in which to construct walling; the ten-foot high walls of a private house had to be a couple of feet in thickness and the towering constructions which enclosed the temples perhaps ten times as thick. It is upon this sheer massiveness which is the keynote of Sumerian monumental architecture that the designers undoubtedly relied for their elevational effects.

A sure sign of competence in the architectural achievements of any age is the manner in which its designers discipline their elevations by the employment of a proper system of punctuation. The Sumerians relieved the starkness of their towering cliffs of brickwork by introducing broad vertical bands which divided the elevations into regular 'bays'. Developing this idea, they flanked the entrance portals with heavy square projections, possibly carried up above the wall-tops as pylons; by this method they invited the visitor to inspect the interior of the edifice and at the same time bestowed a tremendous emphasis upon the only architectural feature—the portal—with which they were acquainted.

As builders in brick they early discovered the secret of the arch, employing it to bridge openings up to about ten feet or so in span and also in barrel vaults covering apartments at ground level. They appear to have also used the arch in an ornamental capacity by constructing rows of blind arcades springing from the wide pilasters with which their elevations were punctuated; their bricklaying skill enabled them to turn these arches in 'orders', one supported upon the other and with each order carried down to the ground on the sides of the pilasters. In their ziggurats they employed the device known as 'entasis' to correct the optical weaknesses of their straight lines.

The monumental courtyard was a planning device much appreciated by the Sumerians. The lofty walls surrounding such magnificent enclosures as the Court of Nannar at Ur are not, however, merely reproductions of the massive fortifications by which the cities were protected, but are actually ranges of rooms set out in the same fashion as in any other courtyard of the period. An enceinte of this impressive scale gave unlimited scope for punctuation by means of vertical features of varying width and projection. The regularity of the material used made it possible for the introduction of refinements in planning the details of the changes in frontage; instead of plain square projections, the edges of these melted into the main wall through graduations of intermediate facets. The fronts of important features—such as those flanking portals—were often embellished with vertical grooves (possibly to hold banner-poles) also contrived by careful bonding of the brickwork (Plate 2).

Roofs and wall-tops alike were waterproofed with a thick layer of mud reinforced with chopped straw. The parapets provided for the protection of those walking upon the tops of buildings were also plastered with mud where the material used was sun-dried brick; where burnt brick was employed, the bonding of this was allowed to run out in the form of a zig-zag cresting so that no open joints were left exposed to the weather. The serrated skyline produced by this curious device was a feature common to Mesopotamian architecture of all epochs.

From about 2300 B.C. onwards the kings of the third dynasty of Ur were raising their great buildings in the rich cities of Sumer. Yet only a century or so after the foundation of this important line, a rival power was beginning to appear on the horizon. In what had been Akkad, a new Semitic incursion from the desert had founded the city of Babylon, from which a new dynasty of Amorite kings was beginning to threaten the supremacy of Ur. At last, under the great king Hammurabi, the storm broke over the Sumerian cities, which, about the year 1900 B.C., came under the suzerainty of Babylon.

The old cities flourished under their Babylonian masters. Ur in particular, greatly venerated as the ancient capital and religious centre, still held pride of place in the Sumerian world that was now become Babylonia. Some of the finest buildings in the country date from this period; the culture of the day seems to have been scarcely affected by what may have been little more than a political revolution.

The architect was an important member of Babylonian society at the beginning of the second millennium B.C. The Code of Ham-

8. The entrance to the acropolis of Mycenae

9. A Doric temple of the fifth century B.C.
(Athens)

murabi fixes the scale of his fees but decrees that he shall pay with his life if his client is killed by his house falling on him.

Great civilizations always seem to soften and become the prey of hardier races. About 1750 B.C., the Hittite hillmen from what is now Anatolia suddenly swept down upon Babylonia and reduced it to chaos. At the same period, however, these new invaders were matching their growing strength against the might of Egypt; the desperate campaigns which the two races fought, for century after century, along the Levantine littoral, cut off Babylonia from the Mediterranean and greatly impoverished the country, which then fell a victim to the Kassites from the nearby Persian hills.

For several centuries the ancient land lingered on, invaded from time to time by predatory races from the desert and the hills. High up on the banks of the Tigris, however, a little city, Ashur, was beginning to hold its own against the dangers which encompassed it. From 1350 B.C. onwards it struggled to increase Assyrian territory, sacrificing the comforts of civilization for the safety which lay in military strength. For six centuries the balance swayed to and fro. At last, in 689 B.C., Sennacherib fell upon and utterly destroyed the city of Babylon.

Less than a century after this spectacular achievement, the empire of Assyria, weakened by the indolence bred of luxury, shrank and faded away into oblivion. A dynasty of Chaldean kings now seized the sceptre, wielding it with such notable effect that the ancient land took on a new and splendid lease of life in what is known as the Neo-Babylonian era. With the splendour of the decaying Assyrian cities as his model, the famous king Nebuchadnezzar restored his capital, and many of the provincial towns, to a state of magnificence far exceeding anything hitherto seen in Babylonia.

The new empire, however, was doomed to be ephemeral. A bare two centuries of fame were assigned to it. Temples, palaces, the high-perched 'hanging gardens' lining the processional way which threaded the city from the gate of Ishtar—all was soon to pass away from the Mesopotamian scene. For two and a half millennia, generations of builders of all races have been industriously wrenching the hard bricks of Babylon, bearing the stamps of great kings, from the beds of bitumen in which they were set. Today even the ziggurat has gone. Only that ancient Sumerian, Nannar, lord of the night sky, remains gazing serenely down upon the tumbled waste of desolation where Babylon once stood.

Although intended as a rival to the Assyrian cities, the Babylon of Nebuchadnezzar, which attained its zenith during the first half of the 6th century B.C., was nevertheless a city constructed in accordance with the best traditions of the architectural style of the land. This is particularly evidenced by the temples, which, even in such provincial cities as Kish or Borsippa, were magnificent structures far exceeding anything to be found in Assyria. Indeed, when we examine the monumental plans of these Neo-Babylonian temples, each with its array of innumerable courts and apartments all confidently gathered together within the compass of the four ponderous external walls, we realize that we see before us the culminating achievements of the Sumerian planners of many centuries earlier.

For Assyrian architecture is but a poor upstart thing compared with that whence it drew its inspiration. The palaces of the proud, cruel monarchs of that fierce race are large enough, in all conscience. But they sprawl in such ill-considered, ungainly fashion over their sites that it is evident that the quality of their design in no way matched the scale of the conception. In respect of their size alone are they to be considered architecturally remarkable; aesthetically considered, they owe their place in art solely to the sculptured dadoes, culled from their Hittite neighbours, with which they ornamented the otherwise unremarkable walls of their more important achievements.

Assyrian architecture is in fact simply the last phase of the Mesopotamian culture which, reaching a magnificent climax about the beginning of the second millennium, had already been deteriorating for many centuries before the Assyrian conquests enabled this brutal race of militarists to fill the ancient cities with their ostentatious palaces. There was no change in structural methods; even the most important buildings were still being built of sun-dried brick. The roofs were formed of mud-packed matting supported by timber beams which, in the absence of any form of medial propping, were as yet unable to span an apartment of any remarkable width.

The principal development was in the expansion of the plan of the Assyrian great house beyond that of its Babylonian predecessor. The little courtyard had now become a great court, with a fine portal, often flanked by imposing square projections like those of a Babylonian temple gateway, giving access to the large reception room of the house. Beyond this, the simple chamber of the primitive house had disappeared entirely, its place being taken by an inner courtyard surrounded by suites of living rooms. Often this second court formed as it were a house by itself, having its own reception room, entered through yet another fine portal, attached to one side.

After the beginning of the 9th century B.C., the palaces of the Assyrian kings begin to follow what is easily to be recognized as a standard form of plan. The outer court expands to a monumental scale and is surrounded by offices and store-rooms. On one side of the great court a fine portal—sometimes flanked by smaller ones, suggesting the beginnings of a portico—gives access to the throne room which occupies the whole of one side of the structure. At the rear of the throne room is a square courtyard, rather smaller than the outer court, surrounded by the king's private rooms. The usual arrangement is to place reception rooms, each backed by an inner apartment in the old fashion, along each of the three sides of the inner court; one of these units gives access to the most private part of the palace, the other two are presumably for the entertainment of important guests.

The building activities of the Assyrian kings seem to have been confined to the erection of these vast structures; each king seems to have begun a new municipal palace in every important city in his realm as soon as he came to the throne. It is therefore not surprising to find that the religious architecture of Assyria is very much inferior to that which appears in the civic buildings. Certainly there is nothing in any way to compare with the Babylonian achievements. Divorced from its attendant host of small apartments—priests' cells and store-rooms for treasure—which help to pack out the perimeter of the ancient temple massifs, the essential features of the plan were the courtyard with the sanctuary occupying one side of this. As the courtyard expanded with the need for accommodating more worshippers, the sanctuary began to elongate uncomfortably; the inner court of the Babylonian temple at the beginning of the second millennium was therefore usually set out on a rectangular plan so that the sanctuary could occupy one of the narrow ends. Thus we find the temple plan settling down as a long rectangular court, with a small sanctuary—

attained through a portal in the centre of one of its long sides—passing across one end of the court. This arrangement, reduced in scale so that the court could be covered over to protect the worshippers from a more vigorous climate than that of Babylonia, becomes the Assyrian temple plan.

It will be realized that a fundamental change had taken place in the arrangement of religious buildings. Hitherto, worshippers had congregated in the open air before the portal of the sanctuary; now they were actually within the temple itself, as in the nave of a church. In most Assyrian examples, the body of the building is entered at the end opposite to the sanctuary, where a narrow room, similar to the ubiquitous 'reception room' found in so many of these ancient planning complexes, is itself reached through a portal situated within an outer court.

The long room entered at one end instead of the middle of a side wall is a planning unit absent from the buildings of the Sumerians. This introduction of an axial approach indicates the influence of the long buildings of the hill-country with their pitched roofs which shed rain and facilitated the removal of snow instead of confining it behind a parapet. The hill-folk, though unable to achieve a degree of civilization comparable with those passing below them in the fertile plain, had long ago introduced the elementary features of their architecture into the country now ruled over by the formidable rivals of the Assyrians, the fierce Hittites of Anatolia.

As the culture of the Babylonians was evidenced by the magnificence of their temples, so the aggressiveness of the Assyrians is indicated by their concentration on earthly pomp. Another aspect of the warlike character of the race is shown by the efficiency of their military architecture. Their cities are all surrounded by massive walls which in their day, if one can credit contemporary illustrations, were of considerable height and well equipped with towers at intervals to assist in the defence. The gates through these mighty fortifications were approached through a pair of chambers echoing the domestic unit referred to above, beyond which a pair of gigantic human-headed bulls flanked the actual gate-passage passing through the wall. Each gate lay between two wall-towers; the twin-towered portal seems to have been the favourite monumental device of the Assyrian architects.

It is possible to sympathize with these warlike people if one takes into consideration the fact that they were for the most part sandwiched between two powerful nations, the Babylonians of the plain and the Hittites of Asia Minor. The latter race were indeed a dangerous enemy to encounter; for centuries they had been defying the might of Egypt and contesting with them the ownership of Syria. We shall see in a later chapter that the Hittites were not lacking in culture; it is indeed from these hardy hillmen that the Assyrians borrowed their most notable contribution to the history of art.

The origins of megalithic architecture and the development of that remarkable feature known as the orthostat will be discussed later. The Hittites employed these standing stones in the form of a dado to protect the base of their mud-brick walls; eventually their artists discovered these dadoes to be excellent situations for the display of sculptured friezes. In Assyrian—or, perhaps, Babylonian—hands, these friezes became objects of such beauty as was never achieved by any other civilization. The vast mud-brick creations which they once embellished have for the most part returned to the dust whence they rose. But the sculptured pageantry remains, imperishably recorded by artists whose chisels proved to be mightier than the Assyrian sword.

Chapter III

EGYPT

Of all the various styles of architecture employed by the great civilizations of the ancient world, none appears today so spectacular as that which for three thousand years graced the buildings of the Nile Valley. It is therefore surprising to find that, despite its long survival and the monumental nature of many of its creations, ancient Egyptian architecture plays in fact but a small part in the history of architectural development. It is nevertheless impossible to discuss this subject without paying tribute to the ancient culture of the Nile valley during the last three millennia before the Christian era.

It is obvious that the civilization which created these wonders was a virile one. The narrow valley, hemmed in by torrid cliffs and basking in perennial heat, is well-protected by desert and sea. Yet the surrounding races—Nubian, Libyan, and Semitic—undoubtedly played an important part in maintaining the vigour of the Egyptians. Interchanges of trade and culture, wars of aggression and defence, even occasional political subjection to a dynasty of foreign rulers—all seem to have kept Egyptian culture flourishing and to have inspired its architects and craftsmen to yet further displays of their skill.

Unlike the pugnacious Assyrians, the dwellers by the Nile seem to have resembled the Sumerians in their willingness to be enslaved by a powerful priesthood. Perhaps no other ancient civilization was so completely swayed by the teachings and behests of its religious rulers. Everything we know concerning the Egyptian of those ancient days points clearly to the pathos of his philosophy, the obsession which governed his life. He had as it were only one foot in this world—the other was reaching, hopefully yet not a little fearfully, towards the far better world which the priests in their mighty temples assured him was waiting in the hereafter. As soon as he could do so, he set about preparing for the journey; as the years passed, much of his estate was squandered upon the project.

His first problem was how to preserve his body after death. For the tenets of this primitive religion encouraged the supposition that, lacking a body, the deceased could not hope to enjoy the life to follow. Thus, for scores of centuries, much ancient Egyptian architecture is governed by this sole aim: the preservation of the earthly body from the natural forces of destruction.

The chief of these would have been the desecration of the grave by animals, especially those jackals and scavenger dogs which then, as now, formed an integral factor of the economy of the country. Some sort of hard covering to the grave was therefore to be desired. From this is derived the low rectangular mass of brickwork—called, from its being used as a seat, a *mastaba*—which illustrates the first attempt at monumental architecture in the Nile valley.

After the unification of Upper Egypt with the Delta country under King Mena in the middle of the fourth millennium B.C., large brick mastabas began to appear in connection with the royal burial places near Abydos—the first capital, situated in Upper Egypt. These strange monuments cover the mouths of shafts leading to tomb-chambers sunk deep in the living rock; the mastabas themselves usually have only a tiny cell-like memorial chapel formed in the solid mass of brickwork of which they are constructed.

At the beginning of the third millennium the capital was moved to Memphis just above the site of modern Cairo. Soon after this event the king, Zozer, who had already completed his mastaba at Abydos, built himself another at Sakkara close to the new capital. It was this mastaba which, becoming the nucleus of a magnificent complex of structures, signalled the inauguration of Egyptian monumental architecture.

The name of the remarkable man who, at the instigation of his royal patron, devised the buildings which for five thousand years have perpetuated his fame as an architect, has fortunately also been preserved for posterity. Many centuries ahead of his era, Imhotep must surely be regarded as the greatest architectural genius the world has ever produced. In after years his country was to produce mighty buildings; never, in all its history, did its designers achieve the refinement of detail displayed by the buildings of the first half of the 30th century created by Imhotep.

A discussion of the details of Egyptian architecture will however be reserved for a later stage, so let us first consider what is undoubtedly the most striking creation of the Sakkara genius. Zozer's mastaba was not fine enough; its broad mass not sufficiently imposing for the memorial of a great king. It was enlarged in area and another mounted upon it. This was done yet again; the Nile valley saw a great mass of brickwork mounting towards the sky as the monument climbed heavenward, spreading its skirts as it did so. Two hundred feet in height, the five terraces of this mighty man-made hill still stand today: prototype of those wonders of the ancient world—the pyramids of Egypt.

As the years passed, and more great kings went to their graves, the pyramids began to gather along the left bank of the Nile. These later structures had their silhouettes smoothed until they formed the perfect pyramidal shape. The finest were covered over with stonework; some, including the greatest of them all, that of Khufu at Giza, were entirely constructed in stone. The Great Pyramid, 480 feet in height, dates from about the year 2900 B.C.; as in many of the later examples, the tomb-chamber excavated in the rock has been replaced by one contrived in the heart of the monument itself. The stones of which the pyramid was formed are enormous; its outer casing has disappeared, but the masonry work of the core thus exposed is of the finest quality.

The line of pyramids, fifty miles in length, which stalks southwards from the root of the Delta along the western bank of the Nile, represents rather more than eleven centuries of Egypt's history. Burial within or under an artificially-constructed tumulus, however, probably continued to be the royal custom for yet another three hundred years or so, the beginning of the 16th century B.C. seeing the fashion changing to interment within tombs cut in the cliff-face above the later capital, Thebes.

Whilst it is of course impossible to ignore them entirely, such featureless structures as these huge masses of brick or masonry are not, however, strictly architectural. Monuments rather than buildings, they merely serve as indications of the burial place of the dead king.

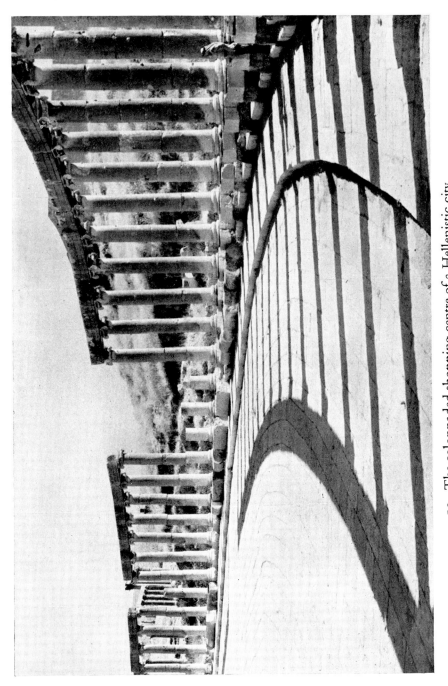

10. The colonnaded shopping centre of a Hellenistic city
(Jerash)

11. The Greeks utilised the natural contours of the ground in forming their theatres
(Pergamon)

Attached to each of them was a chapel in which priests conducted rites connected with the cult of the deified ruler thus commemorated; it is in these buildings that the true architectural style of the period is displayed. Let us therefore attempt to reconstruct the temple plan of the pyramid age of Egyptian history, which is generally known as the Old Kingdom.

As usual, we must first consider the plan of the private house; for the temple of ancient times was the house of the god in whose honour it was provided. The Egyptian houses belonged to that class of building with which we always associate the homes of eastern Mediterranean countries; that is to say the central feature of each was a courtyard. But whereas the Babylonian court always remained an open yard, the corresponding feature in Egypt appears generally to have been covered over from the heat of the high sun. Thus it is a large central apartment, surrounded by private rooms, which forms the nucleus of the Egyptian great house; by the middle of the second millennium B.C. its roof had become a permanent structure raised rather higher than those surrounding it in order to allow of 'clerestory' lighting to the principal apartment.

It will be remembered that the inner court of the Babylonian house was reached by passing across a long reception room. Egyptian houses had two of these long rooms flanking the north and west sides of the central apartment, adjoining which, on the side facing that by which it was entered, is the small private room of the owner. The remaining domestic apartments are collected together on the south and east sides of the house, the outer walls of which form a rectangle nearly approaching the square.

The two reception rooms—the long outer one and the square inner one—are repeated in the plans of most Egyptian temples. The square being a form seldom employed in the planning of rooms—its occurrence in the house plan is due to its having replaced an open courtyard —the inner room of the temple is generally elongated. In small temples, especially those connected with tombs, the inner apartment is generally set along the axis, with the niche containing the statue at the inner end. The outer apartment is always set at right angles to the axis; eventually it becomes an open-sided portico (Plate 6). In larger temples the two rooms are placed side by side, as in a Babylonian temple. The sanctuary is then represented by a small room echoing the private apatrment of the house-owner; a temple dedicated to the worship of more than one god may have a row of sanctuaries side by side.

The covering-over of the house courtyard was a step which would probably have been beyond the powers of the Babylonian builder. The Egyptians achieved it by employing four palm-tree posts to support the roof beams. This principle was extended to widen the span of the flanking reception rooms, which began to develop rows of wooden posts passing down their centres. This employment of the pillar as a structural feature enabling the width of a room to be increased eventually endowed Egyptian architecture with its characteristic 'hypostylar' quality; the wooden posts, translated into stone as columns, became features which were to revolutionize architectural design throughout Europe.

It was not only that the stone column played a vital part in supporting the roofs of temples. The great courts which fronted these buildings were gleaming ovens of white stone, blazing in the heat of the valley; lined with a row of columns supporting a narrow roof they became havens of welcome shade to the waiting worshippers (Plate 5). In this fashion the colonnaded verandah or portico came into being.

After the period of Imhotep's fine designs, an atmosphere of megalomania seems to overwhelm Egyptian architecture. From brickwork and fine masonry the builders turn to the massive walling and giant stones of Khufu's day, with its lack of detail and a general clumsiness of design which is even reflected in the planning. Indeed it is this same heavy-handedness which spoils the creations of the ancient Egyptian architects throughout the centuries. It is only the scale of the work that enables their buildings to succeed at all. Much of their planning consists in the excavation and levelling of vast areas of rock and the setting-out of monumental courtyards; the buildings themselves are composed of a series of features strung out along a seemingly interminable axial line. The largest of the individual apartments, the hypostyle halls, are merely forests of closely-spaced columns supporting stone-slabbed roofs and surrounded by their containing walling. The science and energy utilized in the erection of these masses of stonework is amazing; it is however a moot point whether the resultant artistic effect justified the means employed. The sculptured decoration covering these mountainous structures is astonishingly prolific yet never seems to attain the beauty of form displayed by, for example, that produced by the far less civilized Assyrians.

A magnificent example of the primitive monumental planning favoured at the close of the third millennium is the temple of Mentuhotep II at Deir el Bahri by Thebes. The nucleus of the design is a small pyramid, standing upon a levelled area just below the face of the cliff. The base of the pyramid is surrounded by a temenos wall, the space intervening between this and the central mass being roofed-in so as to enclose the pyramid completely within a hypostyle hall. Behind this feature, a rectangular area has been driven into the cliff face. Half this is occupied by a courtyard surrounded by colonnades; the extreme end becomes a hypostyle hall, nine bays in width and ten in depth, at the end of which is the small sanctuary containing the shrine. It is doubtful whether the architects of the huge temples of later days ever achieved so perfect a planning composition. Monumental in conception despite its quiet simplicity, its effect must have been dramatic to a degree never attained by those who dragged out the axial lines of the later buildings by adding court after court, hall after hall, pylon after pylon, in ineffective straining after immortality.

Not long after the completion of the fine temple of Mentuhotep II the arrival of the 2nd millennium B.C. coincided with that of a new dynasty—the XIIth—upon the throne of Egypt. The capital was moved upstream to Thebes, where the new temple looked out over the valley. The era known as the Middle Kingdom had begun.

The age of pyramids had not yet come to an end. But a new type of sepulchral temple had come into being: a shrine hewn, cave-like, out of the living rock. The situation of this new troglodyte cemetery was at Beni Hassan, half-way between Thebes and Memphis; in it, the kings of the XIIth dynasty began to prepare their burial places. The plan they followed was an innovation; instead of the broad antechamber they prefaced the entrance to the temple with a portico hewn in the cliff-face and displaying a pair of columns also formed in the living rock. These distylar porticoes are of interest as foreshadowing those of classical Greece. Within, the temple itself was a hypostyle hall containing four columns, the whole rock-hewn; beneath it, a shaft led down to the tomb chamber. The most skilful workmanship was employed in the execution of these troglodyte temples; perfectly set out and beautifully finished, their ultimate presentation was perfected by the application of painted decoration. Dating mostly from the first quarter of the second millennium, they illustrate the change in burial fashions from the shaft-tomb to the tunnel driven into the cliff-face.

The second quarter of the millennium was a troubled period which ended in the subjection of the country to the Semitic dynasty of 'Hyksos' kings. It was not until about 1580 B.C. that Ahmose I drove the invaders from the land, founded the XVIIIth dynasty, and launched Egypt into that glorious period known as the Empire. It is this period which accumulated all that buried splendour which is hidden away within the grim rocks of the Valley of the Kings at Thebes.

It was the age of the great temples. Most of these were free-standing structures, set out upon a more-or-less standard plan and added to from time to time. Only one, that of Queen Hatshepshut at Deir el Bahri, rivals in the monumental conception of its plan the fine XIth-dynasty temple of Mentuhotep which it adjoins. While little of the latter remains today, the spacious colonnaded courts of the great queen still gaze out across the site of the white-walled city of Thebes (Plate 3).

Although most of the more imposing temples now to be seen in Egypt represent the period of the Empire, many of these were in fact founded centuries earlier. Altered and extended from time to time, hardly any of them even retain the traces of their original plan. The most famous of them all, the great temple of Karnak by Thebes, was founded as far back as the beginning of the 20th century B.C. but so modified four hundred years later that practically nothing remains of the foundation plan. Twelve centuries more were to pass before the enormous fane, over a quarter of a mile in length, was finally completed.

The elements of the temple plan of the Empire seem to have been the two parallel chambers, each containing two rows of columns, set at right angles to the axis of the building which ended in the small

12. Scenic architecture designed by Hellenistic architects to cover an otherwise featureless wall (Baalbek)

14. The colonnaded skeleton of a Doric temple
(Paestum)

13. The courtyard of a Roman colonial house
(Bulla Regia)

15. The Colosseum, a Roman amphitheatre for spectacles

17. Its huge vault was carried upon a system of abutments joined by lesser vaults

16. The basilica of Maxentius is one of the last of the great Roman halls

sanctuary entered from the inner chamber. In front of the outer doorway was extended a square courtyard, the flanking walls of which
were extended to surround the temple itself within a rectangular
enclosure. The entrance to this courtyard was framed between a pair of
massive structures known as pylons (Plate 5).

The pylon, the invariable guardian of entrances to temple enclosures, is even found in connection with secular buildings. Resembling the remaining wall of an immense and massive tapering tower
of which the other three sides have been removed, it may represent the
Egyptian version of the brick features flanking the entrances to Babylonian temples. It does not appear to have come into use until the era
of the Empire—that is to say about 1600 B.C.—but thereafter continues, becoming larger and larger with the centuries, until the end of
the ancient Egyptian civilization.

Much of the history of a temple such as the huge example at
Karnak is made up by the continual extension of the axis away from
the temple proper by the addition of a series of courtyards, each with
its pyloned entrance. At Karnak, for example, such extra courts
were added at the end of the 14th century B.C. and again in the middle
of the 10th. Five pairs of huge pylons now line the axis of this mighty
edifice.

When discussing the XIth-dynasty temple built by Mentuhotep II
at Deir el Bahri, mention was made of the large hypostyle hall,
containing eighty columns, which terminated the axis of this fine
composition. Covered halls of this size appear, however, to have
played no part in the standard plan of the temple as it existed at the
beginning of the Empire. Yet it could not be long before an opportunity was taken to introduce an example of what was undoubtedly
the most notable architectural achievement of the age into the attenuated complex now forming the temple plan.

In great temples such as those of Karnak and Luxor, the hypostyle
hall was erected between two pairs of pylons, on the site of what had
previously been an open court. That at Karnak, dating from about
1315 B.C., is generally considered to be the finest example of Egyptian
architecture extant (Plate 4). Hypostyle halls of this description are
developments from the interior of the contemporary house, with its
central room flanked by others, rather less in height, over which the

former is lit by means of clerestory windows. The four wooden pillars of the central apartment are represented in the temple by two rows of columns higher than those which accompany them on either side. At Karnak, some of the clearstory windows are still in position.

Vast though Karnak is, it is more an epitome of Egyptian history than a specimen of any particular architectural period. In order to obtain a more accurate illustration of the temple of the Empire, one should turn to two which belong almost entirely to the XIXth dynasty: the Ramesseum of Rameses II at Thebes and the temple of Rameses III at Medinet Habu. Although the first dates from the last decade of the 13th century B.C. and the other is almost exactly a century later, both follow what is clearly a standard plan.

The entrance in both cases is between a pair of pylons, at the rear of which a square court, lined on the flanks only by colonnades, leads towards an inner entrance which at the later temple is also flanked with pylons. The temple court proper is surrounded by columns, doubled on the side next the temple and in the later example on the flanks also. There is, however, a suggestion of decadence in the fact that the fine hypostyle hall of the Ramesseum is represented by a somewhat humbler example at Medinet Habu. Both temples display the two inner chambers, each containing eight columns, with a sanctuary beyond. Subsidiary rooms for storage and so forth fill in the space between the main apartments and the outer wall which contains the whole complex within a rectangular enclosure.

Such, then, was the great temple of the Egyptian Empire at its zenith, which may be considered as including the period from about 1500 to 1200 B.C. Continuous wars against the Hittites and various Syrian peoples seem at last to have weakened the country, and a period of architectural decline then set in; from this it was eventually rescued, at least temporarily, by the arrival of the Ptolemies just after 300 B.C. The Ptolemaic temple plan, represented by those of Edfu and Dendera, varies little in general principles from that of the Empire. A notable feature of each, however, is the wide deep portico giving access to the small hypostyle hall from which the inner chambers are entered; these porticoes are clearly Egyptian versions of the classical temple frontispiece (Plate 6).

Soon after the beginning of the XVIIIth dynasty, a new type of temple appears in Egypt. This is a small rectangular shrine, entered from one end and entirely surrounded by colonnades of plain square piers. Such a very un-Egyptian building as this must surely owe its origin to some external influence, possibly Minoan or even Hittite. Be this as it may, the sanctuaries of some of the contemporary great temples seem to have been also affected. Soon after 1500 B.C., Queen Hatshepshut introduced a chamber which is in effect a copy of the 'periptal' shrine described above but with the colonnades replaced by walls enclosing a processional passage entirely isolating the sanctuary. A century later, Amenhotep III constructed a similar sanctuary at Luxor. Although this type of sanctuary does not seem to have been employed in the great temples of the XIXth dynasty, it reappears once more, this time almost certainly under classical influence, in the temples of the Ptolemaic era.

Before leaving the study of the Egyptian temple plan, reference must be made to the result of the abortive religious revolution introduced by Akhenaten about 1375 B.C. This enlightened monarch— afflicted by one of those inspirations which either change the history of the world or, as in his case, merely ruin the inspired—resolved to abandon polytheism and concentrate upon the worship of one god, which in his case he took to be represented by the sun. Having no further use for the strange figures of animal-headed gods which had hitherto represented the Egyptian pantheon, he dispensed not only with them but with the gloomy chambers in which they had so long lurked. The sun was his god, and his temple the open air; thus Akhenaten's temple at what is now Tel-el-Amarna consisted of merely an outer court and an inner one, the last representing the temple itself. Almost exactly two thousand years later, the monotheist Mohammed was to plan his temple upon similar lines.

While the architects of ancient Egypt, with some exceptions, showed no particular skill in the devising of monumental plans, more credit must be given to their skill in the actual erection of buildings. No civilization has ever achieved—even with the assistance of improved machinery—such stupendous memorials as the pyramids. After the abandoning of bricks as a monumental material in favour of stone, the Egyptian masons deliberately increased the difficulties of their task by the selection of a masonry scale which was itself monumental. Building their walling in true masonry—that is to say, two skins of stonework each independent of the other—they employed such vast stones and laid them so well that the removal of one entire face of a wall would leave the other standing unconcerned. The temple pylon is the pyramid technique introduced into ordinary building.

Next to the wonder of these masonry achievements, the most striking aspect of Egyptian architecture is the monumental use made of the column. Even as early as the beginning of the 30th century, that great genius Imhotep was constructing his wonderful propylaeum at Sakkara with its slender tapering columns like bundles of reeds. Imhotep's columns, however, were not free-standing, but joined together, or to an adjoining wall, by sections of walling.

The free-standing column which is the glory of the hypostyle halls certainly developed from the wooden posts supporting the roof-beams of houses. Translated into stone, these supports sometimes continue to represent the timber post—often carved to imitate a bundle of lotus plants—but more often simply become square piers without capitals or bases. In the rock-cut temples of the end of the second millennium, however, the hewers boldly cut away the angles of these piers until they had become octagonal and, by repetition of the process, sixteen-sided. This sixteen-sided column, with a plain square slab as a capital and a round slab as a foundation, became the 'proto-Doric' column which we find in many of the great Egyptian buildings, notably at both the magnificent examples at Deir el Bahri.

The 'lotus' type of column, however, was meanwhile being developed. Employed at first, like its wooden prototype, solely for internal use—as in some of the pyramid temples—it begins to appear in the hypostyle halls of the temples. Eventually, it replaces the archaic 'proto-Doric' columns in the colonnades surrounding temples. At first 'reeded'—doubtless in recognition of its humble origin as a bundle of slender stems—it later assumes the simple conventional form employed with such dignity in the vast hall of Karnak. At the extreme end of this temple, in the hall erected about 1475 by Thothmes III, the columns adopt the downward taper found in connection with the columns of the Minoan culture; this experiment does not appear, however, to have been repeated elsewhere.

18. A Roman temple with a stately Corinthian portico
(Dugga)

19. An elliptical arch of brickwork covers the *iwan* of the Sassanian palace
of Ctesiphon

20. Roman tenements having balconied upper stories
(Ostia)

It may have been the bud-like form of the 'lotus' column which inspired the Egyptian architects—with, for them, rare genius—to vary the capitals of the two rows of taller columns passing down their larger hypostyle halls by expanding the 'bud' into a bell-like form. These bell capitals first appear with the Empire; at first employed internally; at the beginning of the second millennium they appear in the colonnades surrounding the court at Medinet Habu. The portico at Edfu, begun in 122 B.C., shows the same type of capital clumsily converted into a travesty of the classical 'Corinthian'. A square block of stone is always placed above a bell-shaped capital to prevent its fracture by the weight of the heavy lintels (Plate 6).

Nothing more clearly demonstrates the primitive nature of the architectural sensibility of the ancient Egyptians than the manner in which they distorted simple structural forms in order to introduce the sculptured ornament which seems to have been the method of expression which pleased them best. Columns converted into statues of gods or pharaohs, as at the Ramasseum or in some of the temples to Osiris, seem to us travesties of architecture. Worse still are the 'Hathor' columns, with their huge staring heads, as at Dendera. Clearly, they were a people who appreciated sculpture better than they did architecture.

The purely architectural ornament of the age is indeed exiguous. After the change from the brickwork of the Old Kingdom to the less manageable masonry of later days, no form of punctuation helps to relieve the bare walling. The edges of pylons are generally softened with a roll-moulding, apparently reminiscent of the corner posts of wooden houses. The roll moulding, carried across the top of the wall, is finished above with a simple coved cornice, often ornamented to represent the overhanging foliage of a palm tree (Plate 5).

This cornice is perhaps the most typical feature of Egyptian architecture. It also appears above most doorways, both in domestic architecture and also in the massive pylon-flanked portals of the temples. A disadvantage of the monumental style employed lay in the fact that the ponderous lintels required to span wide openings necessitated equally massive supports on either side. The portals of Egyptian temples are thus either comparatively narrow or, should a wide entrance be required where lateral space was lacking, the lintel might be omitted except for a stump of it projecting from either side of the opening. Egyptian architecture is of course a 'trabeated' style; that is to say, although the vault, constructed in brickwork, was well known and often employed, the only monumental material of the age was stone, and the heavy stone lintel the only approved method of spanning the openings of monumental structures.

The huge temples which represent the labour of two millennia seem today inexpressibly pathetic. It is not only that the glories of the age they represent have long passed away. They seem to know that they are not only architecturally prehistoric, but aesthetically aberrant. These vast piles of stone, rising beside the eternal river, play but a small part in the history of architecture—they are for the most part products not of genius, but of centuries of sweated toil. Approach them closely, however, and you can then understand their meaning. These great man-made cliffs of stone were ... picture-books (Plate 4).

Chapter IV

THE AEGEAN WORLD

As the Taurus Express, on its way from Assyria into the land of the Hittites, struggles across the high passes of the ancient mountain frontier, it begins to enter a very different world. The soft plain which bred the most ancient of the world's great civilizations gives place to a rock-strewn upland threaded by small streams, over which rugged peaks brood above the scanty traces of the most mysterious of all the great empires of the past.

The terraced fields of the Neolithic age cover the north-eastern littoral of the Mediterranean. The men who gathered the stones with which to build the rough walls retaining these fields would be glad to find a large slab of rock lying detached from its bed; such a slab, set on edge, would form an excellent foundation for the upper part of a terrace wall. This is the beginnings of megalithic architecture: that is to say, building with great stones set, not on their beds, but on edge.

These standing stones, called orthostats, were used by the Babylonians and Assyrians, who planted them on one end and inscribed them to serve as monuments or *stelae*. At a certain period—probably the end of the fourth millennium—the Mediterranean littoral was endowed with a magnificent megalithic architecture the finest examples of which may be found in the island of Malta where a remarkable series of temples yet remain standing. The plan of each comprises a pair of chambers set across the axis, entered from a courtyard which, like the enclosing wall of the temple itself, is of an oval shape. Between outer and inner chamber is a magnificent orthostatic portal flanked on either side by niches; the axis culminates in the usual niche or, in at least one example, another small chamber set parallel to the others.

The notable feature of the architecture of these temples is the fact that the orthostats form the foundation to upper stages of walling constructed in huge stones set as ordinary rubble. Within the chambers, the orthostatic dadoes are often beautifully finished, each stone being squared-up to fit snugly against its neighbour; the masonry above may show signs of an attempt at coursing. Clearly the creators of these megalithic temples were builders of no mean skill.

The region in which evidences of megalithic monumental building may be found includes the peninsula of Asia Minor. The natural building material for ordinary houses is ordinary rubble, but by the end of the second millennium the region had come within the sphere of Sumerian influence and was beginning to employ sun-dried brick. The wetter climate, however, made it imperative to construct such walls above a foundation of rubble stone. In permanent buildings of a monumental nature it was desirable to raise the foundation even higher and base the structure upon a stone plinth having the nature of a dado. This was the reason for the association of a megalithic technique with ordinary brick architecture.

Anatolia forms the westward end of that hilly region which seems to have been the cradle not only of modern civilization but also of its architecture, a fact which makes it all the more regrettable that its continued inaccessibility has caused it to remain for the most part still unexplored. Its original buildings must have been of rubble stone; the climate postulates a strong roof almost certainly pitched to withstand a snowfall. That the region had by the year 3000 B.C. already achieved an extremely sophisticated architectural style is shown by excavations conducted at Tepe Gawra near Mosul some twenty years ago.

The buildings at Tepe Gawra were built in the universal brick-work of Mesopotamia. They were, however, regular rectangles of some length and thus almost certainly were covered with a pitched roof. Their internal ground plan is complicated and includes provision for a wide staircase of several flights leading to an upper story —an astonishing development at such an early period. The most interesting feature of each is the open porch or *iwan* set in the principal front of each building: an architectural reproduction of the open-ended reception tent of the nomadic chieftain which plays a large part in the house-plans not only of the Persian highlands and Anatolia but eventually firmly establishes itself in the architecture of Islam. In their elevational treatment the Tepe Gawra buildings were astonishingly advanced, punctuation being achieved by well-spaced pilasters joined by wall-arches constructed in orders. The builders were sufficiently familiar with the arch to be able to vault ground-floor apartments with it; these early barrel-vaults however are always segmental and never spring from above the ground level.

The heart of Anatolia provides a natural situation in which to found a nation. North and south is the sea; east is the rampart of the towering Taurus range. At the time when the ancient civilizations of the Middle East were paramount, no formidable race threatened from across the narrow western straits. At the beginning of the third millennium, therefore, a powerful nation was rising in the peninsula of Asia Minor.

The Hittites were essentially a military race. Culturally they do not compare with the Babylonians, whom they overwhelmed early in the second millennium, or the Egyptians, with whom they fought untiringly for more than a century at a period during which that great nation was at the height of its power. But the sites of their great cities still cover the land, and much of their building may yet be seen. On the architecture of at least one nation, Assyria, they left an indelible stamp.

The culture of the Hittites did not compare with those of their neighbours. The Hittite home was a mere square hovel, additions to which were simply achieved by building on another room in accordance with the whim of the owner. Such buildings may originally have been flat-roofed; there is evidence, however, that external influences eventually brought about the introduction of the pitched roof in the larger houses, which then became planned on more orderly lines so that they could be gathered together under one ridge. This was apparently supported by a wall passing down the axis of the rectangle of rooms which is noticeable as forming the basis of the plans of large houses of the period of the Empire.

The Hittite great house is a structure of considerable significance in the history of architecture. It seems to derive not from the Sumerian or plainsman's house but from the hillsman's type as discovered at

Tepe Gawra. The courtyard, being neither required by climatic conditions nor suited to the hilly countryside, was omitted from the plan; the house proper being a block of apartments covered by a pitched roof of considerable span. In order to compensate for the lack of courtyard accommodation for stabling and other offices the main block was made two-storied in order that these could be sited at ground level with the living apartments on the floor over. Thus we find the *piano nobile* definitely established; indeed it is from these houses that the Byzantine, the mediaeval, and our own houses of today are derived. The main block of the Hittite great house was often flanked by a narrower range, under a lean-to roof, containing smaller rooms of which one was a square newel staircase.

Hittite public buildings have not yet been fully examined. Such palaces as have been explored seem to date from long after the period of the Empire and suggest a Phrygian origin. There were originally no temples; the Hittite gods were worshipped in natural grottoes buried among the mountain crags which guarded their cities. Later in their history, however, they seem to have built rural temples, perhaps at first merely shelters covering some religious object, which eventually became square towers or *hilani;* the *hilani* sanctuary is believed to have been the model for that of the early Hebrew temple.

Essentially a military nation, the chief Hittite contribution to architecture seems to have been displayed by the walls of these cities, the chief of which, Hattusas, became, about the year 2000 B.C., their capital. At first, however, the might of the Hittite army, aided by the natural defences of the country, appears to have been considered a sufficient guarantee; citadels, therefore, were all that were deemed necessary. It was not until the middle of the second millennium that pressure upon the western flank encouraged the Hittites, engaged in their ferocious struggle against Egypt, to encircle their cities with huge walls of mud-brick, reinforced with rubble stone.

The outer wall of the city of Hattusas forms one of the most notable monuments of the Hittite Empire. Built during the 14th century B.C., it was entirely constructed of stone rubble held between two faces made of the same material but with much larger stones. The gates were merely tunnels four or five feet in width, their sides corbelled overhead to form a very acutely-pointed arch. A century later, however, two much wider gates, twin-towered after the Babylonian fashion, were made in this wall. The outer and inner stone facings were carried over the opening by corbelled arches rising from enormous orthostats twice the height of a man and proportionally massive. These features, common to most important portals of the era of the Empire, are often rudely carved to represent lions (Plate 7); here we clearly detect the origin of the famous winged-bull orthostats of Assyria. The mud-brick walling of the better houses of the period were protected by rough dadoes of orthostats; here, again, we observe the source of the Assyrian system of wall-decoration.

The importance of the Hittite contribution to the history of architecture cannot be too highly stressed; thus it is greatly to be hoped that exploration of their cities, so long neglected, will now be vigorously prosecuted. It is true that they were unskilful builders; the rough material they were forced to employ produced untidy mud-and-rubble walling or massive cyclopean piles which could never have compared with the sophisticated creations of Sumerian architects. But the Sumerian tradition perished while that of the Hittites survived to impress the ancient Greeks, to influence the Byzantines, and, at the hands of those experienced architects, to become the ancestor of the domestic building style of mediaeval Europe.

The Hittites were the most European of the ancient empire-builders and built in European fashion. They had neither the arch nor the stone lintel to assist them with construction of monumental buildings. But they had ample supplies of timber and could use it to erect two-storied houses, covered with spreading roofs, and containing wide-spanned apartments the proportions of which compared favourably with the megarons of the later Aegeans.

The Hittites were the first of the early civilizations to build on hilly sites. Thus from the first they ignored courtyard planning as too wasteful of labour in levelling. But for their city walls they demonstrated their skill as engineers by constructing terraces ranged along the contour of the hillside and carried on a system of cells divided by diaphragm walls. From this elaborate site work was developed the great terraced platforms of their successors in the hill-country of Anatolia and Syria where many a temple and castle is founded upon the same system of vaulted undercrofts carrying a level court over a natural slope.

At the beginning of the 12th century B.C., when Phrygian hordes, invulnerably encased in bronze armour, swept across Anatolia and overwhelmed the homeland of the Hittites, the survivors fled across the Taurus to their colonies in northern Syria. During the first quarter of the last millennium B.C. they succeeded in withstanding Assyrian pressure and maintaining their cultural independence. Hittite architecture of this period exhibits the usual monumental portals, now embellished with orthostatic dadoes sculptured in a fashion which was however being copied with far finer results by their powerful neighbours.

The building style of the hill-country, from which the architecture of the Hittites is descended, makes great use of poles cut from the suckers of the poplar tree. Such poles were at first employed as rafters; they can, however, also be used as props. One of their uses was to support a beam carrying the rafter-feet over an external porch or loggia such as could be provided at one angle of a house or in the middle of one of its long sides. Poplar poles were the ancestors of the peristyles of the ancients; the Hittites used them for porticoes.

Learning—probably from the Egyptians—the use of the stone lintel, they then introduced the column as a means of widening their great portals. The Hittite portal, with its central column, was copied by Sargon of Assyria at Khorsabad about 710 B.C., a generation after the final submergence of Hittite power. At Khorsabad, how-ever, two columns are employed; the Assyrians seem to have had the last word in everything.

We now abandon our brief investigation into the primitive culture of the turbulent Hittites in order to examine that of a very different people—perhaps, from the cultural aspect, the most remarkable race the world has ever seen—the mysterious Minoans. Throughout most of the period we have been considering, while Babylonia and Egypt have been struggling to establish their respective civilizations and defend them from enemies without, the islanders of Crete, secure behind their coasts, have been steadily achieving a state of culture far in advance of either.

Three centuries before Hammurabi founded the Babylonian empire, the Cretans were building the first great palace at Knossos; two centuries later, when Egypt was enslaved beneath the yoke of

21. A city gate of Imperial Rome
(Trier)

22. An early church of 'basilican' form in Rome

the Hyksos, the island palace had grown into a structure which would, with the introduction of a few modern conveniences, serve perfectly well as a luxury hotel for 20th-century tourists.

Minoan architecture stands alone in history. Borrowing but little from beyond the confines of the island, it bequeathed practically nothing to the ancient world, from which it vanished almost unnoticed. The Cretans, secure and contented in their little country which appears to have provided all their requirements, probably stayed at home and discouraged visitors.

The period during which this unique civilization flourished occupies approximately the years 1700-1200 B.C. During these five hundred years the Minoans appear to have enjoyed the existence of lotus-eaters. The frescoes with which the walls of their palaces were covered show them flitting through the centuries, gaily attired, seemingly forever dancing, feasting, and being entertained by their heroes and heroines in the bull-rings. No stern Osiris or gloomy Anubis disturbed their dreams; no spear or shield hung on their walls.

But the day came when the savage tribes of Europe, building ships and taking to the sea, sighted the island paradise of Minos. And then the unsubstantial dream which had survived for half a millennium faded away, unmourned, into oblivion. It has been said that the throne room of Minos, as discovered by Sir Arthur Evans, was in a state of such obviously panic-stricken confusion as to make it the most dramatic room ever excavated (Fig. 1).

There is no other architectural style with which one can compare the Minoan. The houses seem to have been of the usual ancient Mediterranean type: a square or rectangle with a flat roof. Stone was the principal building material, good wrought masonry being found even in small houses. Typically, the Minoans passed some three millennia at a bound and introduced half-timber work into the wall-faces, probably in an attempt to make the structure earthquake-proof.

No traditional plan-forms were followed or initiated. Rooms were set out where required; although tidied up into sophisticated rectangular complexes, the house-plans seem to reflect the easy-going nature of the Minoans and refuse to be further disciplined. Buildings were multi-storied; owing to this fact and the rocky nature of some of the sites which made considerable excavation necessary, the architects advanced to modern times and provided light-wells. Loggias and sun-porches were much favoured; some of the larger rooms (incorrectly called, today, megarons) had their outer walls pierced by a number of what would nowadays be called french windows giving access to these.

Fig. 1. A doorway in Knossos

As multi-storied houses required well-planned staircases, the architects provided these; copying at first the Hittite form, the 'dog-leg' type they employed was not seen in Europe until the 17th century A.D. Excavation of sites led to terracing and thence to monumental flights of steps such as those bordering the 'bull-rings'—which were, however, rectangular areas. The principal entrance to the palace at Knossos is reached by passing up a magnificent stairway flanked by monumental buildings, the whole forming a propylæa resembling, on a far grander scale, that leading to the Acropolis at Athens.

The introduction of half-timber work endowed the Minoan buildings with a character quite unlike anything to be discovered again until comparatively recent times. For example, there were actually large windows, subdivided by mullion and transom, formed in the framing. The heavy beams carrying the roofs above loggias and the half-landings of stairs were supported by rows of wooden columns; these themselves were entirely original in design, being tapered downwards instead of in the normal fashion adopted by all other styles. This is probably due to the fact that the column built of stone blocks being unknown to the Minoans, they had never felt the urge to suggest stability by tapering their supports upwards; a wooden post stuck in the ground looks more stable point downwards.

The Minoans do not seem to have employed large building units such as great halls or temples. Their palaces consist of a series of small units, mostly single rooms, collected together without regimentation. Their architectural style is thus a free one, employing no punctuation except in the marshalling of columns and the spacing of openings. In all architectural history, no single style would more generously repay careful analysis than the Minoan. Growing out of nothing, in five centuries it attained, unassisted, a culmination which the rest of the world, forever troubled by material and spiritual strife, in three millennia failed to reach. It almost seems as if, like Icarus, it reached too close to an apotheosis.

The ancient civilizations have marched before us and passed on their way. It is now the turn of the barbarians of Europe to take up the tale. About the middle of the third millennium they began to reach out into the ancient world, their pioneers founding small towns along the Asiatic coast of the Aegean. One of these settlements was Troy; it was well-fortified and lasted five centuries or so—then the Hittites sacked it and kept it in subjection for another five centuries. But just at the time when Ahmose I was founding the XVIIIth dynasty of Egypt, Trojans took advantage of Hittite preoccupation and refounded their city—now to become famous in all the ancient world as the city of Helen.

Within the roughly-constructed but immensely strong walls of Troy were buildings of a class not yet encountered in architectural history. We have become familiar with the ordinary house of the settled agriculturalist who has become a townsman; we have now to consider the results of a sudden transformation to urban status of a pastoral nomad such as inhabited the Europe of those days. These early invaders of the ancient world were probably tent-dwellers by instinct who had barely settled down to the enjoyment of permanent living accommodation before they found themselves the occupants of a fortified town.

The translation of a nomad's tent into terms of architecture has already been indicated by the subdivision of the early Sumerian house into an inner chamber preceded by a reception room which recalls in solid form the side wall of the tent opened up as a sort of loggia. In the well-timbered countries of Europe, the stage may have been reached where the permanent house had become a rectangular structure, perhaps of blockwork, certainly having a pitched roof and possibly provided with some kind of loggia or porch, the roof of which was propped up by fir poles instead of the poplar ones of Anatolia. The ridge of such a building could be carried by the medial wall separating house and loggia. It would not have been a very difficult matter to convert a structure of this class into a house of Mediterranean type.

But these European people were tribal. Their tents were gathered round that of the chieftain who was their protector and whom they served. His abode, also, had to be converted into architecture. The greater tent was more in the nature of a hall having a wide span requiring a row of poles to support the roof-tree which passed down the centre of the building. As no monumental significance was attached to the home of the chieftain, excessive height was not desired; thus a wide roof placed no great overturning strain upon the low walling whence it sprang, even, as must have have been the case, had the walls been of rubble stone. The keynote of the hall was floor-space; in this factor alone lay its claim to architectural importance.

With the arrival of the megaron—the great hall of the Aegean culture—a new class of structure enters the architectural sphere. Each megaron was provided with a spacious fire hearth set between two of the posts obstructing the centre of the building; above it, part of the roof was left uncovered in order to allow the smoke to escape. After the middle of the second millennium, the roof-design of the megaron was modified so as to provide a proper smoke-hole. The roof-tree was doubled to form a pair of purlins, between which the aperture could be trimmed. This change from roof-tree to purlins was of the greatest importance in determining the plan of the great hall of the future; the abolition of the central row of posts in favour of two rows signified an improvement which was nothing short of revolutionary. It was found in practice that by dividing the span into three parts of which the central was not greater than those next the walls, properly-supported purlins could be made capable of sustaining any roof without the

23. A typical Byzantine village church with a central dome surrounded by four projecting wings (Geraki)

24. The nave of the church of the Nativity at Bethlehem

25. Earthquakes have overthrown the columns from the apse of this sixth-century Syrian church (Kalaat Siman)

26. Its form is echoed by hundreds of Crusader churches scattered throughout Europe (Melle)

27. The church of Sts. Sergius and Bacchus at Constantinople is the
ancestor of the churches of western Europe

28. '*Hypsosis*', the piled-up mass of the Hagia Sophia
at Constantinople

assistance of a roof-tree or ridge which might obstruct the smoke-hole; this early discovery of the principle of the cantilever was of the greatest importance when it came to the design of the classical temple.

The megaron of the Aegean civilization is an ancestor of the Parthenon. The early halls, however, were in all probability quite unimpressive except as regards their capacity for accommodating a large gathering within their humble walls. The later megaron had its roof supported by four wooden posts, surrounding the fire-hearth and framing the smoke-hole above this. Even the earlier megaron often had an open portico at one end, a sort of *iwan* above which the gable was supported by a pair of wooden posts similar to those of the loggias of lesser houses. The perfected megaron has an anteroom interposed between it and its porch, the whole coming under the one long roof.

The Aegean culture established itself all round the coasts and islands of the sea whence it derives its name. The most famous of its cities is that of Troy. Its headquarters appear to have been on the Peloponnesus, where two cities, Tiryns and Mycenae, still exhibit architectural remains of considerable interest. Each of these famous sites possesses an acropolis, surrounded by walls of an impressive strength and containing the palace quarter of the city. The principal building is in each case the megaron. At Tiryns, a spacious courtyard spreads before the portico of the great hall; groups of lesser apartments, some of them entered through loggias, are set out around the edges of this yard, which is entered through an elaborately-planned gatehouse incorporating porticoes both inside and out.

The most striking remains visible today are the mighty walls of the acropolis, built, about 1400 B.C., at a time when the prosperous Aegean civilization was already beginning to fear an onslaught from would-be successors. It is interesting to note that the same pressure of barbarians from what is now the Balkans was the reason for the construction of the walls of Hattusas about the same time as those of the Aegean cities. There is nevertheless a great difference between the two styles of military architecture. To begin with, the Hittite fortifications are town walls, surrounding an occupied area and intended to be monumental as well as military. In the case of the Aegean cities, however, the area fortified is that of the acropolis or citadel, occupied only by the palace. Instead of the imposing twin-towered gatehouse beloved of the ancients, there is a cunningly-planned entrance passage, strongly fortified, ending in a simple entry.

At Mycenae, however, the entry is embellished by what is almost the only known example of Aegean architectural ornament, the famous lion tympanum. The gateway is a trilithon formed of two immense orthostats spanned by an equally massive lintel, to prevent the fracture of which by earthquakes a triangular space has been left over it. This space is covered by a corbelled arch in Hittite style, the tympanum being filled by the crude sculpture referred to. The origin of the device—two seated lions guarding a column—is unknown; possibly it represents the badge of the Aegean civilization which produced this monument. It is presumably local; the column is of the Minoan type, but not tapered (Plate 8). The device appears again, centuries later, in a Phrygian tomb in Anatolia.

The Aegean world, together with the Hittite empire, was eventually swept away by the mail-clad tribesmen who poured out of Europe at the beginning of the 12th century B.C. In the Hittite capital may be seen the remains of several Phrygian palaces the plans of which clearly show their European origin. Each has a megaron, while loggia-fronted groups also of Aegean type are grouped, in recognition of some more easterly influence, round a square courtyard entered through a double portal.

While the Hittite empire was withering away before the Phrygians, their kinsmen, the Achaeans, who had already taken to the sea and swept into oblivion the wonders of Minoan Crete, were in process of reducing the empire of the Aegeans. 1184 B.C. is given as the year of the fall of Troy. The fortresses of Tiryns and Mycenae may have held out for a century or even less, but by the end of the century all seems to have been finally submerged.

The invaders who took upon themselves the mantle of the Aegeans began to develop two main regional cultures. First of these was the Dorian, which comprised Greece proper but eventually spread into Sicily and beyond. The archipelago and the coasts of Asia Minor became the land of the Ionians. The Dorians, taking the lead at first, founded the philosophical and social structure which has made the Greeks famous in history; the Ionians, profiting from their closer contact with the ancient world, made the primitive architecture of the Dorians a thing of beauty which was to become thenceforth the basis of European style.

Although the history of classical Greece begins with the first Olympiad of 776 B.C., no notable buildings appear for more than a century after this date. For the Dorians, the building art was in its infancy. Houses were of mud-brick, raised upon foundations of rubble stone. The democratic nature of Greek society discouraged the erection of great houses; the megaron of the Aegeans was but a memory. As the Dorians began to develop monumental architecture, however, and began to search for a type of structure which would serve as a house for their god, it was to the megaron that they turned for inspiration. Thus the great hall which had housed an Aegean king became the model for a Greek temple.

At first the temple followed the plan of the early megaron with its central rows of posts and a deep portico with the gable over supported by one or two pillars or even stone piers. As late as the middle of the 6th century, one of the temples at Paestum in Italy was built with a central row of pillars passing down the centre; this arrangement, however, to all intents and purposes went out of fashion a century or so earlier in favour of the less-obstructed plan seen in the four-pillar megaron.

There are indications that the Doric temple is not a direct descendant of the Aegean megaron but like it shows strong affinity with the great tent of the nomad chieftain. In temperate climates where neither wind nor rain are likely to be too persistent, there is a kind of tent which covers a considerable area and has a roof propped up by several rows of poles within the outer row of which are hung curtains to form walls. Examination of Doric temples of the 6th and 5th centuries B.C, will make it clear that the basis of the design is that of a three-aisled tent having four rows of supports; the walls, like the tent-curtains, are inserted partitions playing no part in supporting the roof.

In the blazing heat of a Greek summer, the loggias attached to the southern side of the house of the period must have been welcome features to the occupants. Applied to the walls of the temple, they both served to keep its interior refreshingly cool and at the same time provided the building with a most distinctive architectural embellishment. From the lateral colonnades sprang the roof, further supported by two internal rows of columns, these spaced so that not more than one-third of the span was given up to the central area. This division into three can be seen in all but the very smallest temples.

Around the inner rows of columns was built the walls of the temple itself. In many of the early examples these were of mud brick, raised upon good masonry foundations and protected, in addition, by dadoes of orthostats. These walls seem to have played no part in carrying the roof except where, as gables, they were carried by the colonnades at the ends of the building and were thus of no great height.

At first the pillar-work of the classical temples was of timber posts, as in the 7th-century temple of Hera at Olympia. A century later we see at Corinth the remains of a temple with monolithic columns which clearly represent the translation from wood to orthostatic architecture. The standard arrangement, however, came to be the column built up of stone drums in the same way as ordinary masonry and tapered, in the traditional fashion of early stone structures, in order to give an appearance of stability. It is these sturdy tapered columns which form the fundamental feature of Doric architecture.

The simple capitals of these primitive columns carried the lintel. At first of wood, its replacement by a stone architrave necessitated a closer spacing of the columns supporting this. On top of the architrave rested the heavy rafters, the ends of which were eventually masked by vertical stones known as triglyphs, between which square slabs or metopes provided an architectural form of wind-filling. Above the rafters, the eaves of the heavy stone-slabbed roof became embellished to form a cornice; this, with the frieze of triglyphs and metopes below it and the plain lintel supporting all, formed the classical entablature (Plate 9).

During the 7th century B.C., Greek culture was developing along the lines which have made it forever memorable. It appears as though the Greeks intended that the stones of their buildings should serve as memorials, not only of the skill of builders, but also of the mental processes of philosophers. From the combination of column and entablature with which their monumental structures were surrounded they evolved an architectural rule, known to us as the Doric Order. This rule strictly regulated the proportions of every detail included in

29. The interior of the Hagia Sophia is a vast unencumbered hall covered by a great dome

31. The interior of a seventh-century Armenian church (Zromi)

30. An example of church architecture of the days of the Crusades (Tarragona)

the design. Scale could vary in accordance with the size of the structure; proportions, however, were unchangeable.

The effect of this regimentation becomes noticeable towards the middle of the 6th century, at which period the internal colonnade was becoming a standard feature of the temple plan. The pitch of the roof made it essential for the inner supports to be higher than the outer. In accordance with the rule, higher columns would have to be thicker; such obstructions were avoided, however, by building two stages of columns, each of which was correctly proportioned and thus actually much thinner than would have been the case had tall columns been employed (Plate 14).

By the middle of the 6th century the Doric temple had become the principal monumental building of the Greeks, both in their home-land and also in the western colonies. It was at this time that the first Parthenon was built upon the acropolis at Athens. The disaster of 480, when the capital was destroyed by the Persians, was followed by the Periclean Age, during which the city achieved the zenith of its architectural expression. In 454 the existing Parthenon was begun. The principal interest in this building, which as the symbol of its era has become endowed with an almost mystic significance, lies in the optical refinements which its architect introduced into his design. Ictinus considered every possible psychological aberration with which the human mind can be afflicted when examining a structure and took the trouble to make allowances for these. When we observe the slightly bulging columns, leaning gently inwards as they rise from the almost imperceptibly curved foundation towards an entablature similarly distorted, we realize that the Parthenon was designed, not by an engineer, but by a philosopher endowed with a deep insight into the minds of his fellow men.

While the Dorians of the Greek homeland and its western colonies were building their temples and perfecting their remarkable architectural style, their fellow-countrymen away in the east were developing along rather different lines. Apart from the vestiges of the somewhat primitive Aegean culture, from which the Dorians took little except the megaron plan and the structural principle which this illustrated, the western Greeks were subjected to few external influences. The Ionians, however, had ventured into the fringes of an ancient land, upon which Babylonian, Hittite, and Assyrian had already left their marks. Throughout the centuries there had always been the menace of the hill-men from Persia; these, after sweeping down again and again for brief incursions into the plains, had at last achieved an overwhelming supremacy over the remnants of ancient races and had founded a mighty empire. It was to the fringe of this successor to the great primæval civilizations that the Ionian Greeks tenaciously clung.

In the hands of the Ionians, the Dorian temple-plan underwent some modifications. The wealthy eastern cities, planted upon east-west trade routes, were soon able to build much larger structures, surrounded by two rows of colonnades and with deep porticoes full of columns like the hypostyle halls of the past. Chief of all these great buildings was the temple of Diana at Ephesus, founded about 560 B.C. Ignoring the primitive Doric Order, the Ionians developed one of their own. Contact with the masonry skill of the Old World enabled them from the start to construct stone columns of a more slender type than those of the Doric buildings; thus the proportions of the Ionic Order are far more graceful. The most noticeable feature of the style, however, is the form of capital employed. The Doric capital was probably simply a modification of that employed by the Minoans. The Ionic capital, however, was a scientific device introduced to broaden the top of the column along the line of the lintel, thus helping with the support of this and enabling the space between the columns to be widened. The Ionic capital, which passed through innumerable modifications before attaining the form in which it appears at Athens, is presumably simply an adaptation of the short length of timber through which a wooden pole may be joined to the underside of a slender lintel. Any people employing loggias supported by poles must have discovered how to use this device; it may be found all over Europe and Asia at this day (Fig. 2).

The development of the Ionic Order had the effect of introducing an element of refinement into the proportions of Greek temples. The huddle of sturdy Doric columns gave place to well-spaced rows of slender shafts, graceful and far less obstructive. Introduced into Athens at the middle of the 5th century, it was at first used only internally, as in the Propylaea, or in porticos such as those of the Erechtheion.

Despite its popularity in the land of its origin, it was fundamentally unsuited to peristylar architecture, owing to the fact that its side view was never intended to be seen. A modified form was devised for use at the external angles of buildings, but even this became unsightly if employed in the internal angles of the peristylar courtyards which were to become such important features of Classical architecture.

Fig. 2. The origin of Ionic architecture

The essential feature of the Ionic capital was the pair of volutes which, by spreading the top of the column, had thereby helped it to support the architrave above. It was these same volutes which were becoming so unmanageable; to reduce them, however, meant that the principal interest would be removed. Experiments upon the expansion and embellishment of the portion of the capital whence the volutes sprang resulted in the creation of a new type of bell-shaped feature, ornamented with fronds of acanthus fern, out of which angle volutes of Ionic form were allowed to emerge on a much reduced scale. The 4th century B.C. witnessed the first shy appearance of this capital—fundamental feature of that Corinthian Order (Plate 18) which is the Greek Baroque—throughout the Dorian world. The Ionians, content with their own magnificent architecture, were less enthusiastic concerning it.

The Phrygians, hot in pursuit of the defeated Hittites, penetrated sufficiently far eastwards to become effectively orientalized. In the Ionian districts, however, the Greek *œcus* or private house remained a block of apartments including a megaron and gathered together under a wide Hittite roof. But the climate of Greece itself encouraged the provision of shady courtyards and loggias; eventually the courtyard house became the standard Hellenic form, acquiring stables, offices, and an *andron* or reception room in the oriental manner.

The Hellenic Greeks were no great planners. In point of scale their buildings were far from imposing; the whole of their greatest temple, that of Diana at Ephesus, could have been erected inside the hypostyle hall which forms but a part of the temple at Karnak. Only a quarter or so of the Greek temple was enclosed by walls; the remainder was occupied by the colonnaded porticoes.

Greek architecture, like that of the Egyptians, is primarily concerned with columnar effect. But the former, instead of hiding its wonders within walls, displays them to the world. Perhaps it was for this reason that the Greek philosophers took such pains in the ordering of their architecture—to the undying glory of their name.

Pathos seems to hang like a cloud over the ruins of Egypt, where the ponderous columns brood over the empty sites of cities which in their day rejoiced, passed away, and were forgotten. But the solitary shaft which soars above the wreckage of a Greek temple seems to be exulting in the certain knowledge that its children have marched, invincible, down the centuries—that there is not, in the whole civilized world, a city street which does not still pay it tribute.

Chapter V

HELLENISM

By the 4th century B.C., the Periclean Age of Athens had become a memory. The Dorian world, with its wide-flung colonies reaching even to southern France, still lingered in the shadow of sturdy temples raised in an antique style. The Ionians, however, straddling the trade routes between the new world and the old, and drawing more and more upon the wisdom of the ancient cultures, were forging rapidly ahead of their western brethren. Hellenic culture, spreading from Athens through Thessaly into Macedonia, had now embraced the whole of the Aegean littoral. The populations of the rich Ionian city-states were continually being reinforced from vigorous Macedonian stock; in return, the Ionians transmitted a modicum of the knowledge they were so assiduously absorbing, so that the Macedonian cities were becoming almost as fine as those of Asia Minor.

It was the Macedonian Alexander who finally paid the debt in full by removing the threat which had for so long hung on the skirts of the eastern Greeks, the utter rout of the Persians in 323 suddenly making the whole of the ancient world a Greek province. The colonizing abilities of the victors were soon displayed. Under the Ptolemies, Egypt experienced a brief return to her former glories; the Seleucids lost little time in spreading Greek culture along the shores of the Levant and deep into the ancient world within.

The Ptolemaic contribution to architecture was probably chiefly represented by Alexandria itself. It is thus greatly to be deplored that this magnificent Greek city has today so entirely vanished. Of all its fine buildings—even the towering pharos which was a wonder of the ancient world—nothing is left today. Save for a few subterranean tombs, no vestige remains even to tantalize us with a glimpse into vanished glories. The famous public buildings of what was perhaps the most beautiful city of ancient days have been utterly lost to us.

Nor can we obtain any clue as to the Alexandrian style of architecture from provincial examples attributable to this period. It is indeed painfully obvious that upon many Egyptian builders, firm in the grip of an architectural tradition which had already survived for close on three millennia, the Greeks made little impression. Attempts to introduce the Corinthian Order, for example, merely resulted in the production of such shocking barbarisms as may be seen at Edfu or Philae, where the wretched Egyptian carvers have tried to apply caricatures of the Corinthian ornament to clumsy bell-capitals of a type which had been designed well over a thousand years before and had since remained happily unaffected by any external influence. These provincial buildings show us, moreover, that neither in planning nor in the ancient art of masonry could the Greeks teach their new protectorate anything it wished to learn. It is therefore possible that the Ptolemaic contribution to Egyptian architecture was to all intents and purposes negligible and Alexandria a purely Greek city entirely laid out and built by Hellenic designers and craftsmen. Most indications suggest that ancient Egypt ignored Hellenism; it therefore seems possible that Ptolemaic architecture never became a style worthy of serious consideration.

It was otherwise with those extensive areas which fell to the Seleucids. Ancient civilizations had vanished, but left behind them a strong tradition of culture. The Greeks arrived to find an excellent source of building-stone ready to hand and no existing masonry style to hinder them in its use. The Ionian city-states, glorying in their wealth and culture, provided secure bases for expansion eastwards; the Seleucid empire was ripe for development.

In order to by-pass the mountain zone which cut off Asia Minor from Syria and Mesopotamia, a new advanced base was set up in 301 B.C. This was Antioch in Syria, eventually to become one of the greatest cities of the world. Beyond Antioch, a belt of ten cities were founded along the fringe of the great desert between Damascus and Amman, the ancient Philadelphia. Eastwards from the Decapolis a chain of new cities maintained the great trade route. In the heart of dead Babylonia, Seleucia rose beside the Tigris; westwards, on the banks of the Euphrates, strongly fortified Dura-Europos provided a link between it and the Syrian cities. Fifty years after its foundation, Antioch severed its political allegiance to Macedonia and became the capital of the Seleucid empire.

In this fashion the culture of the Greeks found its way into the world of the ancients. The old Babylonian civilizations had passed away; their country was already returning to the desert whence it had so long ago emerged. In more fertile Syria, however, a vigorous population maintained something of Hittite, Assyrian, and even Egyptian cultural traditions. It was in the midst of this jumble of Phoenicians, Hebrews, and Aramaic-speaking semi-nomads from the eastern deserts that the Greek cities were founded. In the study of architectural influences it should always be remembered that the political subjection of a country does not usually result in the sudden wholesale adoption by that country of the cultural practices of the victors; the latter, although presumably physically stronger, will almost certainly be far weaker numerically than the population which has been subjected. We cannot expect therefore that the emergence of a Seleucid empire immediately resulted in the complete Hellenization of the Levant and the prompt erection of scores of great masonry buildings in the style which had for centuries been developing in the Ionian lands.

Indeed, it appears that as late as the dawn of the Christian era there was still little change from the long-established regional tradition. Domestic planning continues to develop along Babylonian rather than Hellenic lines. There is no trace of the axially-entered megaron in the plans of great houses; the reception room entered in the middle of one side is the most noticeable unit. The principal innovation is the introduction of the column. Portals tend to give place to porticoes; loggias appear in the courtyards of large structures.

Military architecture was not neglected. Throughout the duration of the Seleucid empire its security was continually menaced by the Parthians, the latest representatives of the predatory hill-men who forever threatened people of the plains. The Hellenistic fortifications of Dura were perhaps the finest the world had yet seen. The wall-tower had now come into full employment as a flanking protection to the face of the main wall; the twin-towered gatehouses had developed from the Assyrian through the Hittite to achieve such perfection as may be seen in the Palmyrene Gate of Dura. A refined, typically Hellenic, form of corbelled arch—legacy of Hittite and Mycenaean —appears in these fortifications of Dura.

The Classical temple does not appear at all in the Seleucid empire; the local population had for centuries employed the plan approved by both Assyrian and Egyptian. Entrances in the middle of the side wall were universal. If an anteroom or portico existed, the sanctuary was set at right angles to this; otherwise the sanctuary itself was entered in the ancient fashion. All buildings were small; there were no sur-rounding colonnades. As the Hellenic house-plan, with its occasional groupings of loggias or porticoes within the courtyard, established itself in the Seleucid world, temple forecourts were sometimes em-bellished in a similar manner.

It was probably the continual menace of the Parthians that delayed the development of Hellenism in the Seleucid realm, which from its very inception had to engage in continual struggle with these deter-mined foes. Only the Decapolis itself seems to have succeeded in maintaining complete independence; to the fact that it did so we may attribute the subsequent magnificent achievements in this region. Eastwards, Dura, Seleucia, and other Hellenistic outposts, with their mixed populations and comparatively feeble ties with the west, were dominated alternately by Greek and Parthian, and therefore never developed a notable architectural style.

While the great capital city of Antioch was alone bearing the standard of Hellenism in its new Seleucid empire, the old Ionian regions were forging magnificently ahead. About 250 B.C., when the Seleucids achieved their political independence of Macedonia, other dynasties—such as that of Pergamon—were arising in the beautiful cities of the Ionians. It was here that Hellenistic architecture reached its zenith, thence to spread throughout the world.

We have already seen how the Greek plan is founded upon two main units, the ordinary private house and the great hall or megaron. The development of the latter into the classical temple has already been discussed; the Hellenistic era produced no further modifi-cations of note until the architecture of the Greeks encountered that of the Etruscans and in combination produced the Roman style.

32. A typical Byzantine church of 'four-poster' type
(St. Luke in Stiris)

33. The twelfth-century Byzantine cathedral at Vladimir in Russia

In the great temple, the Aegean megaron loses itself, to appear no more.

In the Ionian littoral, however, a reduced version of the Aegean megaron appears in a class of private house which follows the Anatolian or Hittite type of plan rather than the oriental. One side of the pitched roof of the megaron is carried down as a lean-to covering a row of private apartments provided along the side of the main hall itself. It is these compact dwellings which form the link between the Hittite house and the Byzantine which is the ancestor of the house of mediæval Europe. For the time being, nevertheless, it was the spacious courtyard surrounded by ranges of apartments which developed into the great house of the period.

It is indeed the ordinary private house which provides the key to the planning achievements of the Hellenistic world. The tent with one side open had become the house with the pillared loggia along one side. One of the achievements of the philosophical Greek mind had been the properly-designed town-plan consisting of a grid of straight streets. The construction of a row of loggia-fronted houses upon one such street might produce a continuous loggia common to all the houses concerned. This is presumably the origin of that important feature, the *stoa,* which dominates Hellenistic urban architecture to such a remarkable degree (Fig. 3).

Stoas were built along the edge of the agora or market place. Ideal as a protection for shoppers, they were also provided on either side of the main streets. In the last two centuries of the pagan era, Antioch, Damascus, and Palmyra were embellished with magnificent colonnaded streets, whose stately columns, stalking beside the way, advertised to the world the glories of Hellenism (Plate 10).

In Hellenistic hands the stoa developed an architectural unit or bay, each of these being a portion of a double passage enclosed by a colonnade to the front and a wall to the rear, with a medial line of columns marking the division into two alleys. Such stoas were employed to surround a temple enclosure; the 'peribolos' forms a striking feature of Hellenistic cities throughout the Mediterranean littoral.

Despite such achievements in monumental architecture, the plan of the great house remained comparatively humble. A jumble of apartments, some of them loggia-fronted, still surrounded the courtyard. Even in the 3rd century B.C., continuous colonnades were of rare occurrence; they never occupied more than three sides of the court and the entrance side, into which a narrow passage led from the street between stables and offices, was left unadorned. The domestic peristyle was yet to be discovered.

Fig. 3. The Stoa of the Athenians at Delphi

The stoa, however, was of the greatest architectural importance. As a peribolos, it was already achieving what was in fact a peristylar form. It is probably from this feature that the Greeks developed that remarkable structure known as the basilica. It will be realized that no single apartment of those days compared in size with the naos of the temple; everything else was of comparatively humble span so that important buildings had to be composed of a series of small buildings. There were thus no great halls in which large gatherings of people could be held.

The climate of the Hellenistic world being of a gentle nature, most meetings could take place out of doors. The stoas surrounding the market place or the peribolos of the temple formed ideal venues for conferences of a commercial, political, or litigious character. Eventually the Greeks evolved a special type of stoa-surrounded enclosure, usually attached to the agora, for this purpose. The small rectangular building they devised was called a *basileios stoa,* or regal portico, later this was shortened to basilica. The enclosed area within was known as the *exæron* of the basilica.

The philosophical Greek mind delighted in problems related to town-planning. Colonnaded stoas formed a comparatively easy way of converting their planning-schemes into three dimensions. One of the most delightful aspects of Greek planning, however, is the manner in which they put their own countryside to use. The little combes and valleys in which they had sat to listen to an orator or view some rustic entertainment were turned by them into architecture. The long valleys became stadia for races of various descriptions. The shorter combes were cunningly converted into theatres; tiers of seating descending the hillside in decreasing semi-circles until the site of the stage was reached (Plate 11). Behind the stage was a long building for the actors and their properties which was known as the 'scena'; the space before it was the 'proscenium' which we know today as the 'stage'. In order to improve acoustics and shut out external noises the scena was provided with two wings flanking the proscenium; hence the 'wings' of the modern theatre. Another place of entertainment was the odeon or music-hall, a small theatre with its scena wall more closely incorporated with the auditorium than was the case with the theatre.

The design of the lofty scena wall of the theatre presented the Greek architects with a problem not encountered in any other building. The monumental factor of height being employed only in connection with the temples of the gods, the walling of even the largest public buildings was on a comparatively humble scale. Temple buildings were embellished, both inside and out, by colonnades, thus relieving the architects from having to devise any form of architectural treatment of the wall-surface itself, as punctuation was adequately provided by the colonnades. When faced with the problem of designing the scena of a theatre, however, the architects were faced with the necessity of providing, not a building, but a solitary wall—one, moreover, very much in the public eye. The architectural embellishment of such a structure set them a task not hitherto encountered. The obvious solution was to face the scena wall with a colonnade; the lofty orders of the temple were, however, completely out of scale with the rest of the structure with its small rows of seating.

The flat roofs employed throughout the ancient world, and adopted by the Greeks for their humbler buildings, form excellent places upon which to take the evening air. Such roofs were therefore in fact part of the accommodation of the house, being in some cases even converted into upper stories by temporary structures which might eventually become permanent. The roofs of stoas formed ideal grand-stands from which to observe interesting occurrences in the street, temple-forecourt, or basilica; the acceptance of this fact resulted in the pro-vision of two-storied stoas with façades composed of two ranges of colonnading. The ordering of these presented no great difficulty as the problem had already been encountered in the interiors of temples, so it was with these two-storied colonnades that the Hellenistic Greeks decided to embellish the scena walls of their theatres.

Apart from the temples with their great Orders, and the two-storied 'scenic' architecture of the theatres, the public buildings of the era were not expected to display monumental elevations. Such buildings were notable only in respect of the area they covered and the refine-ment of the detail by which they were embellished. There being no form of wall-ornamentation, this detail was mainly limited to the use of the Orders in connection with colonnades. The Hellenistic public building was generally entered through a colonnaded portico which took the place of the pylonned portal of antiquity; the rest of the building consisting of a series of small rooms set around internal courts, some of these of a size which enabled them to be employed for the same purpose as the *exæron* of the basilica. The fierce heat of Egypt had encouraged the covering-over of courtyards to form hypo-style halls; the gentler climate of the Hellenistic lands allowed their meeting-places to be hypæthral. This absolution from the necessity of devising means of roofing great halls made the task of the planner of public buildings an easy one; thus a multitude of gymnasia and public bath-houses, as well as civic structures, added to the amenities of the Hellenistic city.

34. The remains of the stairway leading to the upper floor of a sixth-century Byzantine house (Um el Jemal)

35. The verandahs of a Byzantine monastic building in Syria (Qasr el Banat)

36. A ninth-century courtyard mosque in Cairo

37. The forest of columns which fills the sanctuary of the early courtyard mosque (Cairo)

38. The façade of the sanctuary overlooking the courtyard
(Kairwan)

The spectacular achievements of the Ionian architects and their Macedonian emulators mark the transitional phase during which the last vestiges of the ancient Bronze Age civilizations were being cleared away in order to lay the foundations of the modern era. Much had been learned from the ancients; the eastern Hellenists undoubtedly owed most of their advancement to contact with the heritage of past ages. But the old lands were dying. The pioneers of the future were already striving to gaze into the realm which lay beyond the setting sun. And away in the west, where the old Dorian colonies plodded on heedless of the glories of Pergamon, Antioch, and Alexandria, the site for the new foundations was being cleared and levelled to receive upon it the fabric of wonders yet to come.

In the country lying south-west of the Apennines, the colonies of Magna Græcia confronted no ancient civilizations. Their neighbours were the primitive European tribes known as the Etruscans who, by the second quarter of the last pagan millennium, had already become a settled folk living in city states. Surprisingly little is known concerning the early buildings of these people; it seems clear, however, that from the great tents of their chieftains they developed the megaron with its central fire-hearth. The Etruscan form of this is suggested by the well-known rock-hewn tomb at Corneto in Tuscany. The most interesting feature is the manner in which the roof is 'hipped' all round instead of being gabled; the hip-rafters support the trimmers surrounding the aperture above the hearth.

Architecturally the most important Etruscan variation on the Greek type of megaron is seen in the portico. The ante-room of the latter was achieved by means of an internal partition, so that the portico came within the main side walls of the building. The Etruscan portico, however, is clearly derived from the same form of construction as that seen in the flanking loggias of the smaller Greek houses, where the side of the tented prototype had been lifted and supported upon poles. In the large Etruscan tent, however, it was the end wall of the structure which had been raised and supported, to act as a portico extended before the main walls instead of being enclosed within them. Thus the Etruscan feature is a true, open-sided, 'prostyle' portico; the Greek being merely a portico 'in antis', that is to say flanked by side walls or antae instead of lateral colonnades. The latter is merely an entrance device; the former a complete architectural entity.

This prostyle portico appears in the Etruscan temple. The Greek buildings, free-standing and surrounded by their colonnades, were the same at both ends; those of the Etruscans, however, had their entrance fronts clearly indicated by spacious porticoes. Whereas the Greek temple had been enclosed within a peribolos, the Etruscan temple was set at the back of a forecourt which spread before its entrance.

The Hellenization of the Etruscan temple design was merely a matter of adapting one of the Orders to its colonnades. At the beginning of the 5th century B.C. the wooden pillars of the primitive buildings developed capitals similar to those employed by the Aegeans which were in fact the timber prototypes of the Doric capitals to be found in the temples of neighbouring Magna Græcia. In this fashion the Doric Order was introduced into Etruscan buildings. When the Romans eventually translated this wooden Order into stone, they employed two slightly different variations of it. One of these, in recognition of its origin, was called the Tuscan; the other is that which is called today the Roman Doric.

By the middle of the last pagan century, when the city of Rome had established itself as the capital of the new world, the full force of sub-oriental Hellenism was brought to bear upon it. Greek masons and carvers filled the city with fine stone buildings for the most part designed in accordance with the rules of the Corinthian Order. Planning, however, remained unaffected by Greek influences; the simple rectangular Etruscan shrine with its spacious portico became the Roman temple (Plate 18). In the more temperate climate of Rome there was no need for the colonnaded verandahs of the Greeks; half-columns or pilasters were nevertheless applied, at first externally and, later, within the buildings, to provide a system of architectural punctuation to the designs.

The primitive Greek temple, erected upon a levelled site, was set upon a low platform of three steps. The Hellenists, in their researches into the buildings of the ancients, had discovered the method of levelling sites by building-up the lower portions of these upon masonry platforms instead of excavating the higher parts and thus partly burying the building itself. The masonry podium, by raising the temple, greatly added to the dignity of its elevations; thus the designers of the Hellenistic temples usually took advantage of an opportunity to emphasize the height factor in this fashion. Roman temples—which, unlike those of the Greeks, were not orientated east and west—were usually so sited that the entrance portico rose above a high basement the summit of which was attained by means of a wide flight of steps, reminiscent of a Greek propylæa, rising out of the forecourt.

We have seen how the Greek temple-plan was based upon that of the great hall of a chieftain. In the sacred counterpart of the domestic structure, the god was represented by a huge statue set at the back of the *naos*. The Hellenists, however, adopted the ancient symbol of the blocked doorway; in this fashion that important feature, the niche, makes its appearance in classical architecture. The concentration of the Roman temple-planners upon an approach along an axis made the culmination of this with some striking architectural feature an æsthetic necessity; in the forum of Rome, the important temple of Mars Ultor, begun in 14 B.C., shows the niche expanded to form an apse.

The normal method of roofing employed in a Classical temple was timber framed with rafters carrying the covering of marble slabs or terracotta tiles. An important terminal feature such as an apse, however, would require some form of ceiling to hide the awkward jumble of rafters which would otherwise form such a prominent factor in its internal aspect. Hellenism being in close touch with the areas in which the rough dome of rubble was already a common method of roofing small spans, the half-dome or 'conch' was soon discovered to be a suitable device for ceiling an apse (Fig. 4).

Once accepted by the Roman planners, the apse swept everything before it. At one end of the memorial basilica of Julius Cæsar at Antioch an apse was provided to enshrine his statue; soon the idea was developed and apses provided at the ends of such basilicas as were used as law courts in order to give dignity to the seats of the judges. In its greatest form, the exedra, it appears at either end of Trajan's magnificent basilica in Rome; in the provincial example at Leptis in Tripolitania, built about 200 A.D., the arch of the apse is embellished with carving of unsurpassed richness.

In addition to being employed as a planning device, the niche became an important item in wall decoration. The arch being in Hellenistic times a rarity, only employed architecturally as a central feature in an important façade, the niches of the period were flat-topped. The final development was in the form of an 'ædicule', that is to say an elevational treatment in miniature. In the heyday of the Hellenistic Baroque, the first two centuries of our era, niches usually

Fig. 4. The great apse of a Roman temple

take the form of rectangular recesses framed by a pair of small columns and surmounted by an entablature with pediment: the whole, of course, in the Corinthian Order. Niches of this description are often placed, sometimes in two tiers, between the internal pilasters of temples.

It is possibly to the development of the aedicular architecture that the ultimate decadence of the Hellenistic style can be ascribed. All building design must be governed, if not actually by necessity, at least by desirability. The early Greek designers, considering such a matter as inter-columniation for example, were dependent upon structural factors and thus arrived at a solution which appeared visually correct. Architectural wall-decoration should properly be limited to punctuation; anything of the nature of an aedicule may be used perhaps once only in a single design. Sculpture may be used to ornament wall-surfaces, but when architecture is degraded by being employed as if it were sculpture designers are, as it were, being careless of their manners. Architecture is not scenery. Thus scenic architecture is never successful; it is perhaps in the scena walls of such Roman theatres as that at Sabratha in Tripolitania that the beautiful Hellenistic style came at last to an inglorious end.

Yet if their elevations deteriorated, the planning skill of the Hellenistic architects never failed them. Perhaps the greatest of their achievements is that at Baalbek in Syria, where the old world brushed shoulders with the new. Here, everything that could be learnt from the ancients has been assimilated, beautified, and displayed to the wonder of the beholder. The spreading façade of a great propylæa forms the frontispiece; behind this a court, surrounded by colonnades and hexagonal in shape, at once illustrates the fertility of Hellenistic imagination and the scientific knowledge which lay behind it. Beyond, a vast court, enclosed by colonnades broken here and there in order to incorporate a capacious exedra, reaches away towards the temple itself. Accepting the fact that the whole of the structural work is a riot of misapplied architectural detail, not even this can detract from the magnificence of what is a masterpiece of monumental planning (Plate 12).

Chapter VI

IMPERIAL ROME

At the middle of the 4th century B.C., when Hellenizing pioneers set forth from Magna Græcia to initiate their Etruscan neighbours into the mysteries of Greek philosophy, they found them living in strong-walled city states, the entrances to which were flanked, in the fashion of the day, by pairs of massive towers. The entrance gateways themselves were covered, however, not with the corbelled false arches employed by the Greeks, but by true arches constructed in well-turned masonry. This is a fact of great significance in the history of architecture.

It has recently been proved that not only the arch, but even arched vaulting, was in use in Babylonia during the fourth millennium B.C. This need occasion no surprise, for the arch is a natural product of brick-building. Bricks are so light and easily manipulated that even a child can experiment with them; there are a number of ways in which the principle of arched construction can be stumbled upon.

But a knowledge of arched construction does not necessarily imply that its users will develop an arcuated style of architecture. For a start, it is a considerable step from a brick arch to one of which the voussoirs are formed of wrought masonry. Neither the Egyptians nor the Greeks considered brick as a monumental material, hence such arches as they used were for constructional purposes only; the architect of the day considered it his duty to clothe the structural skeleton of a building, not to expose this to the vulgar gaze. Thus, classical architecture was restricted to the use of stone column and lintel, properly assembled in accordance with one of the established Orders.

The Etruscans, however, had no such tradition to restrict the freedom of their architectural development. They knew so much about brick-making that they even employed terracotta ornament in their buildings. Having discovered the arch, they had no scruples concerning its use. Although willing to subscribe to the Orders in connection with religious architecture, they learned the Greek masonry technique and used it in connection with the turning of arches. In this fashion they created the first arcuated style.

The arch is a far more efficient way of bridging an opening than the primitive lintel. Theoretically, its scope is unlimited. Its use, however, presents problems unknown to the designer who follows a trabeated style of building. The architect who employs arches must study their mechanics; he must, in fact, be an engineer. Hence the use of the arch is in itself an encouragement to more efficient building technique; thus it is easy to appreciate the fact that the effect of the revolutionary attitude of the Etruscans was to speed architectural development to a degree that Hellenism might never have achieved.

A race which lives in strong-walled city states sooner or later finds that one of these attains the ascendancy over all. As the last of the pagan centuries drew on towards its close, Rome, long accepted as the leading Etruscan city, had planted its imperial eagles in regions as yet barely discovered.

It was a world in which culture was still Hellenistic. But the Corinthian temple with its massive masonry walls, drum-built columns, and heavy entablature, was now an anachronism. Beside it stood something which would have scandalized Greek architects: a monument in the form of a great arch, rising from massive abutments and erected to commemorate the victorious return of an emperor (see frontispiece).

Throughout the Roman empire the imperial engineers were busy. To make an arched opening in a wall is but a first step; the Romans discovered that arches will support each other and can thus be employed in the form of an arcade. From the many-spanned bridge was developed the aqueduct formed of arcades placed one upon the other; water could be carried by this means to sites which could otherwise never have been developed. Roman bridges carried the Roman roads to the frontiers of the Empire.

In the solution of engineering problems of this nature the Romans accustomed themselves to the use of arcuated construction. It remained for them to develop the arch in connection with ordinary buildings.

The first use of the arch was to bridge an opening in a wall; should this be a very thick wall, such as that surrounding a city, the arch becomes what is known as a barrel-vault to the passage. As far back as the 13th century B.C., the Egyptians not only knew how to construct barrel-vaults but even built them side by side in mutual support. A row of narrow chambers set side by side and covered with barrel-vaults is a constantly-recurring feature in sub-oriental architecture; utilized as store-rooms, ranges of tunnel-like apartments of this description were often constructed on the lower slopes of hilly sites so as to level-up a building-platform above them. Thus the barrel-vault is a useful method of supporting an upper floor.

As the Roman engineers experimented with arches, so they did with barrel-vaults. These now formed an essential factor in theatre construction. The Greeks had carved their theatres out of natural hollows; the Romans raised theirs on level sites with the seating piled up on a system of vaulted corridors and contained by a semicircular wall of considerable height. It was in buildings such as these that the arch became ubiquitous and Roman architecture irrevocably arcuated (Plate 15).

One of the factors considerably affecting the building methods of the day was the increasing use of mortar. While most of the walling of Egyptian and Greek buildings had been formed of large stones set dry and held in place only through their great weight, walls built of bricks must necessarily be bedded in mortar. Brickwork technique varies from that of masonry in that brick walls are built solid, with the bricks set in bond for the full thickness of the wall, whereas masonry walls are built in two skins with a space between these. After it became the practice to use mortar for bedding wall-stones, the medial space was generally filled up by throwing in the chips left over from dressing the stones; the addition of mortar to the mixture provided the wall with a strong core.

The large buildings of the Romans often required very thick walling; this, if entirely constructed of brickwork, would have forced the builders to make vast quantities of bricks. They therefore devised a novel form of brick construction. Employing bricks of triangular pattern in place of the traditional square shape, they laid these on the faces of the wall only, coring the wall as they rose with a mixture of

39. The mosque of Selim II in Adrianople is considered the masterpiece
of the sixteenth-century Turkish architect Sinan

40. A typical monastic church of the twelfth century
(Jerichow)

41. A monastic house of the twelfth century
(Fontenay)

42. The magnificently-conceived framework of masonry which carries the high roof of a great Frankish church (Ely)

43. A twelfth-century Byzantine church as translated into the timber technique
of Scandinavia (Borgrund)

mortar and chippings of various descriptions. By thus copying masonry technique they learned to construct what was in fact a concrete wall faced with brickwork. It was this discovery of concrete which enabled them to construct vaulting, either rough or brick-faced, with the minimum waste of material and skilled labour. Thus, although the architecture of the Romans is, æsthetically speaking, arcuated, in the case of heavy structures only the exposed arches were truly formed; the buildings themselves were to all intents and purposes simply cast in concrete.

Nevertheless the Romans used their knowledge of the principles of arcuated construction to the full when it came to the design of vaults. Not only was it advisable for mechanical reasons to design a solid concrete vault as if it had been an arch; the provision of a framework of arched brick ribs assisted in the construction and saved the use of vast quantities of wooden centering. As the Roman vaulting-systems became more ambitious, so were their engineers encouraged to devise still more complicated skeletal systems upon which to cast their great vaults.

By the end of the pagan era, the barrel-vault had become more fully appreciated by the Roman architects, who were able to construct vaulting systems in which such vaults intersected each other at right angles, as in the case of two passages crossing each other, the lines of intersection, or groins, rising from the salient angles of the crossing. This important development signified the discovery that a vault could be raised, not only upon two walls, but upon four isolated points of support.

It should be realized that these early vaults were not intended to represent roofing systems, but only a supporting device for upper floors. The provision of adequate abutment to even a low vault presented serious structural problems; the raising of a vaulted roof was a task which might have daunted even the most confident engineer of the day.

But imperial Rome needed imperial buildings. The day of the basilica was over. Stoas were all very well for the philosophers of sunny Greece; the business men of Rome needed more substantial structures in which to deliberate. The *exæron* was an anachronism; the need was for great halls in which a multitude could find shelter in

all weathers. Many past centuries had demonstrated the full potentialities of stone column and lintel; what was now wanted was some
device for roofing a span wider than even a timber beam could cross.
The architect must be left for a while to dream of his Orders; the
engineer, who always precedes him, must now be called in to solve
the pressing needs of imperial Rome.

The middle of the first half of the 2nd century A.D. saw a noble
experiment in roofing, that of the Pantheon in Rome. The circular
temple-plan was no novelty; the imaginative Greeks had already
introduced it as a pleasant variation upon the normal, more austere,
arrangement. But whereas the Greek and Hellenistic circular temples
were quite small, the Pantheon is over 140 feet across internally. The
height of the vault is equal to its span. To have constructed an arched
vault of this magnitude would certainly have taxed the ingenuity of
the Roman engineers of the period; the vault of a roof, unlike that
which supports a floor, may lack the safe load above its abutments
which levelling-up for a floor is bound to provide.

The Pantheon dome, however, is not a true vault, but a system of
brick courses corbelled out towards the centre, the actual apex being
left open to the sky. Only a circular building could have been roofed
in this fashion; thus this noble experiment did not represent a very
important step towards the problem of vaulting a great hall. What is
of very great interest is the manner in which the Pantheon roof is
supported from the ground, for the enormously thick walling of the
temple is divided up into eight massive piers, between which the
intervening walling has been lightened by being recessed to form
apses. Over these apses, eight wide arches carry the weight of the dome
down upon the great piers. Thus, for the first time in architectural
history, we find a structure of monumental scale with its roof supported, not upon walls, but carried down through an arcuated system
to rest upon a series of isolated piers.

The Pantheon was the last of the great temples of Rome. There
was some rebuilding of existing structures after their destruction by
fire; the fine temple of Venus at Rome was covered with a huge
barrel vault during the first few years of the 4th century. But the day of
the Olympians was nearly over. The ancient gods of sun and moon,
love and war, health and wisdom, were gathering in the last Syrian

strongholds of Hellenism to prepare for one tremendous curtain-call. The Romans were seeking new deities—gods who would lift from the Roman soul the insufferable weight of boredom that follows a surfeit of peace and plenty. We may find a parallel state of affairs in our own day; the mediæval cathedral which once towered above the roofs of our towns has been replaced by the mass of the cinema building. In the first centuries of our era, the Roman temple shrank into insignificance beneath the arcaded walls of the theatre and the huge hall of the imperial baths.

The first of these vast club-buildings was that inaugurated by Agrippa in 20 B.C. Exactly a century later, the baths of Titus were founded, its plan setting the fashion for subsequent structures of which the most magnificent were those of Caracalla (A.D. 211) and Diocletian (A.D. 302). Although bathing was the ostensible purpose of the thermae, their life centred round the great hall of the tepidarium. This was simply a hall of concourse, in which the clubmen of the Augustan age met and discussed the affairs of the day. No such structure had as yet appeared in the history of buildings; for size, only the pillar-cluttered hypostyle halls of the Egyptian temples could compare with it.

Structurally, the tepidarium represents the culminating achievement of the Roman engineer. Its span—eighty feet or so—was greatly in excess of any rectangular structure hitherto roofed. But with superb confidence the engineers not only covered this vast expanse with a concrete vault but even swept this over a hundred feet into the air. A barrel vault of this magnitude would have been a monstrosity, making it impossible for the upper part of the building to be lit at all and producing a heavy sombre effect only suited to a temple. The engineers of the tepidaria, however, demonstrated their ability to the utmost by employing the cross vault, thus enabling windows to be inserted all round the building for its whole height. The groins of the vault rose from solid masses of masonry; four of these set on either side of the building divided it up into three vaulting-bays.

The engineering skill required to erect a vault of this weight and compass at such a height above the pavement was of no mean order. The overturning thrust against the walls was enormous; these had therefore to be carried some distance outwards from the hall to serve as deep buttresses. As the weight of the vault was carried down its groins on to the eight points of support, however, the engineers lightened the walling between these points by recessing it in the form of apses. In this fashion the apse takes on a new aspect; whereas it had been employed hitherto as a decorative niche it now becomes a structural amenity. As the Corinthian capital is the sculptural hallmark of the Classical Baroque, so is the apse its counterpart in the plans of the engineer-architects of imperial Rome.

The great three-bay tepidarium with its soaring cross-vaults was a building of revolutionary significance in the sphere of historical architecture. Nothing remotely like it had been seen before. Apart from certain decorative motifs, it owed nothing, either structurally or æsthetically, to Hellenistic origins. The concentration of the structure upon the eight masonry piers meant that the greater part of the walling of the building had nothing to support and could thus be safely pierced with large openings for the whole height of the hall. Above the springing line of the vault, the semicircular upper portions of the walling could be provided with large windows so that the whole building could be ceiled with light; henceforth there need be nothing gloomy and oppressive about a vaulted building.

The vaulted hall entirely replaced the old Hellenistic basilica. Those remarkable structures, with their stoa-surrounded courtyards in which business men gathered, and their terminal apses where judges and assessors listened to the pleas of litigants, had served their purpose and become obsolete. Many fine examples had been constructed throughout the empire. In the Roman forum itself, the Julian basilica replaced, in 54 B.C., the original building erected in the year 184; as late as the third quarter of the 1st century A.D., the huge Ulpian basilica, with its two terminal hemi-cycles, was constructed on a new site. In the warmer climate of the African provinces, many fine basilicas were built, the most magnificent being that of Leptis Magna in Tripolitania, dating from about A.D. 200 The Roman basilica was generally two-storied; the larger, double-aisled examples had galleries over the inner aisle only, the roof of the outer aisle being used as a tribune from which to observe events in the forum below. In the last quarter of the 3rd century, the Julian basilica was reconstructed, after a fire, with the columns replaced by piers carrying cross-vaults after the imperial fashion.

Before the end of the pagan era, however, architects were considering the possibility of replacing the exæron of the basilica with a covered hall. The architect Vitrivius, who endeavoured to formulate a system of rules for planning, found himself entrusted with the design of a basilica at Fano in northern Italy, where the climate made the traditional hypæthral type quite unsuitable. The building he produced set a new fashion in the design of basilicas; it was a short rectangle, surrounded by a two-storied aisle, and having the central space roofed over to form a hall. It seems probable that this building, which was erected at the end of the third quarter of the last pagan century, forms the prototype of the European type of imperial basilica, as opposed to the traditional Hellenistic or open-air type still being erected centuries later in the Levant and in Africa.

During the 3rd century, the development of the northern or covered type of basilica, coupled with the expansion of the imperial vaulting technique, resulted in such fine buildings as the basilica at Trier in the Rhineland, a great galleried hall roofed with a cross-vault. In A.D. 310, the three-bay cross-vaulted tepidarium was reproduced in the Roman forum as the basilica of Maxentius. This, the finest of all the imperial basilicas, is one of the most important structures in architectural history. In its plan, we note that all traces of the thick lateral walls have disappeared. Not even rows of apsidal recesses mark the site of lateral abutment; the vaults are carried down upon eight points of support which are built outwards as true buttresses, the first example of the employment of this feature on any large scale. The transference of the thrust of the vaults to lines of support set transversely to the axis of the building is so marked that the structure may be said to be designed on the diaphragm principle, where each bay is separated by an arched diaphragm upon which the whole of the weight of the roof is carried. The spaces between the huge buttresses, covered with transverse barrel-vaults which help to stiffen the diaphragms, are incorporated within the floor area of this vast basilica (Plates 16 and 17).

These magnificent vaulted halls represent the culminating achievements of the Roman engineers. In the embellishment of their buildings, however, the architects of the day were not capable of dealing with the rapid growth of structural knowledge and the emergence of such entirely novel building forms. Falling back on the Orders, they made shift to adapt these to the new types of building. The difficulty was that these Orders had been designed in connection with trabeated architecture; their adaptation to arched openings set problems which were never really solved. Arches made it possible to span far wider openings; thus intercolumniation had to be increased many times over the classical proportion. The Orders were based on the use of the monumental factor of height; most of the Roman public buildings were either comparatively low in altitude or else made up of several superimposed stories, each of no great height. In the case of the huge tepidaria with their enormous bay-spans, the introduction of a solitary giant Corinthian column at each point of support was the best that could be achieved in the way of architectural ornament.

It was in such multi-arched structures as the walls of theatres that the Roman architects managed to produce some kind of order into their designs. The centre of each pier was punctuated with a column; an entablature separated each story. The intercolumniation, which framed the whole of the opening with its arch, was so great that the proportion often approached the square; in such buildings as the Colosseum, however, built during the second half of the 1st century A.D., we can see that the result, if not particularly refined, succeeded in imparting a sense of architectural magnificence to the towering walling of this mighty structure (Plate 15).

Much of the elevational effect of the larger Roman public buildings is due to the use of rusticated masonry. The Hellenistic regions having been subject to earthquakes which frequently injured stonework by 'spalling off' the edges of the stones, the architects of heavy masonry constructions chamfered the edges of each stone before setting it.

Two examples of the Roman use of arches may be mentioned as having an ultimate effect upon European architecture. The first of these is the Syrian device of employing an arch above a lintel, leaving a semicircular tympanum between the two; this is presumably a concession by the lintel-employing Hellenists to Roman engineers who feared fracture of the lintel by earthquakes. A more important feature is the association of arches and columns seen, at the beginning of the 4th century, in Diocletian's palace at Spalato. The structural arches of the Romans invariably sprang from piers; the arrangement noted above, however, although employed chiefly as a decorative motif, reminds us that by the middle of the 3rd century the Hellenistic architects of Syria had already discovered that the classical column could be made to carry an arch.

We have paid tribute to the skill with which the Hellenistic architects spread their magnificent stoa-surrounded courts before the temples of their gods. The buildings themselves, however, were in each case separated entities, each designed on a comparatively simple plan-form and covered by a single roof. The Romans developed the art of planning to an extent that they could incorporate a group of buildings within one planning complex. The finest examples of this architectural achievement may be seen in the thermæ of Rome. The central feature of each was the great hall or tepidarium with its high-vaulted roof towering above everything in the neighbourhood. Along the entrance façade of this huge structure was laid out the swimming bath or frigidarium. At each end of this was an open portico; in the ends of these, doorways provided access from the street. From the centre of the long rear wall of the tepidarium a lobby led to the hot room or calidarium, the floor and walls of which were heated by hot air from a furnace nearby. The tepidarium and the calidarium formed the main bath-building; in the thermae of Caracalla the latter was domed, in those of Diocletian it was designed as a smaller version of the tepidarium. At the ends of the long axis of the tepidarium, doorways led into flanking courtyards set at right angles to the great hall; in these, stoas and exedrae provided facilities for rest and conversation. These courts could also be reached through porticoes set behind the street frontage.

This frontage became an architectural composition of much significance in the life of Rome. Through the four symmetrically-placed doorways passed the teeming multitudes of the imperial city to bathe and discuss the affairs of the day. The two more central of these portals gave access to the swimming bath with the façade of the great hall towering behind it; the lateral doorways led to the quieter courts lying beside its great bulk. Nothing like this imposing complex of buildings had been seen in architectural history; nor would it be seen again for more than a thousand years to come.

To complete this spectacle of architectural magnificence, the buildings of the thermae were enclosed within a setting of gardens, which in their turn were surrounded by a peribolos of colonnades, exedrae, perhaps a theatre or stadium, and a multitude of smaller baths, libraries, and other amenities. The gardens themselves must have been beautiful in their day. A walled garden, where the natural beauty of the vegetation is set against a formal background of architecture, is always a lovely sight; the colonnades and exedrae of the Romans must have provided a perfect setting to the floral acheivements of the Roman gardeners. The Romans were adept at providing a plentiful supply of water to their cities; a favourite scenic device was to lead the aqueduct into an exedra designed as a 'nymphæum' from the encircling walls of which fountains splashed musically into the pool below. Many provincial cities had a nymphæum constructed in the forum or main street to serve as a public water-source.

The Roman gentleman's house had changed little, except in elaboration, from that of his Hellenistic predecessor. The entrance passage of the latter's had now been expanded to form a little court or atrium surrounded on three sides by groups of offices. Access from this to the inner court was through a room called the tablinium, the position of which curiously recalls that of the throne-room which separated the two courts of Assyrian palaces; the Roman tablinium, however, was set with its axis along and not athwart the lines of approach. Within the inner court, the Roman architect might gather the scattered loggias of the Greek house to form a well-ordered peristyle (Plate 13), from which were reached all the principal apartments. Chief of these was the oecus, the family living room, usually set on the main axis directly opposite the tablinium; open to the peristyle, it bore a striking resemblance to the oriental 'iwan'. The dining-room was an apartment called *triclinium*; its three couches arranged in an open-ended rectangle remind one of the system of two parallel tables, joined at their ends by the high table, which form the standard dining-plan of the mediæval great hall.

Owing to the taste of the Roman architects for monumental planning, which implies symmetry of lay-out, the plans of the imperial palaces were probably devised with more regard for this than would permit of any standard arrangement of the apartments themselves. The triclinium, however, becomes the banqueting hall, and the tablinium the throne-room. The disposal of these appear to be chiefly influenced by the desire for symmetrical arrangement about a main axis.

Imperial Rome was not all palaces, temples, fine houses and monumental public buildings. With all this extravagant planning it was inevitable that the dense population of the city should so outgrow the available building sites for it to become necessary to erect multi-story blocks of tenements: another feature of its imperial architecture that had never been seen before and would not be repeated in domestic building practice until modern times. Indeed, these great brick apartment houses, with their large window-openings spanned by segmental arches, would not look in the least out of place in an industrial town of today (Plate 20).

In all the Roman world there was no city to equal in grandeur the imperial capital itself. Yet Roman cities, many of them containing fine buildings, rose and expanded over the whole of the Mediterranean littoral, westwards to Gaul and Britain, and eastwards to the desert frontiers of the ancient lands. Temples, basilicas, and thermae surrounded the thronged market-places; planning, however, was seldom on the monumental scale seen in Rome itself. In Europe, the provincial Roman house was often constructed in well-joinered half-timber work set upon a brick foundation; the larger houses were sometimes built round a courtyard but many rural farmhouses were planned in more primitive fashion as a range of rooms connected by a loggia.

Although the Romans themselves were efficient builders in timber, their writers pay tribute to the excellence of the timber architecture of Gaul, the Rhineland, and other western regions subjected by their armies. Although nothing but the most meagre descriptions exist of this architecture, it is clear that the buildings of western Europe were at that time more resistant to the weather than those of the Romans. This was possibly due to the use made of wooden-posted loggias surrounding the plank-built outer walls of the west. In any event, it is quite certain that during the first half of the first Christian millennium a notable timber architecture had been developed in Europe.

The territories lying beneath the sceptre of Imperial Rome witnessed the greatest building boom in all architectural history. Great cities rose in desert and jungle, vast grids of dwellings interspersed with public buildings. The building potential employed on all this was necessarily for the most part unskilled; rubble stone, timber, or brick were the materials in common use. In order to achieve an external effect worthy of the imperial age it was necessary to clothe the walling in plaster, a practice which set a fashion for subsequent building throughout the Mediterranean littoral where the climatic conditions were such as not to throw too great a strain upon the weather-resisting properties of an impermanent covering of this nature. From this habit of plastering walls was developed the art of painting decorative motifs upon them. The curious craft of the mosaic artist was employed as a cheap method of ornamenting floors.

The culture of the Romans cannot be compared with that of the ancient Greeks. The former were of a more practical turn of mind —of a mind, moreover, to carry their culture with them on the points of their swords. The Roman pioneers were not philosophers, they were soldiers. Their military architecture was not restricted to the walls protecting their cities. Their frontiers had been thrust to the limits of the world of their day; along the Roman *limes* a chain of forts, yet another architectural innovation, secured the limits of the empire against the intruder. The Roman fort, like everything the Roman planned, was a strictly-ordered affair; standing four-square, its angles were flanked by sturdy bastions of masonry or brick-faced concrete. Experienced as a result of years of siege-warfare against Parthians and Persians, the Roman engineers knew of the dangers of mining; the square Greek wall-tower with its weak angles was therefore replaced by the solid semicircular bastion. Even in their military structures the Romans lost no opportunities of architectural expression; the city gate, in particular, was generally designed to advertise the magnificence of their imperialism. Giving full rein to their talent for arcuated construction, the Roman architects doubled their gateways to allow for two-way traffic and sometimes even added smaller gates for pedestrians. One of their greatest achievements is the Black Gate at Trier with its tiers of arcading, punctuated by classical Orders, in the finest tradition of imperial architecture. The pair of slender round towers, each four stories in height, by which this noble frontispiece is flanked, introduce yet another completely novel feature into building history. In these arcaded towers we see the germ of the monumental architecture of mediæval Europe (Plate 21).

Chapter VII

EARLY CHURCHES

The first quarter of the millennium which began with the birth of Christ saw the development of a new class of religious building, each devoted to the worship of a single omnipotent god. While the cult of the ancient domestic deities continued to be the state religion of the regions forming the Roman empire, many humble people in the Hellenistic Levant were beginning to turn to new philosophies. The earliest of the new monotheistic religions was the Jewish; later this developed into the Christian.

In an earlier chapter we discussed the sanctuary of the pagan temple and its fundamental feature, the niche or blocked doorway containing the cult statue. The religious revolution introduced by the Hebrews made it necessary for their architects to revise the plans of temples to suit the requirements of a cult which eschewed the representation of the Divinity by a statue. The basis of the Hebrew religion being the Mosaic Law, the niche within the Jewish temple was made the repository of the parchment scroll upon which this Law was inscribed. The recess, which was fitted with a pair of doors for the protection of the sacred object within, was known as the *aron;* each Jewish synagogue has one such Holy of Holies provided in the centre of the wall nearest to Jerusalem.

The first synagogues were the reception rooms of private houses; these were, it will be remembered, rectangular apartments entered in the middle of one of the long sides by a portal leading out of the courtyard. The latter was of course an essential feature of any temple plan as privacy of worship could not be achieved if the doorway of the sanctuary opened directly out of the public street. Thus we find the Jewish synagogue adopting the traditional temple-plan of the region except for the modification of the niche to form a cupboard for the sacred scrolls which had replaced the cult statue.

The Hellenization of the synagogue plan resulted in the introduction of the columnar Orders as ornament. The Jewish buildings were of course very humble in scale and in no way compared with the temples of the state gods; thus the architectural adornment of the former was of a domestic rather than a monumental nature. The courtyard of the Hellenistic synagogue sometimes received the addition of a three-sided peristyle like that of a large Greek house.

The most significant factor governing the synagogue plan was a result of the absolutely revolutionary nature of the form of worship taking place within them. The sanctuary of the pagan temple had been a guarded place, admission to which had been considered as a concession connected with the performance of rites. There was never any intention of admitting a large number of worshippers in a body. Worship in a synagogue, however, was performed by its whole congregation gathered together within its walls. Thus the latter building, whatever its status, had to be of a size which would contain this congregation. A mere private sanctuary was not enough; the synagogue had to be a hall of assembly. Thus we once more see the necessity for the provision of a completely roofed building which would hold a considerable number of people. The problem of the civic basilica was being repeated in the temple.

An important feature of the perfected synagogue plan was the *bema,* a raised platform set in the middle of the floor and serving as a kind of large pulpit. To the bema were brought the sacred scrolls; around it the congregation gathered to hear the reading of the Law. The focus of the synagogue plan was thus centralized upon the bema instead of being aligned axially towards the niche as in the pagan temple. Thus we find a new feature in the planning of buildings, centralization taking the place of alignment upon an axis. The result was the adoption in Roman times of a synagogue plan based upon the modified Hellenistic basilica with its roofed exæron surrounded by a peristyle. The entrance doorway might be lateral or axial; the latter eventually became the accepted classical form. The *aron* was in the wall facing the entrance; before this an enclosed courtyard, often peristylar, assured its isolation from the busy world without.

44. The curved wall of the high apse of a twelfth-century church is carried upon columns to give access to the *chevet* beyond (Conques)

45. An elaborate twelfth-century *chevet* resembling the half of a circular church
(Paray-le-Monial)

In the early days of Christian worship this too was held in the reception rooms of private houses. There was one feature of a Christian church, however, which had hitherto been excluded from religious buildings. This was the altar which in pagan temples had been used for sacrificial purposes and had thus been of necessity set in the open courtyard before the doorway of the sanctuary. The altar of the Christian church was the table upon which its most sacred rite, that of the Communion, was celebrated before the whole congregation gathered within its walls. It is not improbable that the altar was originally set in the midst of the building as in the synagogue; it is clear, however, that by the end of the 3rd century the normal Christian church had become aligned on the axial plan with the altar set at its western end so that the celebrant could face the east when confronting the congregation before him. In early domestic churches the entrance doorway was lateral; later the more obvious terminal entrance opposite to the altar became the accepted arrangement. The courtyard was of course an essential feature of the early church-plan.

During the centuries whilst these two humble types of building, the synagogue and the Christian church, were spreading stealthily throughout the old Hellenistic world, Imperial Rome was striding upon its way oblivious of the significance of these elementary prototypes of monotheistic religious architecture. One of the outstanding features of the Imperial architecture was a craving for the purely monumental type of building. An important utilitarian structure is noticeable by reason of its extent; a monument by its exaggerated height. In the case of a building which is all monument and serves no useful purpose at all, the achievement of height may be the sole aim of its designer.

Most monuments are connected with the illustrious dead. The simplest form is perhaps the piled cairn of stones or the mounded tumulus raised above the tomb-chamber of the primitive chieftain. Sometimes the chamber itself is a *dolmen* of great stone slabs set in megalithic fashion; another version is the lofty rubble dome of the *tholos* type of tomb seen in its highest form in the Aegean mausoleum known as the Treasury of Atreus. A refinement is the construction of a stone dado round the base of the tumulus; in megalithic architecture this takes the form of a row of orthostats. The tholos may have the base of its protecting tumulus protected by a circular retaining wall of good wrought stone; when this has been developed in the form of a solid masonry drum we arrive at the form of the tomb of Augustus or the better-known example which now forms the Castle of St Angelo but which was originally the tomb of Hadrian.

The tomb-chamber enclosed in a mass of masonry may be seen in the mastabas and pyramids of Egypt, the latter being, of course, the mightiest examples of purely monumental architecture in the world. In Hellenistic days, the tholos enclosed in a square mass of masonry becomes the mausoleum type of tomb seen at Halicarnassos or Cnidos; these magnificent monuments are embellished with Orders and completed by pyramidal roofs surmounted by statuary. From the great Hellenistic mausoleum was developed the normal type of Roman tomb in which the ground plan is reduced so as to accentuate as much as possible the monumental factor of height. Hundreds of these striking monuments still rise above the ruined sites once seething with the bustling life of the Roman empire but now returned again to desert and oblivion. The Palmyrene towers form perhaps the most notable collection of tombs of this class.

Concentration upon the vertical factor in design was bound to result in a greater interest being taken in the centralized plan based upon the square, circle, or its intermediate polygonal forms. We have seen how the development of the circular Hellenistic temple resulted in the construction of the Pantheon with its huge corbelled dome. The combination of an arcuated style with circular planning was bound to lead to the development of the true dome. That the Romans, even before the end of the pagan era, knew how to construct domes over small spans is illustrated by their introduction of the apse into the temple of Mars Ultor. A considerable improvement in dome construction was achieved when the engineers devised the method of first setting up a series of brick ribs upon which frame the 'web' of the dome was eventually applied. This had the effect of lightening the whole construction and also enabled the dome to be set upon a series of points instead of a continuous springing line. Yet it was probably not until the middle of the 3rd century that they felt able to throw a properly-constructed—as opposed to corbelled—dome over a main span. The thermae of Gallienus which date from this period had a nymphæum, now known as the Minerva Medica, covered by an eighty-foot dome perched upon a series of ten wide arches. The noticeable feature of the plan of this structure is the extreme slenderness of its supporting piers; between them the floor space of the building has been considerably increased by the introduction of a ring of apsidal projections. In this nymphæum we can detect the first steps towards the enlargement of the floor area of a hall by raising its walls upon a series of arches giving access to an adjoining system of subsidiary structures.

For three centuries after the Crucifixion, Christianity remained an obscure cult, observed in private houses and small chapels of no architectural note. The recognition of the religion in 313 affected only the Holy Land; even here it is doubtful whether the cathedral built at Tyre was a building of any great size. Ten years later, however, the acceptance of Christianity as the state religion of the Roman empire, brought about a revolution of staggering magnitude. It is doubtful whether any political or social change has ever affected architectural history to a comparable extent. In 330, pagan Rome was abandoned as the capital in favour of Byzantium, which became the Christian city of Constantinople. The emperor devoted himself to the newly-discovered religion; most of the remaining thirteen years of his life were spent in the eastern parts of his empire.

Constantine's first thought was to erect monuments over the Holy Sites. Calvary, the Sepulchre, and the Grotto of the Nativity at Bethlehem were each marked by a building the design of which was intended to represent the greatest achievement in purely monumental architecture the engineers of the day could devise.

The structures required lacked any precedent for their design. Each was to be, not a temple to some remote celestial divinity, but a shrine enclosing an actual site of immense religious significance. It was to be a monument of a class which could not be mistaken for anything but what it was.

A truly monumental structure is above all things lofty. If it is to be an actual building and not a mere shaft or slender tower its base must spread to support the mass as this rises; thus it must adopt a conical or pyramidal form as opposed to the ordinary broad low mass of the structure required for accommodation only. It is this piling up of structural mass which, at first adopted by the designers of Constantine's memorial chapels, forms the principal aim of the later Byzantine builders, the greatest of all architectural engineers. Professor T. B. L. Webster of University College, London, has suggested that the word *hypsosis* might be employed to suggest this motive which inspired the Byzantines and, despite the reactionary influence of the Roman Church, eventually appeared once more in the mightiest of all Christian shrines, that of St Peter's at Rome itself.

Thus it was the urge of *hypsosis* which encouraged the designers of Constantine's chapels to erect lofty structures rising above circular shrines more cunningly planned than anything yet encountered in architectural history.

In the case of a rectangular building, the restrictions which might be imposed on floor area by the permissible span are easily countered by extending the building along the main axis of its roof. In circular structures, however, the diameter of the building is completely controlled by spanning problems and no expansion can be achieved except by piercing the lower portions of the main walls in order to incorporate the floor areas within subsidiary structures. This means that the main walls have to be carried upon a series of isolated points of support.

For two centuries past, the engineers of Rome had been experimenting along these lines until their familiarity with arcuated constructional problems had enabled them to achieve the almost completely pillar-supported nymphæum of the Minerva Medica. Three quarters of a century later they had finally solved the problem, as may be seen in the beautiful tomb-chapel of the emperor's daughter, Constantia, built in 330. Such was their grasp of the constructional principles involved that they were able to dispense entirely with piers and support the dome—which it is true is only half the span of the Minerva Medica—upon a series of twelve arches rising from coupled pairs of Corinthian columns. Thus the building is in fact completely surrounded by an aisle; the roof of this, which is a barrel-vault, acts as an abutment to the thrust of the dome.

The architects and masons of the Holy Land, living in a region still steeped in Hellenistic building traditions, could never have achieved anything of this nature. They had had no experience of domes; even the arch was a feature upon which they looked with misgivings. They had probably never attempted to carry a wall upon a series of isolated props, employing their magnificent Orders for the support of roofs only. In the temenos of the temple of Jupiter at Damascus, however, is a small structure, now carrying a Moslem 'treasury', consisting of a ring of columns supporting an entablature planned as an octagon. This little structure, which dates from the 3rd century and appears to have been a well-head, suggests that the Hellenistic architects may not have been very far away from discovering the use of colonnades in place of the solid ground stories of buildings. Be this as it may, it is known that at least two of Constantine's monuments to Christianity, the churches of the Nativity and Ascension respectively, were planned as octagons and were surrounded by aisles. It can therefore be assumed that the walling of the central feature was carried upon colonnades. The contemporary tomb-chapel of the Emperor's daughter in Rome itself is circular in form and has its *hypsosis* carried upon arcades, unsuited to a polygonal plan.

We have thus followed the development of ancient religious architecture from the axially-planned temple to the culmination of pagan design in the great Pantheon of Rome which set the fashion for Constantine's hurriedly-constructed shrines. From the high-domed *hypsosis* was to spring a line of glorious structures, the lofty churches of the Byzantines which spread throughout Europe and held the field for centuries until western Europe became submerged beneath the reactionary forces emanating from the Church of Rome. For, leaving the Orthodox Church to raise its small but towering shrines towards the heavens, the Church of Rome became content to build churches, which, if less ornamental, would at least accommodate more people.

It is necessary once again to call attention to the magnitude of the new building problems resulting from the conversion of the Roman empire to congregational worship. The monumental chapels erected by Constantine were but tokens—what was so suddenly needed was a series of great churches sufficiently spacious to contain as it were the whole of the population of the empire at once. The principles involved were simple enough; a rectangular structure with an altar at

one end was all that was required. It was size alone that set the problem.

The Roman engineers, accustomed by now to the great hall of the
public baths as the climax of their skill, could not cope with this
sudden demand for the speedy erection of covered accommodation
for multitudes wishing to gather for worship. Thus it was left to that
Hellenism which had nurtured the new religion to provide the
necessary buildings. All thoughts of lofty domes and wide-flung
vaults were abandoned at the outset. The new churches were to
continue as they had begun; simple rectangular halls covered with
wooden roofs. The inventions which had been introduced in connection with the open supports of walls carrying heavy domes would
certainly prove suitable for application to the far lighter structures
contemplated.

In this fashion was devised that simple unpretentious structure
which has come to be known—from its resemblance to the civic
building—as the basilica. The main walls were supported upon a
series of columns, carrying either arches or an entablature. The central
nave was flanked by two or four aisles (in the latter case a row of
arches had been introduced to stiffen the rafters of the lateral roofs)
above which the walls of the nave rose as a clerestory pierced with
windows. Despite their floor area, these early churches were humble
enough in elevation. Neither structurally nor æsthetically can they be
classed as great architectural monuments; yet the wonder is that,
considering their complete novelty and the time available for their
production, they were ever conceived at all.

The problem of the accommodation of worshippers thus solved,
Constantine lost no time in adding great congregational naves at the
western side of the monuments he had raised over the holy sites (Plate
24). This association of a church with a sacred feature suggested the
provision in all religious buildings of some treatment which would
add to the dignity of the wall beneath the altar. The obvious form for
this to take was simply a repetition of the apsidal niche which had in
turn formed the terminal feature of pagan temple, civic basilica, and
Jewish synagogue. The basilical type was that upon which the
Christian apse was modelled, the seat of the bishop taking the place
of that of the civil judge. Sometimes the effect was increased by add-

ing the whole of the end of the civic basilica with its cross aisle or transept to the church; a final embellishment was to introduce the Jewish bema, expanded to a size that would accommodate a choir of singers to lead the chanting, and set it before the altar. The balustrade surrounding the Christian bema recalled that separating the judiciary area before the apse of the civic basilica from its exæron. It is from this balustrading or *cancelli* that the area occupied by the priest in a Christian church eventually becomes known as the chancel.

An essential feature of the early church was the courtyard protecting its principal entrance. Developed as this was from the courtyard of the private house, it had been known from earliest times by the domestic name of atrium. Its architectural history had followed along domestic not monumental lines; thus it never became a great temenos enclosing the whole building or even spread before an imposing portico. The side next the church was the first to be covered with a loggia or *pastos*, to be followed by lateral wings after the Hellenistic fashion. In its final Roman form the whole atrium became peristylar. As in all courtyards connected with religious buildings, the side next the church remained the most important and tended to become expanded into an entrance portico or narthex.

The first of the series of great 'basilicas' inaugurated by Constantine was the metropolitan cathedral of St Peter, begun in 326. It has, of course, entirely vanished beneath the mass of the present great church. Nor are there any other churches remaining in Rome of this date or the century following it. The large Basilica Ursiana at Ravenna, begun in 370—the first to have its apse at the east end—has disappeared; all the original churches of Constantinople were long ago replaced by Byzantine structures. After the emperor's death in 337 a period of reaction against the new religion brought ecclesiastical architecture to a complete standstill. Fifty years after the foundation of St Peter's, however, the huge church of St Paul without the Walls was constructed; rebuilding after a disastrous fire in 1823 has unfortunately destroyed its ancient character but the general proportions of the church are unaltered and it offers today the best illustration of a great basilica of the dawn of Christianity.

After the end of the 4th century no more of these vast five-aisled churches were built; thenceforth the plan of even the most important church had become simplified into that of a nave flanked by a pair of aisles and terminated by a spacious eastern apse containing the altar. As the length of the building now served to endow this with adequate privacy, the atrium fell into disuse; the narthex, taking its place, achieved thereby an added responsibility and additional architectural embellishment as compensation for this. Three churches, all dating from 425 or thereabouts, may be cited as examples of the standard Roman church of the period. The first of these is the charming basilica of St Sabina at Rome (Plate 22). At the church known as Eski-Juma in Salonica we can detect indications of the sturdier technique which was to develop into the Byzantine style.

The sudden unrehearsed admission of large numbers of persons into the new churches had caught the architects unawares so that they had been able to devise no proper scheme of architectural ordinance other than that produced by the colonnades themselves. The bay design of the Hellenistic basilica with its widely-spaced columns supporting nothing heavier than wooden roofs had given place to an intercolumniation of somewhat archaic proportions, while the exteriors of the buildings had perforce had to rely upon their ranges of windows for any form of punctuation. Smaller churches with consequently proportionately less congested points of support enabled some sort of attempt at bay design to be attempted. This can be seen in the fine basilican churches of Ravenna: St Apollinare Nuovo, begun during the closing years of the 5th century, and its namesake at Classe which dates from some forty years later.

Probably the finest series of basilican churches were those erected in the beautiful cities of the Decapolis in the Holy Land itself. The basilica represented the highest form of architectural expression known to that Hellenistic culture which had produced the Christian Church. Thus the land of basilicas soon acquired the taste for stately churches built of well-wrought masonry—instead of the plastered brick or rubble of Rome—and boasting long naves flanked by ranks of fine Corinthian columns. In the 6th century there could have been little doubt as to which country was the Holy Land of Christendom. But in 636 the Moslem flood swept away before it all the gathered culture of the centuries. Today, thirteen centuries have completed the ruin. The columns of Jerash and her sister cities now lie in their ranks as

47. A Russian bell-tower with an elaborate steeple in the style of the 'tent-churches' (Yaroslav)

46. An example of the Byzantinesque central feature of a twelfth-century western-European church (Toro)

48. A typical twelfth-century bell-tower
(Cuxa)

they fell, and desolation has overwhelmed the glories of the Christian homeland.

After the burst of ecclesiastical building which marked the reign of Constantine, Rome began to slip rapidly away from her position as arbiter of architectural fashion. The emperor himself had abandoned his great capital for its successor on the Bosphorus; the imperial engineers soon followed him to pastures new in which they began to lay the foundations of what was to be the grandest building style the world was ever to experience. As the 5th century fell away, the ancient glory of Rome faded with it, to be replaced by the semi-barbaric power of the Gothic capital at Ravenna. What the Lombardic architects made of the Roman basilicas will be seen in a later chapter; for the present it will be necessary to follow the imperial engineers to Byzantium, where the new Roman capital rubbed shoulders with the ancient world of strange races with long memories of bygone culture.

The eastern Romans, heirs of the Seleucid Hellenists, had found themselves neighbours of the invariably troublesome hillmen of the Persian mountains. In the middle of the 3rd century B.C. the Parthians had replaced Seleucia on the Tigris with a new capital at Ctesiphon nearby. By the Christian era they were established in a strongly-fortified city at Hatra within easy striking distance of the Decapolis itself. At the beginning of the 2nd century A.D., Trajan was ignominiously repelled from the walls of Hatra, which did not fall until taken by people of the Parthians' own race, the Sassanids, in 250.

The architecture of the Parthians is of interest as it forms a complete contrast with that of the Hellenistic Seleucids who were their neighbours and who played such an important part in the development of architectural style. The former were a people of Persian origin and still clung to the open-ended *iwan* which had become the architectural representation of the chieftain's tent prepared to receive visitors. The iwan was often a recess in the centre of the front wall of a house; the Persians being competent brick-builders and quite familiar with the arch in all its forms, larger examples were often vaulted in this material. The palace of Sapor I, the Sassanian monarch who defeated the Parthians, at Ctesiphon possesses the mightiest iwan of all; its towering parabolic vault, thrust into a pseudo-Hellenistic façade, dates from the middle of the 3rd century A.D. (Plate 19).

Introduced to stone as a building material, the Parthians developed an original method of construction for roofing their iwans. This was to throw across them a series of sturdy arches like a skeleton vault; each arch was so close to its neighbour that stone slabs could be laid across between the flat tops of the spandrel walls and a flat roof thus achieved. It was a strange form of construction and produced a very uncouth interior cut up into vertical slices by the massive, low-sprung diaphragm arches.

By the end of the 3rd century A.D., the Parthian vault had crossed the desert into Syria and was being used in the numerous cities which were rising on the eastern fringe of the Hellenistic world. In these timberless regions the problem of roofing was a serious one; by a combination of the Parthian arch and their own corbelling technique the Greeks were able not only to solve the problem but also to produce a fine series of buildings comparable with any in the world of their day.

The unit employed was the square, divided into two by a sturdy arch of considerable span and rising from a few feet above the ground. From the top of the spandrel wall above the arch the builders corbelled out to match similar corbelling set upon the walls flanking the arch until they could bridge the gap by stone slabs. By this means they could not only construct roofs but also intermediate floors; thus multi-storied buildings appear in many of the cities of the Syrian desert.

Within a century of the Crucifixion, many of the adherents of the new religion, proscribed within the Roman empire, were able to find a home in northern Babylonia, where an episcopal see was founded at Arbela by the Tigris. The churches they built followed the original arrangement of pagan temple and Jewish synagogue: the sanctuary being set across the axis of the approach to the building. When at a later date the apse became a customary feature of all churches, this was built out, on the site of the niche, from the centre of the long wall opposite to the entrance doorway of what had become the nave of the church. A long narthex passing across the front of the building brought it still more into line with those in the Romanized regions.

The Hellenistic Christians, emigrating eastwards from pagan persecution, founded a considerable number of cities along the western borders of the Syrian desert. Within the walls of these cities—all of which were destroyed by the Moslems in 636 and are now desolate ruins—great numbers of churches were erected. One of the most important is the group of ruins now known as Um el Jemal, which contains no less than seventeen. The earliest of these are rectangular halls covered with low-sprung Parthian vaults; the church of Julianos, dated 344, is an imposing structure, vaulted in ten bays. By the end of the 4th century, however, the basilica with its two rows of columns or piers seems to have become normal even in these remote cities.

In the domestic architecture of these Syrian cities the arch remains ubiquitous. Their spans are considerable and their abutments ill-designed; only their lack of elevation has enabled them to survive. By the 6th century, however, knowledge of the arch seems to have progressed sufficiently for it to be employed in arcades taking the place of the colonnades of the basilica. These Syrian arcades must not, however, be confused with those of the contemporary Roman basilicas. The supports of the latter are lofty columns set comparatively closely together, whereas the wide Syrian arches spring from low massive piers.

Christian colonization of the desert fringes led to the selection of these areas for the enjoyment of that austere monasticism which seems to have played such an important role in the life of the early Church. By the end of the 5th century the Syrian monasteries had become well-planned groups of buildings set round a courtyard and flanked by a basilican church. An important feature of the latter—and one quite new in architecture—was its slender bell-tower, clearly the prototype of those which were eventually to become such treasured features of the landscape of Europe.

In the same fashion as the Christians of the Seleucid areas made their way eastwards, so did those of Ptolemaic Egypt set up their monasteries along the desert fringing the Nile. Building technique was at a low ebb at the time and mud brick the only material available; thus the early Coptic monasteries in no way compared with those of the Syrians. It was not until the great days of the Byzantines that Coptic architecture came into its own.

The Christian religion came without warning upon a world which for century after century had progressed steadily along accepted lines of evolution. In as it were an instant the pagan temple, developed at the hands of generations of architects, became utterly obsolete; in the same instant was born the Christian church, a building that none had heard of until the moment. Every makeshift device is seen in the conversion of all kinds of buildings to serve the new religion. Here and there the exæron of some old Hellenistic basilica was roofed in to provide a church; an ancient temple at Syracuse was hurriedly converted.

Once the new basilical plan was established, classical temples were pulled down wholesale and their materials reused for building churches. Builders found themselves saddled with piles of second-hand columns collected for use in a church about to be erected. The use of the arch in place of the entablature had its advantage in that there was no further necessity for holding to the established proportions which had been fixed by the Classical Orders. The builders had thus only the columns themselves to adjust to fit the new structure. In some cases a second capital had to be placed above the original in order to enable the column to attain the desired height. The difficulty of placing the springing of an arch upon the delicately-carved capital of a Corinthian column was often countered by placing a kind of corbel capital called a pulvin intermediately between the two; the pulvin both kept the weight of the arch away from the frailer parts of the capital and also, if necessary, broadened the area of support to take a wider wall than it might otherwise have done.

Even to regions which knew no stone architecture the churches of Rome penetrated. Long after the imperial cities of Britain had fallen away into ruin, the faithful Roman monks returned to the scene to carry the Christian religion to a countryside the eagles had failed to hold. When at the close of the 6th century St Augustine was sent to convert the Anglo-Saxons, western Europe was building in timber only. All traces of the native structures have long ago perished, but we know that the wooden houses of the Gauls and Teutons were such as to command the respect of the Romans who saw them. In particular we are told of the wooden loggias by which the walls, formed of vertical planking, were protected from the wind and the rain which swept over a countryside sterner far than that of Italy.

But St Augustine and his monks worked laboriously to salvage bricks from the ruins of Roman cities, and with this material they showed the wondering Anglo-Saxons how the Romans built their churches. The buildings were humble enough in all conscience, being just little rectangular shrines with apses projecting from the east wall. The ruins of several of St Augustine's churches yet remain; one of them, at Bradwell, Essex, is still covered by a roof, so that those who wish may worship in a church that was built more than thirteen centuries ago. One feature is missing; the Roman monks, in tribute to the work of western builders, surrounded their churches with timber loggias or porticoes, long since carried away by the tempests of the years.

Chapter VIII

THE BYZANTINES

The Roman Church, founded and nourished in the ancient Hellenistic world, never had a chance to show what its architects could do. The collapse of the social order to which they belonged sent the architects of Imperial Rome eastwards to seek their fortunes in the new capital at Byzantium. Thus it came to pass that the eastern or Greek Church gained, after a bare two centuries, what the Roman Church had to wait for more than a thousand years to attain.

The heirs of those who had designed the magnificent *tepidaria* of the imperial thermae must have been shocked to see the architectural barns which represented the cathedrals of the new religion. The architect of the great basilica of Maxentius would surely have wept could he have seen the design approved by Constantine, only twenty years later, for St Peter's. Structures such as these with their flimsy walling and timber roofs seemed ephemeral indeed when set beside the achievements of the imperial engineers. So it came to pass that while some of the architects of the 4th and 5th centuries were filling the cities of the empire with austere basilicas, others were dreaming of massive piers of concrete carrying wide-flung arches, and glorious domes sweeping towards the sky. Spacious basilicas notwithstanding, the engineers knew that the centralized plan could not be consigned to oblivion; indeed they were certain that in it lay the future of architecture.

The Romans had evolved the dome—elevational counterpart of the circular plan—by stages of development succeeding from the arch through the barrel-vault and the cross-vault. Roman engineers had studied the principles of abutment and the technique of ribbed construction and concrete infilling, thus their domes were built as if they had grown out of the wall from which they rose.

All this had been achieved by long experiment and practice; the technique involved was acquired, and not indigenous to the land and its culture. In the ancient world, however, the tall beehive dome built of coursed rubble stone corbelled across the span had been known for three millennia. The circular hut or *tholos* had passed on its way from the Persian foothills through Babylonia to the shores of the Aegean. In northern Syria, the peasant's hut was a stone dome of the sort we may still see today.

Persia was the home of the dome. During the first quarter of the first Christian millennium the Persians had been perfecting a fine brick architecture based on the vault and dome for roofing purposes. They had learnt how to raise their tall domes—which, unlike the shyer Roman hemispheres, needed far less abutment—upon the tops of walls. Experimenting still further, they then discovered how to build a dome over a square apartment by throwing four small 'squinch arches' across the angles and thus producing an octagonal foundation which could easily be swept into a circular plan (Fig. 7).

In the middle of the 3rd century A.D., the Persian Sassanids swept across Mesopotamia and into the Seleucid world which was just beginning to learn the principles of arcuated construction. About a century later, the Sassanid domes began to appear in northern Mesopotamia and Armenia, regions in which the Christian church had by then become firmly established. It was at the time when Constantine was founding his centrally-planned churches in the Holy Land that the eastern dome began to show signs of becoming an accepted architectural feature.

There was yet much to be learned before the domes of the eastern buildings could be fitted upon the Hellenistic walling of those 4th-century churches with their pillar-supported main walls surrounded by aisles. At the beginning of the 6th century, however, the Syrian builders had solved the problem, as the octagonal church of St George at Ez Zorah, completed in 515, demonstrates. This little octagonal building is covered by a tall eastern dome carried upon eight wide arches rising from slender piers and completely surrounded by an aisle.

The Armenians experimented along their own lines. A feature of the Sassanian buildings was the manner in which the walls carrying the dome were sometimes removed and replaced by four wide arches carried upon piers left at the angles for the purpose. Sometimes, as if to show their confidence, the builders even removed the lower parts of these piers and inserted short columns; thus it appears as if the whole weight of the building and its roof were carried by these. The Armenians developed these experiments still further by removing the screen walls filling the great arches and adding four apsidal projections roofed by the usual 'conches' or semi-domes; in this fashion they increased the floor area from the original square to a quatrefoil.

The first great church to be built upon a centralized plan was the cathedral of Bosra in Syria. Only the aisle walls of this important building—the prototype of the Byzantine great church—remain to-day; the main central structure has disappeared. The nucleus of the cathedral was a square tower, probably carrying a tall dome, and clearly buttressed by the four apsidal projections described above. The important feature of the building is the remarkable fact that the walls of these four apses were supported upon a series of Corinthian columns; the whole weight of the roofs was carried upon these sixteen columns and the four comparatively slender angle supports constructed at the angles of the central square below the dome. Thus the surrounding aisle was completely incorporated within the floor area of the cathedral. In this building, which was completed in 513, we at last see the welding together of the Roman architectural monument and the Hellenistic aisled basilica.

The accession of Justinian to the throne of Byzantium in 527 was the signal for a burst of church-building rivalling that of Constantine. The church of the Nativity at Bethlehem was rebuilt to a more sophisticated design, Constantine's octagon being removed and replaced by a structure the plan of which was based upon that of Bosra cathedral. The surrounding apses were each carried upon two columns instead of four, the western apse being omitted to allow of the fine five-aisled nave which remains today. The wall of the aisle surrounding the fine domed 'triconch' was curved in sympathy with the central structure. Only foundations remain of this very interesting conception, which survived until the end of the 12th century but was

49. Light and graceful arcading carries the roof of the twelfth-century cloister
walk (Soria)

50. A great church which illustrates the early form of the French Gothic style
(Laon)

then replaced by the present somewhat undistinguished east end, roofed throughout with timber roofs.

The importance of Justinian's church at Bethlehem cannot be underestimated. While concentration upon the centralized structure covered by a great dome prevented the architects of the capital from paying any consideration to what was rather a hybrid conception, Justinian's plan spread throughout the boundaries of the empire. It was the central feature or *hypsosis* which seems to have captured the imagination of church-designers all over Europe; in timber, stone, and brick the square or circular towers, with or without the flanking projections, appeared in their hundreds throughout the countryside. It was as though every parish in Christendom wanted a copy of the church at Bethlehem for its very own. The 'triconch' became the *haikal* or sanctuary of the Coptic monastery of the 6th century, the nave of which was however a long open atrium, surrounded by deep loggias, like the court of an Egyptian temple. Even in the 12th century the arrangement appears once more in the great churches of the Rhineland.

The results of the Byzantine experiments is best demonstrated by the church of Sts Sergius and Bacchus founded in 527 in the capital itself. The dome of this most perfect of the centralized churches springs from a ring of eight piers carrying the usual wide arches, as at Ez Zorah. In the greater church, however, the four diagonally-placed arches lead into apses of the Bosra type, supported upon columns and serving in this case to convert the octagon into a form which produced a floor space closely approaching the square. Thus the architect had succeeded in bringing his dome down, first—by means of the normal spherical pendentives—upon the octagon and thence through the conches of the four apsidal recesses to enclose an area larger and more conveniently arranged than would have been the case had he been content to employ a circular or polygonal ground-plan (Plate 27).

Contemporary with this church are two others situated in two of the most important of the cities of northern Italy, Ravenna and Milan. The first of these, St Vitale, is a simple octagon surrounded on each face—excepting that adjoining the main apse—by the usual apsidal projection supported upon columns and giving access to a surrounding octagonal aisle. St Lorenzo at Milan is an enlarged version of

Bosra cathedral, having four apses in place of the cluster of smaller ones seen at Ravenna. The angle supports, which are far sturdier than in the Syrian church, have been modified since their original foundation, but it appears that they were so arranged as to convert the square into an octagon before the base of the dome was reached. Thus the apses are really sprung from the cardinal sides of an octagon set within the main square itself; the four remaining sides were probably lightened by niches. The outer wall of the aisle surrounding this somewhat complicated structure is adjusted so as to echo the shape of the main building itself.

The domes of these two western structures are of far lighter construction than that of Sts Sergius and Bacchus and the eastern churches generally. The latter were constructional and intended to serve as roofs, whereas the former are simply ceilings and have timber roofs above them as protection from the weather. The heavy domical roof was not employed by the Byzantines west of the Adriatic; timber was the normal roofing material of western Europe.

The aisles of these 6th-century churches were not merely added in order to increase the accommodation within the buildings; the vaulting with which they were covered assisted in buttressing the comparatively slender piers supporting the main structure. The upper surfaces of the aisle-vaults provided floors to galleries above; thus the aisles of most of the larger Byzantine churches are two-storied. The gallery was a feature greatly admired by the Hellenistic Greeks; the inner aisles of the civic basilicas were frequently made two-storied so as to surround the *exæron* with a gallery overlooking it. The use of the Parthian type of vaulting by the Syrians and the fashion for creating multi-storied houses often resulted in the loggias attached to these being similarly treated. Basilican churches of the 6th century were sometimes provided with galleries over the aisles, St Agnes without the Walls of Rome being an example.

Byzantine architects were pre-eminently concerned with the mechanics of building. Hitherto the structure had been mainly the concern of the builder, the architect simply being, as his title denotes, the master-builder. But by the 4th century the Byzantine designers had ceased to be described as architects and were become engineers, a clear indication that their function was deemed to be, not the elevational presentation of a building but the calculation of the mechanics governing its erection.

The aim of the Byzantine engineers had been to erect great churches covered by lofty domes. In this they had succeeded in so far as the elevational aspect of their designs was concerned. They were nevertheless restricted in their planning schemes by the centralization forced upon these by the spirit of *hypsosis* and, what was even more important, the requirements of domical construction. They were confronted with the problem of building a dome over a church *nave* planned as an axial building. The solution was found in time for them to display their ability to the utmost in the design of the great cathedral of the Byzantines, the Hagia Sophia at Constantinople itself, begun in 532. The basis of its plan is that of the basilica of Maxentius at Rome with its three huge vaulting bays. The central bay they covered with their dome, spanning over a hundred feet; four gigantic lateral buttresses provided the necessary abutment to the wide arches supporting this *hypsosis*. In place of the two terminal bays, however, they erected a pair of enormous apses joined to the central area by its two transverse arches; these apses were supported on large piers and roofed by semi-domes as if each were half a domed church separated by the central feature. The principle of the construction was that which had already been inaugurated in Bosra cathedral; at Hagia Sophia, however, the two lateral apsidal projections were omitted in order to convert the plan from the centralized to the axial. Smaller apsidal projections, carried by columns, completed the squaring-up of the main floor-space of the cathedral, which was surrounded by the usual galleried aisles. Between the pairs of lateral buttresses the two wide arches were filled by screen-walls carried upon the arcaded fronts of the aisles and galleries. The whole glorious structure is a triumph of engineering and the manner in which the masses forming it have been piled together give an impression of stability not to be equalled in any other building in the world. The Hagia Sophia may not have the whimsical charm of the graceful Gothic cathedrals; not one of these, however, can display the overwhelming dignity of the Byzantine masterpiece. (Plates 28 and 29).

After the completion of this great church in 537, the ecclesiastical architecture of the Byzantines seems to have reached a state of exhaustion. The imperial architects had attained their desires; there seemed to be nothing more to do. In any case, religion was beginning to take second place to politics, so that public buildings were becoming of more moment than churches. Constantinople, capital of Christendom, was once more assuming its true role as a wealthy, pleasure-loving city, into which were poured the treasures of both Europe and the Orient. Byzantium was becoming a city of palaces; it is a great misfortune that the long Turkish occupation of this wonderful city has removed all traces of its ancient splendour save for those churches which have been converted into mosques. Even in the mid-7th century, when the whole of the Hellenistic regions became lost to the Moslems, the Byzantines could never have imagined that such was to be the ultimate fate of their glorious buildings.

The loss of the Byzantine palaces is all the sadder for the knowledge of their glories we have from documentary sources. An indication of the state kept by the emperors is found in the magnificence of their throne rooms which seem to have rivalled the great churches in scale and structural elaboration. Thus by the middle of the first half of the sixth century the throne room was an octagon surrounded by eight apses; a century later it was even a triconch similar to that hitherto used for the sanctuaries of the most venerated churches.

The utter collapse of the Hellenistic world which took place in the middle of the 7th century was indeed a sad loss to architecture. Driven from Syria and Egypt, the trabeated style, with the Orders which had been its most notable adornment, was swept into oblivion; the former to reappear only in the form of a 19th-century essay in archaism, the latter to be set aside until their renaissance during the 15th century. Hellenistic Rome, its architecture long since swallowed up in a vortex of concrete vaults, from which a few arcaded basilicas endeavoured to emerge as if striving to perpetuate the spirit of the Classical tradition, was now completely involved in the semi-barbaric life of western Europe, seething under the pressure of the great migrations.

From the 7th century onwards, the principal Byzantine sources were sub-oriental in origin. At the eastern end of the Black Sea, where the Hellenistic masons had for some time been rubbing shoulders with the Iranian dome-builders, a fine building style was now in existence. This Armenian architecture may be described as westernized Sassanian. Persian brickwork had been replaced by good Greek masonry, while the tall domes were now constructed in rubble concrete. The arch rising from piers is ubiquitous; the classical column does not appear at all. The masonry technique and ornament strongly suggest that employed by the Syrian builders of the 6th century. There are, however, no basilicas; the plan of every church is ruled by its central dome.

The Armenian dome is obviously Sassanian in origin. Considerably taller than a Roman dome of the same span, these eastern structures seem generally to have been provided with a ring of small windows just above the springing. As early as the 6th century the lower part of the dome was being adjusted externally so as to provide a vertical drum in which these windows were set. The hemispherical Roman dome, having to be provided with heavy loading above the abutments, projects but little above the masonry surrounding its base. In its Byzantine form the dome is so efficiently buttressed that it can be constructed as less than a hemisphere; in other words, it becomes a saucer dome. It will be observed that the curves of pendentives pass more smoothly into those of a saucer dome than one of hemispherical section.

After the completion of the great churches of the Justinian era, the Byzantine architects ceased to raise their vast domed roofs over their buildings. For one thing, the Church was beginning to lose the tremendous popularity it had enjoyed—if somewhat spasmodically— during the last two centuries of Byzantine patronage. The smaller churches which were being built throughout the Byzantine realms were being erected to far more economical designs.

It seems probable that during the 6th and 7th centuries the lead in church design was being given by the architects of Armenia, with their combination of Sassanian and Hellenistic technique. The Sassanian dome was customarily supported upon four wide arches occupying almost the whole of the sides of the square upon which it was raised. In order to provide adequate abutment, these arches were made very broad on the soffit; thus the plan of the building approached the cruciform, with each of the four arms of the cross roofed by what were in fact short barrel-vaults.

At the time of the Moslem invasion, the Armenians had already developed their architecture to a finer degree than might have been seen in the Balkans, Asia Minor, or any other more purely Byzantine regions. Although the buildings were small compared with those of Constantinople, Antioch, or Ravenna, Armenian mason-craft seems to have been of a very high order, possibly owing to the emigration of Syrian masons under the threat of the impending invasion. Certainly there is a very strong resemblance between the architectural ornament of the Syrian buildings and those of Armenia.

The Armenian plans, being based upon the dome, are entirely different from those of Syria. The earliest churches, as at Mastara, have the dome buttressed by the usual four apsidal projections but carried upon squinches of Sassanian character. By the middle of the 7th century, however, the pendentive has come to stay. The quatrefoil plan with its apses carried upon arcades and surrounded by an aisle, as at Bosra, is seen in the church of St Gregory at Zwarthnotz, where the dome is carried upon four massive piers.

Armenia, land of domed and vaulted churches, was at this time short of building timber. To save centering in arch-construction, the architects of the beginning of the 7th century began to reduce the soffits of their sturdy arches to a width less than that of the walls they supported; in this fashion they invented the ordered arch and, at the same time, the ordered pier which was to develop into the type of structure supporting the Gothic cathedrals (Fig. 8, also Plate 31).

Despite the undoubted masonry skill of these 7th-century Armenian architects, they had not the engineering knowledge of the Romans which had enabled the latter to cover their buildings with vast cross-vaults and domes. The Armenian dome, stilted or raised upon a drum for lighting purposes and not very securely buttressed, seldom grew to be very large on plan, and thus always tended to restrict the span of the building. In order to increase the accommodation of the church it was thus necessary to lengthen it by greatly increasing the depth of the east and west arches leading out of the central space until they had become barrel-vaulted appendages. The eastern of these formed a chancel, the western a 'west nave'. Both were flanked by low arches opening into very narrow aisles; these in their turn led into the north and south arms of the central space, isolating the supports of the dome into four piers. Fine cruciform churches of this nature are common in Armenia, the cathedral of Thalish, built in 688, being a perfect example. A century later, the Byzantine architects produced a massive copy of this type of structure in the church of St Irene at Constantinople. The central space of this fine building is covered by a spreading saucer-dome raised upon a low, windowed, drum; another saucer-dome covers the west nave. The aisles are galleried in the Byzantine fashion.

During the 8th and 9th centuries, the Byzantine lands—that is to say the peninsulas of Asia Minor and the Balkans—became covered with small churches of no great architectural merit. The plan followed was based upon a square of four massive piers supporting a central dome flanked by four deep arches which were in fact the short barrel-vaulted arms of a cross (Plate 23). The isolation of the four supports of the dome makes it appear that the central structure was surrounded by an aisle, which in fact only exists at the angles of the building unless the lateral arches flanking the dome were filled with galleries; these, however, were disappearing, even in Byzantium itself, after the end of the 8th century.

The Armenian church-builders, the refinement of whose style is clearly illustrated by the dignified church at Thalish, were meanwhile proceeding along lines of their own. The central dome is still the most important feature in the elevation of the Armenian church of the last quarter of the millennium; indeed its drum becomes taller and elaborately ornamented with external arcading. On plan, however, the dome has ceased to exercise its original influence; the long church with the western extension from the central area has become standard.

Notable advances are made in the masonry details of these buildings. In particular the ordered arches become lighter and more graceful; by the end of the 10th century they have attained the pointed form. The compound pier takes on the complicated plan associated with mediæval European architecture. By the end of the millennium the Armenian church was a building which had achieved a surprisingly advanced stage of design and construction.

This style had no effect upon the architecture of the Balkans and Asia Minor. In these regions, where churches were not large, the centralized plan continued to maintain its supremacy; by the 10th century, however, the angle supports of the dome had become trans-lated into four columns which replaced the original massive piers (Plate 32). At this time there is also a tendency towards the elongation, not of the nave, but of the chancel which was now being interpolated between the central space and the apse.

As early as the 6th century the Byzantine church had abandoned the use of the atrium, presumably owing to the lack of space in cities for this spacious forecourt. The eastern part of its peristyle, the nar-thex, was, however, invariably retained and formed an essential part of the church plan. By the end of the 10th century the narthex was often being returned along the flanks of the building to form a kind of external cloister or loggia round three sides of the central cruciform mass of the building. This innovation is possibly connected with the loggias which formed such an important feature of early timber architecture in western Europe; it may be seen in the 12th century at St Mark's, Venice.

Notwithstanding the debt to Hellenism acknowledged in the fine masonry buildings of the eastern Byzantine world it was the use of Roman brick which enabled the engineers of westward-spreading Byzantinism to indulge in their taste for *hypsosis* as displayed by high-flung vaults and domes. Thus the monumentalism of design was not equalled by the same dignity in elevational presentation which might have been achieved had the buildings been erected in wrought stone. We therefore find considerable interest being displayed in methods of covering brickwork, either by plaster or with a mosaic of small pieces of assorted material. From the amazing designs of the mosaic artist was developed an artistic style which found expression in painted decoration; walls, vaults, and domes being treated to some form of coloured ornamentation which greatly helped to brighten the interiors of buildings removed from the sunny regions of the Classical world.

The ecclesiastical building boom of the Justinian era was at its height at the middle of the 6th century which saw the erection of the great cathedral itself. Byzantium's most important contribution to the development of architectural history was quick to make its appearance in the western empire founded by Charlemagne at the end of the 8th century. The emperor's cathedral at Aachen, a belated copy of

51. Only the nave and transepts of the towering cathedral of Beauvais were ever attempted

52. The builders of the Gothic cathedrals of France strove to attain height
(Bourges)

a Byzantine octagon of nearly three centuries earlier, set a fashion for centralized planning which was to play a fundamental part in the development of the church-plan in western Europe and at the same time effected the introduction of Byzantinism as the foundation for its mediæval architecture. It was not however until the Ottonian revival of the 10th century that the humble provincial architecture of the West—much of which was executed in timber—was able to develop its potentialities.

In the closing years of the first millennium, the conversion of southern Russian to Christianity brought Byzantine ecclesiastical architecture into vast new regions. The first important building was the cathedral of St Sophia at Kiev, built in 1036. The plan adopted was developed from the small Byzantine church of the period, with its dome rising above a cruciform mass which on plan appeared as a surrounding aisle. The cruciform effect was disguised in elevation by raising the parapets of the external walls to a common altitude; this squaring-up of the building so as to give the effect that the dome rises from a cubical mass is to be seen in many Byzantine churches and became universal practice in Russia. At Kiev cathedral the narthex with its wings has been incorporated within the building as an outer aisle; thus the building has five aisles on each of its axes.

The spread of Christianity, and with it Byzantine architecture, along the trade route across Europe to the Baltic resulted in a similar cathedral being built at Novgorod in 1045. Thus it was clear that Russia was destined to fall within the orbit of the domed style of south-eastern Europe; indeed, so strong was the initial grasp of the Byzantines that the country entirely escaped the Gothic period which for three centuries absorbed the rest of the continent. The building technique introduced at Kiev and Novgorod depended upon the use of the brickwork common to the Byzantine style; a century later, however, the Russians developed a fine masonry style in the region lying east of Moscow. The finest of the churches of this period—and probably the finest ecclesiastical building in Russia—is the Cathedral of the Assumption at Vladimir which dates from 1158; its plan follows the elaborate version of the centralized arrangement initiated at Kiev.

Throughout the history of its ecclesiastical architecture, Russia has remained true to the dome as its principal elevational feature. The form adopted was the late Byzantine type of no great diameter and raised upon a lofty drum. The normal Byzantine church seldom had more than one dome; the Russians multiplied their domes to a sometimes fantastic extent. Thus the central domes of most large churches were flanked by at least four others, either axially over the short transfeature, an arrangement first seen in Byzantium in the middle of the first half of the 9th century. The bulbous dome, the origin of which is still not ascertained, but which is probably of Persian origin, appears at least as early as the 13th century.

In 976 the basilical cathedral of St Mark in the island-city of Venice was gutted by fire. The rebuilding took the form of giving the church a new interior planned upon the same lines as that of St Irene at Constantinople, erected some two centuries earlier and the last of the great churches of Byzantium. Later the Venetian church was enlarged by removing the screen walls closing the ends of the arches flanking the central dome and building large square transepts, each of which was designed upon the same principle as one of the two great domed bays of the original church. The short chancel separating the central area from the apse was also roofed with a dome, completing a cruciform building displaying five domes.

In western Europe, the Byzantine style had impressed itself upon a series of little churches in which the central feature had been a low tower, supported upon four simple square piers, covered with a pyramidal cap of timber in place of a dome. At the beginning of the 12th century, however, a stronger line was being followed in the heart of France, where interest in barrel-vaulting had reached the stage at which it was being employed for the roofing of the main spans of churches. In the opening years of the century the cathedral of Angoulême was designed as a long aisleless structure of four great bays, each covered with a Byzantine dome complete with its pendentive supports and rising from four massive piers of masonry. In 1120 the church of St Front at Perigueux was planned in five bays arranged in a cross; in this example the angle piers are separated into four portions so that each bay is a reproduction of a small Byzantine church with the dome-supports isolated fron the outer walls.

The buildings of the great days of Byzantinism were founded upon wide deep arches springing from sturdy piers of brickwork or masonry. The trabeated style of building had vanished from Europe. With it had disappeared the Classical Orders, which were not even employed as wall-decoration. The column, however, was far from being obsolete. The Byzantine column is a somewhat different type of object from that which formed the principal feature of the classical temple. Since the days of the first arcaded basilicas the column had been turned out of a single lump of stone instead of being built up in several drums as in the lofty shafts which supported the classical entablatures. Thus the Byzantine column is a shorter, slighter affair than its predecessor.

In the great churches of the era of Justinian, the walls of their apsidal projections were supported upon masonry columns of Classical type. With this exception, however, the column was seldom used as a primary support until the 10th century. The proper function of the turned Byzantine shaft was to form part of an arcaded screen such as that supporting the front of a gallery. It is these arcades which form the principal architectural ornament of the church interior. As early as the 7th century, the Armenian churches, which did not employ the column at all, had their walls punctuated externally by ranges of tall arcades rising from slender shafts, sometimes coupled in pairs. Thus it will be seen that in essence the Byzantine building technique employs piers as primary supports and columns for secondary purposes only (Plate 27).

The capital of the Byzantine column follows no ordinance as did those of the Classical styles. The general principle seems to be a modification of the Doric echinus to accommodate a slender shaft to a considerably wider wall. Thus the average Byzantine capital is square on plan with its underside swept together to meet the top of the circular column. These 'cushion' capitals were sometimes placed one above the other, the upper, or 'dosseret', being wider than that below so as to assist the transference of the wide wall to the slimmer column. In fine buildings the capitals were often beautifully carved; the ornament is quite free and much of it is no doubt of oriental origin.

Every great architectural period has its typical building. The Classical Greek temple gave place to the Roman tepidarium which in turn became forgotten under the spell of the glorious Byzantine cathedral. Yet the buildings of this period were not all churches, nor was the contribution of the Byzantines limited to ecclesiastical architecture. It was in the plans of their houses that the New Romans displayed the modernism of their outlook and their liberation from the shackles of an outworn Classicism.

We have seen how the Hellenistic house of early days expanded to surround a formal courtyard, itself a relic of a now archaic orientalism; we have also seen how those ardent admirers of Hellenism, the imperial Romans, perpetuated the courtyard principle and added yet another, the atrium, before the entrance to the noble peristyle. Yet despite the ubiquity of the Roman colonist it was nevertheless not the Roman type of house which was to become the ancestor of the dwellings of mediæval Europe.

Notwithstanding its wings spreading into Greece and Syria, the real homeland of the Byzantines was what is now Anatolia, land of snows and the pitched roof which sheds them. Thus it was the compact Hittite type of house which became that of the Byzantines. We have seen in Chapter V how the Aegean house had became a rectangular nucleus of rooms comprising a set of small apartments flanking the megaron and covered by a lean-to roof formed by producing one side of the main roof. The Byzantine house was simply a two-storied version of this having the megaron raised to the first floor which thus becomes a *piano nobile*. At the same time this main block becomes an approximately cubical mass, irregularly roofed, and of a tower-like form entirely different from anything hitherto found in domestic architecture (Fig. 5).

Access to the *piano nobile* was by a wide stair leading to the door of the megaron and either passing up one of the outer walls of the structure (Plate 34) or enclosed within the lesser division of the plan. In the warmer parts of the empire the main front of the building was protected from the sun by a loggia, two-storied so as to provide a balcony or verandah before the megaron. Stabling and offices were scattered about irregular courtyards, seldom enclosed and provided with loggias here and there for purposes of intercommunication. An interesting feature is the provision of projecting hoods over windows in order to exclude the rays of the noonday sun.

Perhaps no historical style of architecture was so productive of innovations as the Byzantine. With the introduction of the *piano nobile* the staircase became a feature of paramount importance, often being enclosed within its own forebuilding. In monastic houses the stair-tower was generally raised to form a tall structure of monumental proportions, used as a campanile and certainly the ancestor of the church towers of Christendom and the minarets of Islam. The 6th-century towers of Byzantine Syria still form one of the most imposing series of monuments to be found in the ancient world; sculptured bands of Greek lettering, extracts from the Scriptures, betray their origin.

Fig. 5. A sixth-century Byzantine house

Byzantine architecture, in every way Greek in spirit rather than Roman, displays the culmination of the practical achievements of the Classical era. The clumsiness of the Doric gives place to Ionic grace and blossoms into the appealing beauty of the Hellenistic city. It was left to the Byzantine Greek to exploit the possibilities of *hypsosis* as he piled his great church towards the clouds. In doing so he set the key stone upon Classicism and at the same time prepared the foundations of the age to come.

From embattled Byzantium—its 5th-century walls are protected by square Greek towers and not the semicircular bastions of the Roman *castra*—went forth the cultural colonists who instructed the peoples of the sunset lands in the art of civilization. But Byzantium itself was falling, a last outpost of the ancient world already threatened by tremendous pressure from unimaginable sources. Byzantium today is represented by its great cathedral and a few desecrated churches, while its triple walls, target of bitter sieges and bearing the scars of savage earthquakes, remain the most magnificent spectacle in all military architecture.

Chapter IX

ISLAM

The 7th century saw the Byzantine empire at the height of its glory but with its power waning under the influence of luxury and indolence. Thus the Moslem onslaught of the third decade of the century caught it unprepared; it may well have been touch and go as to whether the rush of the tribesmen was to stop short of Constantinople itself. In fact it was only the mountain barrier of the Taurus which stopped the desert warriors and saved Asia Minor from succumbing with the rest of the ancient world. In a few weeks Sassanids, Seleucids, and all the rest of the relics of past civilizations disappeared; Romanized Egypt soon followed. During the remainder of the century, the invincible Semites filtered through the decaying cities clinging to the southern shores of the Mediterranean; as the 8th century was born, Isalm had reached the Atlantic and was spreading into Europe. Here, however, it encountered no tired old civilization but a rising new power, soon to lay claim to the sceptre of Rome itself; the hammer of Charles Martel smashed the vanguard of Islam against the anvil of the Pyrenees and Europe was saved.

In less than a century the Moslem gains had been enormous. The old lands of the Middle East were now at the mercy of the infidel; his ships were soon to rove unhindered through the Mediterranean. Of the old cultural centres, decaying Rome and stunned Byzantium alone were left to brood over the realization that their empires had passed into the hands of barbarians. The new world force which had arisen was entirely lacking in any form of culture; the exponents of Islam were desert tribesmen used to living in tents of goat-hair. Yet within a few months of their victories they were raising buildings in the territories they had conquered; in a few decades they had laid the foundations of one of the most beautiful of all architectural styles.

The race which thus spread itself from India to the Atlantic was in reality a religious community. Inspired to tremendous feats by the influence of their faith, they were quick to set its seal upon the lands they annexed by erecting shrines to Islam. Their problem was that the religion itself was but newly born and knew nothing of temples; moreover the Arabs of the desert had no knowledge of building in any form. The latter difficulty was soon overcome by employing builders already practising in the conquered territory. The problem of planning a temple to Islam was one which could not be settled so easily.

In 623, when Mohammed built his house at Medina, his followers prayed within its courtyard, facing the wall nearest to Jerusalem, holiest of monotheistic cities. When the weather was hot, the worshippers begged for shelter from the rays of the sun; the humble loggia with its row of poles supporting a roof of rush matting was the first sanctuary of Islam. From that moment the plan of the mosque was settled as a courtyard with a loggia along one side to form a sanctuary. One feature was lacking to produce the effect of a temple; the niche for the statue of the god. Mohammed would not allow the use of idols of any form; on his death, therefore, the niche was placed in the wall of the mosque nearest his grave in Mecca. Thus the worshipper can always imagine the figure of the Prophet, risen from the tomb, standing within the *mihrab*, attentive to the prayers of the faithful.

Orientation towards Mecca is an essential factor in the planning of mosques. Mohammedan worship merely consists in saying one's prayers facing towards the *qibla*, or Mecca direction. Thus the ideal arrangement of a Moslem congregation would be a long rank of worshippers standing side by side. This requirement, not encountered hitherto in religious architecture, was met by setting out a huge courtyard having one side—the *qibla* wall—towards Mecca; along this qibla wall a deep loggia provided shade for the worshippers as in the original mosque at Medina. In actual fact, the other three sides of the courtyard were also provided with loggias, generally much shallower in projection than the sanctuary itself to provide overflow accommodation as required (Plate 36).

The 7th-century mosques were indeed extensive structures. From Mesopotamia to Morocco the vast courtyards appeared, surrounded

53. The soaring pillars of a Gothic cathedral of Spain
(Seville)

54. A late-Gothic church of western Europe
(Hertogenbosch)

internally by deep loggias which swelled before the *qibla* wall of each into a spacious pillared hall. In both plan and elevation these early mosques were simple enough; the new religion preached austerity and its temples were merely intended to give privacy and shelter to worshippers. Only the *mihrab* niche, provided in all mosques large and small, introduced an architectural feature unconnected with structural requirements.

The structural problem facing the 7th-century mosque-builder was that of supporting the roofs of the sanctuary, and its supplementary loggias if such existed. Bay design was easily introduced by setting-out the building upon a rectangular grid. The new territories of Islam contained plenty of basilica-type churches with column-supported arcades; it was only a matter of persuading the local builders to re-erect these arcades along the lines set out by their new masters.

There is something curiously naïve about these 7th-century mosques. Most of the materials comprising them are second-hand. The sanctuary of an important mosque often being many times larger than the biggest church in the district, a number of churches had sometimes to be looted to provide enough columns for one mosque; thus the latter often unashamedly exhibits a complete hotch-potch of oddments in the supports of its arcades. The arches are quite plain and unaffected; if the columns are too low they may be carried up as piers before the arch is turned. The roof was of timber; the whole supporting structure is generally so light that wooden tie-beams are introduced resting upon the capitals of the columns and passing in all directions (Plate 37).

The sanctuary of the early mosque differs from the church nave in that the axis of the former lies athwart the direction faced by the worshipper and thus, though comparatively short in depth, may be of great width. Hence the early mosques have their sanctuaries planned in a great number of aisles, separated by arcades as in a church, but far greater in number. At Cordova there are nineteen; seventeen is not uncommon. There is always a central aisle, aligned on the principal *mihrab;* often it is wider than the others, as in a church. In the great mosque at Damascus, probably designed by a Byzantine architect, the sanctuary consists of a spacious church-like structure of three wide aisles passing along the *qibla* wall; this arrangement was followed in planning those mosques erected in Cairo before the end of the first millennium.

The Damascus mosque was built in the early days of the 8th century, at the height of the Omayyid epoch which during the first half of this century contributed so much to the glory of the growing culture of Islam. In its early stages, Islamic architecture owes most to its immediate predecessor, the Byzantine; thus there is more than a suggestion of the basilica church in the sanctuary of the mosque. In some of the great mosques of the 'sunset-land'—the Moghreb—the *qibla* end of the centre aisle is given a dome covering the space before the *mihrab*; these early domes are small and rise from drums in the same fashion as those of contemporary Byzantine churches.

In the middle of the 8th century all this was changed by the rise of the Abbasid dynasty in Mesopotamia and the subsequent suppression of the Omayyids. Henceforth the principal architectural influence was Persian. The open-ended *iwan* appears in domestic planning at this period. Development of the trade route from east to west resulted in the founding of chains of caravanserais or *khans*: courtyards surrounded by loggias giving shade to the traveller and his animals. The *khan* is one of the most typical buildings represented in Islamic architecture; soon it becomes two-storied, with sleeping galleries above the stabling.

The most important architectural feature introduced by the Abbasids was the Persian arch, pointed in form and rising from square piers of brickwork instead of the column of antiquity. By the 9th century this had become universal in Islamic architecture; the Cairene mosques of Ibn Tulun and El Hakim are examples of its use.

Courtyard frontages of earlier mosques, such as that of Kairwan, were often at this period being provided with new arcaded façades designed in the Persian manner with pointed arches rising from brick piers (Plate 38). Thus Islamic architecture was at last breaking free from its Byzantine shackles and second-hand constructional devices; oriental in its roots, it was adopting the most eastern of the building styles then available.

The style of the great mosques, with their hypostyle sanctuaries filled with a forest of columns, reached perfection in the western lands of the Moghreb beyond the sphere of Roman penetration. Here there were no second-hand columns to be looted from the ruins of other days; the Moslem architects built sturdy square piers and turned their curious horseshoe arches above these. The origin of this form of arch —which was used by the Byzantines of 6th-century Anatolia—is uncertain, but it may be due to the greater ease with which its centering can be supported while the arch itself is being built; in normal arches the centering must be supported either from the ground or upon the slight projection afforded by the impost or the abacus of a capital whereas in the horseshoe variety the lower parts of the curve can carry the centering.

The 8th century saw the covering of the Mesopotamian plains with the huge semi-oriental palaces of the Abbasid caliphs—that of Samarra, begun 836, covered 432 acres—set out on monumental plans and surrounded, where water-supply permitted, by densely-populated cities rivalling in their extent those of their Babylonian predecessors. Most of the building was executed in sun-dried brick, so that hardly anything is left today. No trace remains of the Baghdad of Harun-er-Raschid, which in its day covered some twenty-five square miles. Only some of the more isolated palaces, built of burnt brick and founded upon remote sites far removed from the dwellings of those seeking building materials, have survived as illustrations of the Abbasid style of architecture; Ukheidr is perhaps the most notable example.

During the third quarter of the 8th century, Islam, threatened in the east by the Mongols and with its westward drive finally checked by the rising Christian empire of the Franks, began to fortify its frontiers. The Mohammedans had as yet no proper military architecture; the Persian wall of enceinte was a tall curtain of no great thickness punctuated with innumerable slender half-round buttresses which served as substitutes for the wall-towers without which no fortification is secure. Western Islamic defences of this period were similar but the buttresses were square after the Byzantine fashion.

The century ended with the reigns of two great rivals, Charlemagne, emperor of the Franks, and Harun-er-Raschid, caliph of Baghdad. Under the latter and his successors the 9th century passes in a surge of Abbasid glory while palaces and teeming cities rise

along the ancient rivers of Babylonia. Persian architects, newly converted to Islam, introduced monumental planning of a class never
before seen in architectural history; the perishable nature of the sun-
dried brick employed in the actual carrying out of the work has,
however, caused most of their achievements to return once more to the
desert plain.

The 10th century saw the rise of powerful dynasties in the Moghreb.
An impressive style of military architecture, Abbasid in origin but
with Byzantine modifications, begins to spread in a line of fortified
palaces and walled cities reaching from 'Ifriqua'—now Tunisia—to
the limits of Mauretania. Soon the Berbers are building their huge
uncouth qasbas on the mountain spurs fringing the Sahara. By the
end of the millennium the Islamic empire had established itself from
the tip of the Moghreb to the mountains of Persia. All its cities had
been provided with great mosques surrounding spacious courtyards
and expanding on the qibla side into vast sanctuaries in which a
tangle of arches cluster above a forest of columns. Even in the
Abbasid east, where dome and vaulted iwan were finding their way
into Moslem domestic buildings, the largest mosque exhibits no
architectural feature except for the arcades supporting the flat roof of
the sanctuary. Puritanical Islam has not yet developed the monumental factor in its religious buildings.

The 11th century began with pressure upon eastern Islam from the
Mongols, who overran Persia and began to threaten the power of the
Abbasids. More important to the history of architectural development
was the conquest by the Seljuk Turks of the last Byzantine foothold
in Asia. By the end of the century Armenia and Anatolia had become
Turkish; ancient Iconium, today Konia, became the Turkish capital
and seat of a new and important architectural style deriving much
from the Byzantine traditions of the region.

The 12th century is one of the most important in the history of
architecture. In the classical regions, the Roman and Byzantine styles
had deteriorated into feebleness, their places being taken by the vigorous but half-barbaric so-called 'Romanesque' of western Europe and
the uninspired 'basilican' style which still obtained along the northern
shores of the Mediterranean. In Africa and south-west Asia, the
immensely vigorous but still ingenuous Islamic empire, muddling

along with a kind of second-hand architecture, was beginning to seek a style of its own upon which to build. The Crusades of the 12th century, which hurled both Byzantines and Franks into the Islamic world just at that point where western architecture impinged upon the Persian styles, resulted in an interchange of ideas which benefited Christian and Moslem alike and launched both creeds into the great adventure of the Middle Ages.

The situation of the Holy Land caused the clash to take place in the eastern Moslem world. Thus, for the Moghreb and Spain the 12th century was one of great mosques with spacious courts surrounded by elaborately foliated arcades which were to influence in their turn the Gothic architecture of Christendom. In the east, however, the tale is one of fortification against the Crusading armies which threatened the cities of Syria and Egypt. These 12th-century Moslem fortifications are fine works based on the best Byzantine models, from which the square-towered curtains of Christian castles were also being copied; tall gatehouses flanked by large towers protected the entrances to Moslem cities of the days of the Crusades. The new fashion in Islamic military architecture—so different from that illustrated by the oriental castles of the 9th century—soon spread to Spain, where the great cities of the Moslem frontier were surrounded by town walls of a strength never before seen in Western Europe.

The era of the Crusades marks the rise of a new Turco-Byzantine culture in Anatolia, where the city of Konia began to take the lead in Islamic architecture. Like all converts, the Turks had taken fervently to the Moslem religion; their origin, however, led them to develop an entirely different style of religious architecture from that followed in the regions conquered by the Arabs. The courtyard, from earliest times indigenous to these areas, was unsuited to mountainous districts where sites were rocky and hard to level; the Persian house is a compact block of apartments instead of a hollow square. Thus the great courtyard—which the climate of Anatolia rendered inconvenient as a place of worship—is absent from the Turkish mosques, emphasis being placed upon the covered sanctuary.

The great courtyard mosque is the very essence of early Moslem architecture. As the creed of Islam spread its arms across the world it carried these vast sprawling structures with it. In the 12th century they are still appearing in the western Moghreb; by the 16th they have covered Persia and reached distant India. They do not, however, represent the more enlightened taste of the central Moslem world, in which most of the large cities were already provided with a great mosque representing what in a city of Christendom would have been its cathedral. The sanctuaries of these mosques were continually being enlarged—sometimes at the expense of the courtyard—in order to accommodate still larger congregations under cover. Thus even in the older regions of the Moslem world the end of the first millennium saw its architects beginning to concentrate upon the improvement of the sanctuary. What they felt was the need for buildings which would compare in architectural significance with the Christian cathedrals. The vast columned halls of the early mosques, though spacious enough, were too insignificant in stature. The need for a height factor in the design had become apparent; thus the abandoning of the great courtyard was soon to be followed by that of the pillared sanctuary in favour of something which, although less extensive would be loftier in elevation.

One Friday morning in 637 the Moslem troops had worshipped their prophet in one of the grandest apartments the world has ever seen—the great vaulted *iwan* of the Sassanian palace at Ctesiphon (Plate 19). It was an experience that Islam never forgot. To the Moslem mind that mighty man-made cavern must have represented the most glorious of all architectural achievements—a truly perfect sanctuary of the true Faith. Structures such as this were far beyond the powers of that ordinary Moslem architect. It was not until the Abbasids began to incorporate Persia within their empire that the art of roofing large spans with vault and dome began to appear within the Moslem world. Thenceforth the vaulted *iwan* finds a place in eastern Islamic domestic architecture.

Mongol pressure upon the Abbasid empire, culminating in its utter destruction in 1258 by Hulagu, drove many Persian architects and craftsmen across the barrier of the Taurus and into Asia Minor, where they added their skill and knowledge to that of the Byzantines who had for so long been covering Armenia and Anatolia with beautiful buildings. From this combination of east and west was born the most perfect of all western Islamic styles, the Seljuk.

Inspired by the Crusades, Islam began to foster interest in its creed through the medium of the religious school or *medressa*. These buildings, which began to appear during the 12th century, were planned on similar lines to the Byzantine monastery; each consisted of a series of apartments gathered round a small internal courtyard at the *qibla* end of which a vaulted *iwan* provided a sanctuary in which prayers could be said.

The Byzantine and Persian architects who together created the fine Seljuk buildings developed the *medressa* plan until they were able to produce a Moslem building designed in as orderly a fashion as the contemporary Byzantine church; the finished structure being covered with elaborate ornamental detail in which Greek, Armenian, and Persian elements were mingled in rich profusion. Thus for the first time Islam produces a compact building instead of an agglomeration surrounding a courtyard and at the same time discovers elevational design and external ornamental treatment.

The Seljuk architects made much of the dome. Both in the Moghreb and in Cairo, the Byzantine dome perched upon its drum had become an established feature over the bay immediately before the principal *mihrab*; the Seljuks, however, employed their domes not merely as architectural features but actually as roofs over apartments of considerable span. Thus a favourite practice was to support the vault of the sanctuary by flanking it with a pair of tomb-chambers roofed by wide domes of Byzantine rather than Persian pattern.

The squaring-up of the courtyard seen in the Sirtsheli *medressa* at Konia, erected in 1242, hints at what was to be the aim of the Seljuk architects; just twenty-five years later the *medressa* of Fahreddin Ali in the same city was constructed with what had been the internal court covered with a dome. Thus the mosque had at last drawn level with the Christian church and become a completely covered-in building, suited to a sterner clime than that which had seen its inception.

The tidying-up of the elevations of these Iconian buildings as well as their plans was assisted by the fact that the rooms surrounding the internal court were usually arranged on two stories the combined heights of which equalled that of the sanctuary and its flanking chambers at the *qibla* end. Thus once again the architects could take advantage of contemporary Byzantine achievements in church design and compress the *medressa* into a compact block instead of a collection of buildings of assorted heights. Among the Persian contributions to the elevational features was a magnificent portal set in the wall opposite to the sanctuary and echoing in scale and proportions the great arch of the latter.

The culmination of the Seljuk style which took place during the 13th century was only the result of experiments undertaken during the great days of the Crusades, at which period the small compact mosque was already appearing in the crowded city of Cairo; the little El Ahmar mosque, which dates from the second quarter of the century, being an example. By the 13th century, the inevitable mixture of Byzantine and Persian elements was influencing Cairene architecture; the results suggesting, as usual, that the partnership was one of Byzantine engineer and Persian craftsman. The ubiquitous Cairene domes are, however, clearly oriental and not Roman, and the planning schemes of 13th-century Ayubid sultans are on the lavish inconsequential scale of the orient. As in the Seljuk style, the domed tomb-chamber and vaulted sanctuary play important parts in the design; in the mausoleum of Sultan Kalawun the dome is supported upon eight columns and surrounded by an aisle after the fashion of a Byzantine church.

In the ordinary Cairene mosque of the 14th century and onwards, the lofty vaulted sanctuary entirely supersedes the spacious pillared hall. In the building of Sultan Hassan in 1356 the courtyard was reduced in area so that the whole series of pillared porticoes which in early days surrounded the court of the mosque could be replaced by four great *iwans* of which that on the *qibla* side is larger than the others. Behind the *mihrab* is the domed tomb-chamber of the sultan. The funerary mosque of Sultan Barkuk, founded at the extreme end of the century, still retains the porticoes; the large sanctuary is flanked, in Seljuk fashion, by a pair of tomb-chambers covered by domes.

The mediæval mosques of Konia and Cairo do not illustrate the taste in religious architecture of the greater part of the Moslem world in which the Arabian courtyard still reigned supreme. Architectural development of these buildings was concentrated upon the central portion of the sanctuary in which was situated the principal

55. By chains of vast castles the Crusaders protected the route from Asia to Europe
(Anamur)

56. The feudal hall is the principal domestic building of mediæval Europe
(Winchester)

mihrab. The Moghrebin device of covering the bay before the *mihrab* with a dome (Plate 38) similar to that of a contemporary Byzantine church was improved upon at the end of the 13th century by removing four of the columns and expanding the dome to cover nine roofing bays instead of one. In this fashion considerable vertical emphasis was given to the most important part of the plan.

At the same time the domed sanctuary also began to make its appearance in the midst of the Persian courtyard mosques. Here the problem was more difficult, for the reason that the vaulted *iwan* was becoming more fashionable and in some cases had already been inserted amongst the columns of the pillared hall which spread before the *qibla* wall. The solution was to place the dome upon the inner portion of the *iwan*, the outer end of this remaining as a great porch to the inner sanctuary enclosed beneath the dome. From the 14th century onwards this combination of domed *maqsura* preceded by a cavernous porch becomes the normal form of oriental sanctuary; in some eastern mosques there is one of these features on three sides of the great court.

The vast Persian porch eventually found its way to the side of the court facing the sanctuary, where, inserted into the courtyard wall, it loomed above the entrance façade like a gigantic doorway, fearsomely out of scale with the wall in which it is set but obviously intended to echo that of the sanctuary within. By means of such somewhat surprising architectural devices as these, the designers of courtyard mosques attempted to introduce the monumental factor into their schemes. The enormous mosque of Ispahan has four vast pillared halls each entered through one of these great portals.

In 1452 the capture of the ancient Byzantine metropolis by the Turks and the conversion of the Hagia Sophia into a mosque signalled a revolution in Islamic religious architecture. Henceforth all Turkish mosques were modelled upon the Byzantine cathedral which still represented one of the finest achievements of mankind. The courtyard mosque passed away for ever from the central Moslem regions; henceforth, even in the Moghreb, the plan of the mosque began to imitate that of the Byzantine church, with little but its orientation towards the *qibla* to indicate the difference (Plate 39).

Mediæval Moslem architects never attempted to emulate the striving towards *hypsosis* so noticeable in connection with contemporary Christian religious buildings. They were perhaps more concerned with structures of a practical nature. As merchants and traders they maintained good communications with all parts of their vast domains, providing magnificent bridges over water-crossings and building forts to protect the route. One of the most important of the Moslem buildings is the the *khan* or caravanserai, a large courtyard, often fortified, provided for the protection of trading convoys. Arcaded loggias provided shelter for pack-animals; by the middle of the mediæval period a first-floor gallery was often provided for the accommodation of the travellers themselves. It is these two-storied courtyards, which by the 13th century had also appeared in large private houses, which are the origin of the Italian *cortile* and the Spanish *patio*; they were modelled upon the many attractive examples to be found in the Mediterranean regions of the Moslem world.

Mediæval Moghrebin architecture seems to have been little affected by the influences, mostly Persian, to which Seljuk and Cairene architecture was submitted. Throughout the Middle Ages the great courtyard mosques, their pillared sanctuaries ever expanding, spread their vast expanses in the heart of the cities of the sunset land. Certain types of structure, however, exist in the Moghreb which are not found in other parts of Islam. One of these is the *rabat* or fortified monastery by means of which bands of military religious held the Berberine frontier. These structures were compact rectangular buildings consisting of apartments arranged in two stories around a small inner court; originating during the 11th century they later developed into the Moghrebin type of *medressa* which during the 14th century became a common and attractive feature of western Islamic architecture. A building similar in type to the rabat is the *kasr* or semi-fortified house which, spreading throughout the cities of Spain, is known to us today in its familiar, if corrupt, form of 'alcazar'. The *kasr* is a courtyard house of two or three stories in height, generally rather forbidding in its external aspect but often provided with internal cloisters, sometimes two-storied on the model of the *khan* or caravanserai. It is this type of Moslem house of the 12th century which is the origin of the Italian palazzo of Renaissance days.

Notwithstanding the charm of their internal courts and cloisters the Moslem architects produced no proper external façades. There is a grimness about their buildings which completely belies the beauty of their internal appointments and has thus caused them to be neglected by the students of elevational architecture. The Moslems were a military race; their whole culture had been founded upon the sword. Taking their cue from their Byzantine predecessors, they soon became experts at military architecture, as the walls of their cities, from the 11th century onwards, illustrate; they were probably some two centuries ahead of their Frankish rivals in this respect.

It was not only in military architecture that mediæval Islam led the world. The domestic buildings of the Moslem empire had early equalled in splendour those of their Byzantine predecessors; by the 8th century, Persian influence had raised the Abbasid Arabs to a cultural level far above that of their Christian rivals. It was this very strength of the Persian element in Islamic culture which enabled it to develop independently of the Byzantines, so that long past the end of the Middle Ages even the Moghreb lands were still essentially oriental in their outlook.

The Persian type of house, although also a development from the nomad's tent, varies somewhat from that which is found in Babylonia. There is the same single apartment fronted by a loggia representing the raised side-wall of the tent. The house of the Persian hill-dweller, however, was covered by a pitched roof in place of the flat mud roof of the plainsman; thus any enlargement of the former had to take into consideration roofing problems unknown to the latter. For example it is difficult to build a series of apartments covered with pitched roofs round a courtyard; thus courtyard houses were not originally a feature of Persian architecture.

The early Persian house was expanded by simply building an apartment across the end of the structure and its loggia so that the resulting plan would be rectangular and the roof would merely have to be extended longitudinally to cover the addition. Thus the enclosed part of the house would form an 'ell' with the loggia completely filling the re-entrant angle; this type of house appears in the hill-country and its foothills from the fourth millennium B.C. to the present day.

The addition of an apartment at the opposite end of the house to balance the plan results in a building having two wings with an enclosed porch between them. This is the nucleus of the Persian great house; it appears in a humble form four thousand years or more before Christ. The front eaves of the simple roof were usually supported across the gap between the wings by two wooden posts so that the portico was distylar; it is important to note, however, that the entrance is in the long side of the building and not, as in a classical temple, at one end. The portico enclosed between wings is found in

Fig. 6. A typical Islamic loggia

some Hellenistic public buildings where it is certainly a Persian importation. Before the Sassanian developments in brick domes and vaults Persian building technique employed a multitude of wooden posts to support the roofs of large apartments; the most famous example of this hypostylar architecture is the great hall at Persepolis; it clearly illustrates the porches flanked by wings and also filled with a forest of wooden posts.

It was the winged house with the enclosed portico which set the fashion for lesser Moslem domestic architecture. The wooden beam and pair of posts soon became a triple arcade of dainty design such as remained popular throughout the centuries and may still be seen today throughout the Moslem world (Fig. 6). By the 8th century Byzantine influence had introduced the *piano nobile,* so that the arcaded porch was transferred to the first floor where it formed a charming tribune or *makad* removed from the bustle of the street below. When the small internal court eventually found its way into the large multi-storied town houses of the mediæval period, one or more tribunes of this type were usually provided within this. The arcaded *makad* on the *piano nobile* also found its way into European architecture, notable examples being those of the 15th century Venetian *palazzi* (Plate 74).

It should be emphasized that throughout the mediæval period the Islamic civilization was very far in advance of the Christian and the architects of the latter were only too glad to learn from their Moslem colleagues. The flat roof of the oriental house is a favourite place for taking the air without appearing in public—an important factor in a society favouring the harem system. Such roofs usually acquire a variety of temporary shelters erected to provide shade or privacy; as these become permanent and are absorbed into architecture we find them represented by graceful loggias perched on the roof-tops. From these are derived the exquisite upper galleries which surround the exteriors of some Italian palaces and play a yet more important part in the domestic architecture of Spain. Islamic influence in the Balkans following the fall of Constantinople may be detected in the open galleries seen occupying the summits of many a tall farmhouse in Roumania and elsewhere.

The introduction of the internal court in large houses may have been originally due to the popularity of yet another Persian feature, the *iwan* or open-ended apartment, which could only have been used in conjunction with a private courtyard. The 9th-century Abbasids made great use of these magnificent apartments. Following, albeit unconsciously, the plan of the inner court of an Assyrian palace, their architects sometimes set a group of three great iwans together; this device they probably developed from the Byzantine triconch found in the bishop's palace at Bosra in the 6th century and the great Omay-yid palace of Mshitta in the 8th. At Ukheidr, the cluster of three *iwans*— called by the Arabs a *beyt* or house—appears again and again as an independent building unit. By the 12th-century it has become the principal apartment of some large houses, echoing, perhaps, the throne room of the Byzantine palace. The principal *iwan*, sometimes all three, would be raised slightly above the central area in a manner suggesting the dais of a Christian great hall.

In the densely-packed cities of Islam the erection of multi-storied houses became a necessity. Here again the Moslems were far ahead of European architects in the design of tall city buildings; the courtyards of late-mediæval *khans* or caravanserais with their tiers of arcaded stories are generally most impressive. In tall private houses having internal courts roofed over the ground story there was sometimes an upper court with a surrounding loggia, cloister-fashion, at first-floor level.

The cloister type of courtyard, ideal in torrid climates for providing shade for worshippers within temple courts, is not necessarily found in the domestic architecture of the same regions. The cloister is in reality a device for protecting those passing between courtyard rooms from the elements of sterner climates. In Spain, where winter conditions unknown to central and eastern Islam made such provision desirable, the Moslems had already been in contact with the wooden loggias of western European architecture; hence the beautiful palace-cloisters of 14th century Islamic Spain, the finest examples of timber architecture remaining in Europe.

The keynote of Islamic domestic architecture is luxury. The interiors of their great houses were elaborately ornamented with faience, an art in which the East has always excelled. Although in the Moghreb and other regions susceptible to Moslem influence the roof of clay tiles was commonly employed the form of covering upon which Moslem architecture had been founded was the flat roof of clay-concrete, a material of great weight requiring a closely-set system of heavy beams upon which to support it. From the beams carrying these roofs, and also those of upper floors, which were of similar construction, the Islamic architects developed glorious ceilings elaborately coffered and painted; during the late 15th and 16th century their designs were gladly copied by the palace architects of Spain and Italy.

Despite the beauty of their architectural ornament, the Moslems never really developed a truly monumental style of building. Only in such strange features as the domed sanctuaries of the later mosques and the cavernous porticoes associated with these did their architects make any effort to raise their buildings skywards in true monumental style. One remarkable architectural feature remains, however, entirely Moslem—the minaret. The origin of the minaret remains obscure; it seems, however, that it was intended to represent the Moslem counter-part of the Byzantine bell-tower.

Minarets are of two main types. The Moghrebin minaret, developed from contact with the Christian world, is merely a tall slender tower; it appears in Spain during the 12th century and by the 14th has spread throughout the Moghreb in a series of fine monuments. The Crusades may have introduced the same type of structure into Syria. The oriental minaret may be described as the architectural expression of a spiral staircase. In Abbasid days the stair was constructed round a central core; by mediæval days it had become enclosed within a more slender structure. The Cairene minarets are elaborate architectural achievements suggesting Byzantine assistance; Turkish minarets indicate an origin in the Classical column with its projecting capital providing a gallery at the summit.

The Moslems were not normally tower-builders, but attention must be called to the magnificent series of funerary towers which were built in Persia during the 11th to the 13th centuries and which were to influence the design of Russian bell-towers at the end of the mediæval era (Plate 47).

One of the most notable Islamic features is the horse-shoe arch which appears in pre-Moslem days in Spain and soon becomes ub-iquitous throughout the Moghreb. Rising from square piers, it entirely replaces the classical form of column-supported arch throughout the western Moslem world. In the 12th century, when contemporary European architects were beginning to lighten the orders of their heavy arches by means of mouldings following the line of the arch, the Moslems relieved the austerity of their smaller plainer arches by providing a series of miniature arches or foliations passing round the soffit. The Persian arch follows the usual trend in arcuated architecture and becomes lowered in pitch; by the 13th century it has become four-centred, continuing so for the rest of its history.

The most striking feature of Islamic architecture is certainly the dome. This is not the wide-spreading variety met with in Roman and Byzantine architecture, but the full-blooded Persian construction which lifts itself into the air in true monumental style. The oriental dome is not merely a form of roofing; it is an architectural feature of para-mount importance. At the end of the 14th century, the Persian dome is often enlarged on plan so that its span becomes greater than the drum upon which it stands; this device, which is achieved by means of corbelling, results in the bulbous form so typical of the late-mediæval dome of eastern Islam. The origin of this form is not clear, but as the Persian dome is the product of a more rigorous climate than the rest of the dome-employing regions it may be that the overhanging sides of the bulbous variety assisted it to throw off snow clinging to it.

Fig. 7. The 'squinches' by means of which Islamic builders raised a dome above a square

Islamic domes, being of Persian origin, never rose from the Roman pendentive employed by the Byzantines but from the more primitive squinch arch which spanned the angles of the square and converted it into an octagon (Fig. 7). An ingenious system of brick corbelling, with each individual brick set normal to the wall-face and thus diagonally to the splay, resulted in the creation of another essentially Islamic architectural feature—the honeycomb pendentive. This remarkable device eventually attained a high degree of elaboration, especially in the cavernous porches of later mediæval mosques and in palace interiors.

Despite the vast amount of building undertaken by Islam during the millennium which covered its period of prosperity, it cannot be denied that the architecture of the Moslems never attained the perfection of that of its Christian rivals. In architectural ornament, however, it has never at any time been surpassed. This is due to two primary factors, the first of which is the skill and devotion of the oriental craftsman who worked with a patience foreign to his European contemporary. The second is the nature of the Moslem religion, which forbade any representation in ornament of any living thing, vegetable as well as animal. Thus Islamic artists were forced to invent their own ornament, basing their designs first on geometry and later developing their art into that fascinating maze of elaboration which we call arabesque. By the 14th century, however, Moghrebin ornament, divorced from oriental support, was deteriorating towards standardization so that a form of reticulated treatment is common at this period. One of the most important features of Islamic architectural ornament is the use of the Kufic lettering as a sculptured decoration of walls.

As builders in brick the Moslem architects were faced with the problem of concealing this humble material beneath a cladding of some sort. Plaster was of course ubiquitous but lacked the pictorial frescoes of contemporary Christendom. The enforced restriction to repetitive ornament suggested mass production; this was effected with notable success by the use of wall-tiles of glazed faience which were also used to waterproof the outer surfaces of domes. The use of screens of beautifully-wrought joinery as internal partitions led to the extension of this craft to provide panelling for the ornamentation of wall surfaces. As the Middle Ages progressed timber framing covered with plaster was introduced to produce architectural effects within the building. Never at any time during architectural history has Moslem interior decoration been equalled for richness and complexity; a curious fact when one realizes the fundamental disadvantage under which the artists worked.

Islamic architects were keen engineers and took great pride in their public works, as is illustrated by the many beautiful bridges which remain from their era. Above all, they remembered their desert origin and paid great attention to the water supply of their cities; also every mosque had its fountain at which the faithful performed their ablutions before prayer. This exceptional interest in the science of irrigation enabled them to become the finest gardeners in the mediæval world; thus they were able to provide their lovely palaces with a deservedly beautiful setting.

Chapter X

THE FRANKISH LANDS

Although architecture as we know it was late in reaching the sunset lands of Europe, we have the evidence of 6th century Roman writers that their Gaulish contemporaries lived in timber houses of an excellence which astounded the sophisticated rulers of the ancient world. Although every vestige of this style of building has long ago vanished we can form some impression of its nature by comparison with the timber buildings of later days. The forests of western Europe being full of excellent hardwood, it can be presumed that a properly-framed construction was employed (blockwork being the product of those who dwell in regions where only fir is obtainable). Whatever form of framing was employed, the walling would probably have consisted of planks set on end and fixed into horizontal members above and below.

As we pass from the Mesopotamian deserts towards the Frankish lands, we find that the enemy of the builder is of a very different calibre. It is no longer necessary to provide shade from the blazing sun of noon; yet the sterner regions of the west are ruled by an element almost unknown to the founders of architecture. No flat roof of the ancients could support the weight of a winter's snowfall, against which the western roofs must be steeply pitched so as to encourage those miniature avalanches which alone can keep the loading safe and the whole structure from collapse.

Snow shed from roofs and piling against the feet of walls will soon bury these to a considerable height. Wooden walls are not the best method of protecting the interior of a building half-buried in snow, thus the early western builders seem to have continued their roofs out over the walls in the form of loggias. It was these features which so excited the admiration of the Romans. As the house had to be entirely surrounded by loggias if full protection was to be given to the walls, we may assume that the hipped roof was also a feature of these early timber buildings; the gable end is primarily a masonry construction.

We know little of the religion of these people except that much of the cult was of natural features which were thus worshipped in the open air. Thus Christianity, reaching the sunset lands of Europe, had to bring with it the church-plan of more enlightened regions. From the great days of the 6th century onwards, tiny buildings constructed in a fashion hitherto unknown began to appear in the west. These early churches were but small rectangular buildings with an apse projecting from the east wall. Dignity was however achieved by accentuating the vertical dimension to an impressive height; in many cases the churches were surrounded by wooden loggias so that they should not lack the principal architectural feature of the local building style. In the late 6th century churches built by St Augustine in south-eastern England the end bays of the loggias were built up with solid walling to form a pair of sacristies or *parabemata*.

During the next century, these *parabemata* developed into square porch-like projections resembling embryo transepts, roofed at right angles to the nave and producing on elevation a cruciform effect faintly suggestive of the contemporary Byzantine or Armenian church. Small churches of this type may be met with during the 7th and 8th centuries in several places within the Frankish area; the church at Bradford-on-Avon in England, dating from about 700, is an example which displays considerable refinement in its masonry design.

Whereas the main doorways of the Roman churches were at their western ends, the Byzantines preferred the lateral entrance. The western church-builders, having to cope with a climate which tended to produce draughts sweeping down the length of a building, generally followed Byzantine practice; only in very large churches is the more monumental western doorway employed.

In Ireland and the western parts of Britain, the Roman church was able to weather the stormy centuries following the withdrawal of the Legions and pursue a humble but persistent development at a time when the rest of western Europe had relapsed into paganism. The principal result of this Celtic phase upon the church plan seems to have been the abandoning of the classical Roman apse for the less

57. The end of the Gothic period produced a series of magnificent bell-towers
(Verneuil)

58. The elaborate frontispiece indicating a portal is a feature of late-
mediæval Spanish architecture (Salamanca)

59. A brick-built castle of the Teutonic Knights in north-west Europe
(Marienwerder)

60. In stone-less northern Europe the Gothic builders made good use of brick tracery in their façades (Prenzlau)

sophisticated and more easily roofed square chancel, the first appearance of this feature in architectural history.

It is a curious fact that the spread of Christianity through the efforts of the Roman missionary monks of the Dark Ages cannot be coupled with a corresponding introduction of Roman culture throughout the converted regions. But Rome itself was at that time a decaying city, displaying only the ruins of great buildings and possessing no means by which to repeat architectural achievements of earlier days. Thus no architects followed in the wake of the churchmen, whose religion was represented materially only by humble little shrines of the very slightest architectural pretensions.

The cultural capital of the day was undoubtedly Constantinople; thus contemporary ecclesiastical architecture followed the Byzantine pattern. The plan of the important provincial church at the middle of the first millennium was the centralized structure consisting of a square *hypsosis* supported upon four props and surrounded by an aisle. In the original Byzantine areas the central feature was crowned by a small dome perched upon a drum; in the west it was simply raised above the aisle roofs as a low tower covered with a pyramidal timber roof. During the 8th and 9th centuries these simple 'four-poster' churches were spreading throughout the Frankish lands. In the Rhineland, the cathedral of Trier was founded upon this plan. The well-known church of Germigny-des-Prés, founded in 810, yet remains an almost perfect example of western provincial Byzantine; it was copied, a century later, by Alfred the Great in the church he built at Athelney to commemorate his great victory over the Danes. Hundreds of timber churches, in which four sturdy oaken posts took the place of the masonry piers, must have been burnt during the troubles of the 9th century; 11th and 12th century examples yet remain, however, in south-eastern England, notably at Stock in Essex. The contemporary 'stave-churches' of Norway illustrate the modifications in design necessitated by the use of softwood (Plate 43).

The supremacy of Byzantine culture in the Carolingian world is shown by the design of the cathedral built by Charlemagne at Aachen in 796; it is copied from that of the great Byzantine octagons of the 6th century. The wonder of these masterpieces of church architecture was ever in the minds of the builders who worked in the dawn of the

Middle Ages. Thus we still have Mettlach abbey church, built in 987, and the foundations of the octagon at St Augustine's Abbey at Canterbury, built about 1060. Even after 11th-century churchmen had denounced the inconveniences attending upon the over-centralized plan it was still determinedly followed by the Knights Templars; the Temple Church in London is a notable example.

For practical purposes, however, the Frankish world adopted the centralized plan in its square form, the great church of the 9th century being a square tower supported on four massive piers and surrounded by an aisle. In some cases, such as at Werden-an-der-Ruhr, the north and south aisles had galleries above them supported by intermediate piers, the origin of the 'duplex' system of the later Ottonian bay design. The central feature was crowned by some kind of pyramidal wooden roof sometimes elaborated to form a steeple. This tower-like *hypsosis* frequently took the form of an all-wooden construction carried upon four huge posts; in such churches the first stage of development was to dispense with the obstructive props and carry up the walls of the surrounding aisle so that the whole building formed a tower; the timber roof which differentiates the architecture of the western Byzantine region from the domed eastern style made the covering of wide spans a comparatively easy matter.

In larger churches, the central feature was originally surrounded, not by a simple aisle, but by a group of four short projections resembling embryo transepts and leaving only the angles of the building to be covered by lean-to roofs, more in the fashion of the normal small Byzantine church (Plate 23). It is from these structures that the cruciform plan of the western great church develops. The octagonal church could only have been enlarged by the construction against it of some ill-fitting appendage; the four great arches of the four-poster led into embryo excrescences which invited extension to form the arms of a cross. Thus the nucleus is established and the course of its expansion assured.

During the 9th century—the 'Siècle de Fer'—the Carolingian world succumbed to a holocaust which swept away many of the little Romano-Frankish churches and also the 'four-posters' with which the Byzantines had established their architectural supremacy in western Europe. With the opening of the 10th century the stage was set for the finest period of Frankish architecture—the Ottonian Renaissance.

The power behind the new Roman Empire was the Roman Church; its pioneers the Benedictine monks, soon to be reformed under the ægis of the great Abbey of Cluny. Thus, the inevitability of Byzantine cultural supremacy notwithstanding, Roman ecclesiastical tradition was bound to assert itself. It did so by insisting upon the planning of churches upon an axis rather than around a focus. The determination of the architects of the day not to be deprived of their monumental designs resulted in a compromise between the two styles which was to influence the whole of mediæval European architecture. To the west of the Byzantine nucleus appeared the Romanesque nave.

In the case of rural churches this addition was easily effected. Important churches with their western entrances upon a market square or main street had perforce to be extended eastwards. Thus the great Ottonian churches of the 10th century were developed by constructing an entirely new building, with its own towered nucleus, joined to the original structure by the new nave, the bay design of which repeated that in the older building and thus produced the 'duplex' system of alternate sturdy and light supports so characteristic of Ottonian ecclesiastical architecture. The original church then formed a towered western annexe—often transepted—to the great church; this feature appeared in a number of 10th-century English buildings and may be seen today throughout Germany. This planning concept signalled an important advance in the history of church design not only by introducing the western tower but also by inaugurating the monumental entrance known as the west front. In some cases the westernmost of the three appendages to the western tower was made apsidal in form; these western apses seem however to be practically limited to Germany.

While the powerful German episcopacy of the day seem to have welcomed the advertisement afforded by the towered façades of their cathedrals, the monastic founders do not seem to have deliberately constructed these western annexes. Early 11th-century abbey churches such as those of Limburg and Hersfeld concentrate attention upon the eastern nucleus, containing the monastic choir, by greatly exaggerating the length of the transept in order to provide sites for lateral altars. In northern Spain, the contemporary church of Ripoll also shows this enormously attenuated transept. Even central Italy, for the most part indifferent to Byzantine building fashions, produced in 1063 the vast cruciform galleried cathedral of Pisa. By the end of the century, however, the main transept of the western churches had everywhere established itself upon a somewhat less exaggerated yet nevertheless still impressive, scale.

The plan of the monastic church revolved about the choir in which the monks gathered to sing their offices. At first sited beneath the central feature, as the cruciform plan developed it became moved into the western arm, leaving both wings of the transept communicating across an unobstructed crossing. Eastwards of the latter was a short presbytery or chancel, terminating in the inevitable apse. At the west end of the choir was a screen-wall, beyond which the nave stretched away towards its western doorway.

When, during the 10th century, the Romanesque nave began to appear as an important part of the large Frankish church, it did so in its aisled form. The main walls of the structure were not, however, supported upon rows of classical columns in the Roman fashion. Either the Byzantine pier was employed or else—also in accordance with Byzantine architectural practice—piers alternating with columns or circular pillars. This device of the duplex bay plays an important part in the interior elevation of the Frankish church; Durham is perhaps the finest example. By the end of the 11th century all four arms of the church were sometimes broadened by the addition of lateral aisles.

The development of the plans of smaller churches follows much the same lines as in their greater brethren. The addition of a nave to the original four-poster or tower church often ends in the removal of the western arch of the latter so as to throw nave and central space into one. The transepts, if any, then remain as appendages to the eastern end of the nave instead of flanking a crossing as before the merging of the two took place. Thus the 'pseudo-cruciform' plan, common throughout the Frankish lands during the 11th century, finds its way into the smaller church; if the building is aisled the presence of transepts will be further emphasized by the increased size of the eastern arches of its internal arcades.

In an earlier chapter we noted that the Byzantine colony in Ravenna had lost no time in evolving a westernized variety of the architecture of the metropolis which had appreciated from the outset the convenience of the Roman 'basilican' type of nave. This union of the two fashions was to result in the creation of the Lombardic style which, from its headquarters in the great city of Milan, had by the beginning of the 11th century spread throughout the Frankish empire. Thus the tentative experiments of the Ottonian renaissance were closely followed by a wave of building which represented the culmination of Frankish architecture.

The century opened with a fine series of Rhenish cathedrals. As it wore on, western Europe lost itself in a building mania, exhausting its treasures in the erection of vast churches, planned on a scale never before contemplated, exhibiting range upon range of sturdy arcades and soaring cliffs of masonry constructed with a precision leaving nothing to be desired (Plate 42), the whole being crowned by a towering central feature rising high above the roofs of all other structures.

One of the greatest of these mid-11th-century churches is that of Tournai in Flanders, seat of much of the commercial wealth of Frankish Europe. The seizure of England by the Duke of Normandy and the transference of vast tracts of English property to the Benedictines brought about intensive rebuilding programmes; at the turn of the century the Anglo-Saxon masons were demonstrating their skill by producing such magnificent churches as Durham, Peterborough, and Ely, in their day the largest churches in the world.

On the mainland, Normandy was being covered with new monastic churches designed in the same noble fashion. Farther south, the huge church of St Sernin, Toulouse, spread its vast bulk across one end of the pilgrimage route across the Pyrenees which terminated in the equally mighty church of St James of Compostella. Frankish architecture had arrived at maturity.

It is perhaps unfortunate that this western European style has been classified as Romanesque. It is so clearly of Byzantine origin. One of the most notable features of the design of the larger churches is their two-storied aisles, an arrangement hitherto only encountered in the Byzantine great church. In Frankish architecture they appear con-

currently with the Ottonian renaissance of the 10th century; by the
11th they have been abandoned by the Germans to become, however,
important factors in the design of the magnificent English abbey
churches.

Galleries play no part in the development of the Roman or 'basilican' church, though it is true that a small number of these buildings
were designed with two-storied aisles shortly after the inception of this
feature in the normal Byzantine church. In the western churches, however, great play is made with the galleries and their arcades; a common
treatment being to divide each opening into the church into a pair of
arches separated by a small column. This diminutive version of the
duplex bay—the *bifora* or double opening—is a typical feature of the
Frankish style; it also appears in windows, especially those of belfries.

In very large churches such as that of Tournai the portion of nave
wall against which the aisle roof abuts is sometimes ornamented
internally by a blind arcade. French architects call this the triforium,
a term which is employed in England—quite incorrectly—to designate the galleries over the aisles. In the great churches of the 11th and
12th centuries it was the usual practice to provide a narrow passage,
set in the thickness of the clerestory wall at the level of the sills of the
windows, in order that access might be attained to these for cleaning
purposes. The inner face of the wall above each window was carried
by a triplet of arches or *trifora:* thus it was that this passage was known
as the triforium (Plate 42).

A fundamental feature of the western Byzantine style was the tower-
like *hypsosis* rising above the surrounding roofs. As the church
expanded in all directions so that its outer walls receded farther and
farther from the crossing below the tower, it became essential to raise
this at least high enough for windows to be set in its side walls above
the roof-slopes abutting against these. Hence the tower becomes a
'lantern' lighting the crossing below. In the Ottonian churches, the
crossing was carried up to form a square tower; the Lombardic type
of lantern, however, resembles the octagonal drum of a Byzantine
dome covered with a pyramidal timber cap instead of a dome. Except
in England, where the Anglo-Saxon masons stoutly supported the
Ottonian tradition, the Lombardic type of central feature became
accepted throughout most of western Europe.

The roofs of these early lanterns formed the most striking external features of the great buildings they adorned. It is greatly to be deplored that none of them remains today, as it is clear from contemporary descriptions and illustrations that they were elaborate constructions in all probability representing the finest achievements of the Frankish carpenters. The finest examples seem to have been those of the Anglo-Saxons; it is an architectural tragedy that they had to be removed during the 12th century owing to their structural inadequacy as keystones to the magnificent buildings above which they soared.

The lightening of bay design within the church below and the resultant increase of lateral thrust from the arcades abutting upon the four great piers of the crossing tended to overturn these and bring the whole of the centre of the church to ruin; thus most of the original lantern towers collapsed within a generation or so of their erection. Those which remain owe their survival to the addition of a belfry story during the 12th century which weighted the four crossing piers sufficiently to enable them to resist the thrust of the lateral arcades.

One of the factors which greatly increased the structural problems of the Frankish engineers was the popularity of masonry vaulting. The original purpose of a vault was to support a floor; the floors of the Byzantine galleries and those in the Frankish churches were always carried upon vaulting. The Byzantines, however, had from the first employed the vault as a roof, thus presenting to the interior of the building a smooth stone ceiling instead of a tangle of timber beams. It thus became a matter of honour to the western architects that they should strive to provide great churches completely covered with stone ceilings which would conceal all this rustic untidiness.

The first vaulted naves appear in the south and east, where masonry skill was better developed and timber technique less universal. The system employed was the ordinary barrel vault, common to most early Spanish churches and appearing in Burgundy—where the use of the pointed form greatly minimized the thrust—before the end of the 11th century. These wide vaults were constructed upon sturdy arches crossing the building at intervals; a device which restricted the use of centering to these arches and enabled the interspaces or webs of the vault to be laid without resort to the elaborate system of timberwork necessary in the case of vaults not so subdivided.

The barrel vault is an unsuitable covering for wide spans as it produces a gloomy space, hanging above the building, in which it is almost impossible to provide windows. The Romans had already discovered this defect and countered it by the invention of the cross or groined vault; it was this type of construction which covered the aisles of the Frankish churches and supported the floor of the gallery over. The introduction of skeletal arches set diagonally along the lines of groining once more resulted in a great saving of timber centering; it is the development of the 'vaulting rib' which made possible the high vaults of the cathedral naves of western Europe.

The covering of the central span with a heavy stone roof the weight of which was brought down through the vaulting ribs upon a number of isolated points of support made it necessary to pay far more attention to the planning of the building, not merely for convenience, but with an eye to structural requirements. The naves of the Roman churches had been set out along an axis; in the case of the western churches the cross axes, also, had to be considered. The result was the adoption of Byzantine methods of construction and the setting out of the building as a series of squares, each covered, not by a dome, but by a 'quadripartite' vault. At each angle of each square was a massive Byzantine pier. As this implied a bay design equal to the span of the building it became necessary to introduce intermediate pillars to carry the main wall of the nave, resulting in the duplex bay system which thus became firmly established in western architecture. The perfection of the whole system is seen in the early 12th-century churches of St Ambrose at Milan and St Michael at Pavia.

The headquarters of Frankish mason-craft was Lombardy. The Lombard instructors, who travelled to the limits of Christian Europe, were architects in the truest sense of the word. Not content with planning and calculating, they were able to influence the development of elevational design. Under their influence it became the custom to introduce non-constructional features merely for the purpose of architectural effect; more particularly in connection with the horizontal punctuation of elevations by means of vertical projections emphasizing the bay arrangement, a function which had hitherto been left for the windows to suggest.

During the 10th century it became a common practice to introduce

61. The towers of an English Gothic cathedral dominate the landscape (Lincoln)

62. By the end of the mediaeval period the cloister walk had been provided with a stone-vaulted ceiling

63. A German 'hall-church' having aisles equal in height to the nave
(Landshut)

64. The east end of a 'hall-church'
(Soest)

vertical pilasters, narrow and of slight projection, to the outside of church walling. Internally the same function was fulfilled by slender shafts passing up from the centre of each pier and rising to the whole height of the building (it may be noted in parenthesis that the presence of these shafts of punctuation, which appear as early as the 10th century, does *not* imply any intention of the builders to construct a vault). The external pilasters were sometimes elaborated to form a blind arcade; a typically Lombard device is the scalloped band supporting a parapet set at the same face as those of the pilasters, a feature often seen repeated on the stages of towers.

The tower is a feature peculiarly Frankish. While from earliest times this class of structure had been employed as a fortification, it was the western Byzantine style which developed the monumental form of this finest of all architectural features. Some attention has already been paid to the lantern tower which grew out of the original nucleus of the four-poster church. It is now necessary to consider the tower after its deliberate removal from the centre of the building to serve as a monumental feature at the western or entrance end.

The western tower rising from a spreading transept provided the churches of the Ottonian era with magnificent frontispieces; the noble example at Ely indicates that even as late as the 12th century no finer method of indicating an entrance had been devised. While the difficulties of erecting a structure of this magnitude over the end bays of a wide nave eventually caused the west tower to vanish from the greater churches, its position as the terminal feature of the normal parish church of western Europe was thereafter assured.

The diminutive tower or turret played an early part in Frankish architecture as a circular staircase turret provided to reach the galleries of large churches. Coming into architectural prominence at the end of the 10th century, these stair turrets first appear as attachments to the middle of the gable end of the transept across which, in these early churches, the aisle gallery was usually prolonged. At the same period, some builders were beginning to absorb the campanile into the church plan by building it over a bay of the aisle; in large churches they erected the towers in pairs flanking the short presbyteries, thus greatly augmenting the elevational dignity of the most important arm of the building.

Owing to the octagonal plan of the Lombardic lantern, turrets built in the angle of the crossing did not impinge upon the central structure. In Flanders, Normandy and England, where the square lantern had remained in favour, the pairs of turrets were sited over the terminal bays of the aisles. Sometimes, as at Tournai and Winchester, the transepts were so embellished. In Normandy, however, the pair of turrets over the end bays of the nave aisles developed into the twin towers which were to supersede the single great western tower of 11th-century Germany and ultimately to play a vital part in the most impressive elevational spectacle known to western ecclesiastical architecture.

In the great days of the Frankish empire, when the Church was all-powerful and the whole building potential of Christian nations was being absorbed in the erection of vast cathedrals and monastic structures, very few masons were available for domestic operations. The great hall of the tribal chieftain—now become feudal lord—was merely a barn-like structure of carpentry, in some cases dignified by the long porticoes or loggias which even as late as the 12th century were still so much admired. The Carolingian palace seems to have been a group of single-storied buildings set round a courtyard in which the great feudal hall attempted to ape the Byzantine basilica.

The residential apartments of the Frankish palaces were situated in long narrow structures having a loggia passing along the front wall of each. Towards the end of the millennium the stone-built Byzantine house, with the *piano nobile* raised above a ground floor used for storage purposes only, had reached the Lombardic areas. For the most part, however, the Frankish house continued to be a timber construction, very liable to destruction by fire. Hence the 11th-century invention of the private castle, which was a timber house surrounded by a defensive perimeter of thorn hedge or palisade, often augmented by earthwork.

The early Benedictine monasteries consisted of groups of timber huts surrounding a small church, but the powerful abbots of the 10th century and onwards were usually able to employ masons for building their houses. Monastic houses were of the normal two-storied type, with common room below and dormitory above (Plate 41). The long building often projected from the church as a prolongation of the transept. The monastic hall or refectory was a simple aisle-less structure, frequently sited parallel with the nave of the church; a smaller but architecturally more magnificent hall was that in which met the chapter or governing body of the house.

Apart from the great scale of the Frankish buildings at the turn of the first millennium, there was nothing architecturally remarkable in them as structural achievements. They were simply great piles of stonework, laboriously raised after but elementary calculations. Little engineering skill went into their design. The one innovation, ignored by the Byzantine architects but appearing in the west at the middle of the 11th century, was the turning of arch-rings in expanding orders so as to economize in the timber centering which must have proved an expensive item in the erection of buildings containing such a multiplicity of arched openings as characterizes the Frankish style. From the ordered arch was developed the compound pier; this invention, also ignored by the Byzantines, was to play a vital part in the creation of the Gothic style.

Early Frankish architectural ornament is not remarkable. As few columns were employed there was no development of the capital. The circular pillars, built-up in masonry courses, were capped with a moulded band. Only the small ornamental shafts needed capitals; as these were often employed in the angles of ordered piers or the edges of openings it was important that their projection was kept as small as possible. By knocking off the corners of a Byzantine cushion capital the Franks were able to produce the 'cubiform' capital which had practically no projection at all.

There was little architectural sculpture available and that was of amateur quality. Thus the carved ornament is primitive and mostly based upon chip-carving motifs employed in decorating timber buildings. For the same reason the Corinthian capital so beloved of architects for more than a thousand years is either missing from the little Frankish shafts or else is quaintly distorted into shapes the Romans never dreamed of. But it is not by virtue of their ornament that the great churches are known throughout the civilized world today.

Chapter XI

THE CRUSADES

At the close of the first millennium the cultural development of the Frankish realms had brought all Europe west of a line joining the Adriatic to the Baltic within the architectural fold. Its capital was still Byzantium; Christian and Moslem alike acknowledged the magnificent building style which had inspired tall churches and the vast architectural glades of the mosques. In church and mosque the Byzantine dome, perched upon its lantern drum, published to the world the site of *mihrab* or high altar.

Yet throughout the Christian world one factor always remained insistent; the spiritual appeal of Rome. The cultural importance of 11th-century Rome, like its political power, was of little significance. Yet the Frankish emperors, ruling from their remote capital in Aachen, insisted that their dominion represented the successor of that pagan empire now represented by the ruin-sown wastes from which rose the shadowy city which even today is called 'Eternal'.

The glorious Byzantine cathedral of the Holy Wisdom was still Christendom's principal architectural achievement. But the great sprawling barnlike church of St Peter remained the nerve-centre of the Western Church—the Church Militant which was to convert the heathen and defend Christendom against the might of Islam.

The fact remained that the Roman missionary had no Roman architect to accompany him on his expeditions. Rome might hold the keys of heaven; it was, however, a heaven which had long been established upon Byzantine lines. To set beside the soaring domes which rose above the roofs of the world, St Peter had nothing but the simple basilican churches lined with their austere ranks of silent columns. The slender campanile, it is true, might point the way to the stars and draw attention to the church lying at its foot; yet it was but

65. A great Gothic church of north Italy
(Venice)

66. As yet ignorant of cannon, the towers of the late-mediæval castle aspire to great heights (Sirmione)

a humble structure owning little which could endow it with true monumental significance.

The defect of the Roman ecclesiastical style which had for so long hindered its development was the persistent employment of the Classical monolithic column as a means of supporting the main walls of an aisled building. Such columns have to be turned on a lathe; there is therefore a very definite limit to the size of this feature. In many places where facilities for stone-turning were absent, second-hand columns had to be procured from ruined structures. It is impossible to create an architectural style from such material.

The 6th-century churches of Ravenna probably represent the zenith of the style, which continues however well into the second millennium without any appreciable change in character. Thus Torcello cathedral and S. Miniato at Florence (1013) show little architectural improvement upon the first churches ever built. Only the changeover from the closely-spaced columns which carried the entablatures of the early buildings to the more graceful arcades of their mediæval successors serves to indicate the passage of those seven centuries during which the Byzantines had revolutionized architecture.

But the appeal of the Corinthian column was too strong for this beloved feature to be engulfed without a struggle within the mass of a Byzantine pier. The Roman monks who, in the 11th century, began to colonize the valley of the Loire brought it with them and introduced it into their great churches. Thus at St Benoît-sur-Loire one finds a church resembling in mass an ordinary Frankish building of its era but containing within it, instead of massive piers, serried ranks of Corinthian columns arranged as in a 'basilican' church of Rome.

One result of this introduction of the column as a primary factor in western church architecture was the invention of the device of carrying the aisles of the presbytery round the back of the great apse in order to imitate the 'chevet' of the great church at Bethlehem (Plate 44). It is a simpler matter to carry the walls of a curved apse upon a row of columns than upon thick piers; but a problem is introduced in the bursting effect of the thrust of the arches which actually transfer the load from wall to column. The vaulting of the ambulatory will carry this thrust down to the aisle walling but then this will be tending to burst under the pressure. The problem was eventually countered by buttressing the aisle wall with a ring of three or five small apsidioles to produce the type of chevet which was later to prove such a glorious feature of Gothic architecture (Plate 45).

By the end of the 11th century it had become clear that the continued employment of the column, even in the drum-built form which had replaced the original monolithic variety, was merely hampering the elevational development of churches. Early in the 12th century attempts were made in Lombardy, France and England to build huge masonry columns which were in fact simply large circular piers; one has only to visit Gloucester to appreciate the grotesque results of such efforts to retain an obsolete feature. Yet it was through their adherence to the principle of the tall support that the mediæval architects, by modifying it after the fashion of the compound pier, were able to develop the moulded Gothic pillar; thus it is certain that from such primitive-looking beginnings as Piacenza cathedral they evolved the graceful pillars of 13th-century Venice or Florence.

Monolithic columns, capped with cushion capitals, had been employed in the Ottonian churches of Germany, but only, after the Byzantine fashion, in association with piers. Round about the year 1100, the Benedictine monks succeeded in introducing the basilican form of nave into a number of their German churches; the capitals of the columns instead of being of the usual Corinthianesque type, are cubiform in the Frankish style. Such churches are not, however, typical of German ecclesiastical architecture, which never wholly adopted the Latin fashion of building.

Where the column survived was in galleried churches having a main arcade of no great height. Western England, colonized by the monks of the Loire, adopted the circular masonry pillar and employed it effectively in a number of great churches whence it spread to the parish churches which were rising throughout the countryside during the 12th century. In north-western France, the drum-built column had captured the imagination to such an extent that it soon became the universal form of support. The second half of the 12th century witnessed the rise of a series of galleried churches, lined with ranks of Corinthianesque columns and ceiled with high-flung vaults, prototypes of the glorious Gothic cathedrals of France.

The mysterious spiritual power of Rome is best illustrated by the events following the migrations of the Gothic tribes which resulted in the sack of the city in 410. Rome it was that proved the conqueror, converting the fierce invader so effectively that the new Gothic dynasty did much to restore the churches and resuscitate the culture of its capital at Ravenna. From their new-won lands the Goths were quick to absorb the elements of the culture they found therein. No 7th-century architect of Ravenna could have designed the lovely little church of S. Juan de Baños in the Asturias, dedicated by a Visigothic king in 661. Nothing could be more satisfying than the graceful arcades, rising above their slender columns, which line the little basilica. The final touch is given by the loggias which surround three sides of what must have been in its day one of the most charming churches in the world.

Architecture, once carried from Ravenna into Spain by the Visigoths, appears to have made great strides. That the country was a breeding-ground for masons is evidenced by the glories of its Islamic architecture. That Christian Spain was capable of executing fine masonry buildings is illustrated by the Church of S. Maria de Naranco, originally built in the middle of the 9th century as a presence chamber for an Asturian king. The most striking feature is the barrel-vault, perched high above walls punctuated internally by a blind arcade resembling that of a basilican church and externally by a series of pilaster strips which project as if they were intended to serve as buttresses—features which did not appear elsewhere in western architecture until three centuries later.

It was yet some time before the Spanish church-builders attempted to raise a barrel-vault over the nave of an aisled building. Indeed it is obvious that the dainty column-supported arcades of such a church as that of S. Miguel de Escalada, completed in 913, could never have withstood the thrust of such a feature. By the end of the century, however, the Frankish pier had reached the Peninsula and the future of Spanish ecclesiastical architecture was thus assured.

The Spaniards have a tradition of good building. Their country is blessed with a good supply of building stone and clay for brick-making; as heirs of the Romans and neighbours of the Moslems they have had excellent opportunities for developing an architectural technique. More favoured than their northern neighbours they had no need to develop the subtle forms of engineering devised by the Gothic architects; the Spanish buildings convey a sense of greater permanence by reason of their massiveness. Spanish roofs are solid vaults covered with interlocking tiles of Roman type; such coverings are weighty and would always have prevented the development of a graceful style of architecture.

At the beginning of the second millennium Christian Spain was happily placed to absorb all the best features of western architectural practice. To begin with she had been endowed by the Visigoths with the basilican plan, which was simple, unsophisticated, and capable of almost unlimited horizontal expansion. The vast arcaded halls of the southern mosques were at hand to illustrate what could be achieved in this respect. She had taught herself to use the barrel-vault; by adopting the type of massive supporting member employed beyond the Pyrenees she could perch her vaulting upon sturdy arcades unknown to her Moslem neighbours. One charming little feature she could share with both Christian and pagan; this was the lantern dome which alike illuminated altar and *mihrab*.

One of the most perfect of churches is that of S. Vincente de Cardona which dates from the middle of the first half of the 11th century. In essence it is an aisled basilica of the same genus as the almost contemporary Florentine church of St Miniato. But sturdy compound piers and ordered arches are substituted for the light Italian arcades, while a Spanish barrel-vault replaces the timbering of an open roof. Above the easternmost bay, from which springs the apse, rises an octagonal lantern, flanked by embryo transepts reaching only to the aisle walls and providing just that touch of spatial punctuation so notably lacking in the basilican churches of contemporary Italy.

The church of S. Vincente de Cardona is not to be compared for size with the vast buildings which, a generation later, were beginning to rise in scores throughout the Frankish lands. But these great shrines were the mightiest manifestations of Christendom, each served by a horde of monks and thronged by congregations gathered in from the surrounding countryside. There were also other sites, of more than parochial importance, upon which stood churches unconnected with monastic houses and supplying the needs of seasonal worshippers such as pilgrims journeying to some great shrine. It was these pilgrimage churches which adopted the design illustrated by S. Vincente as their standard. From the middle of the 11th century to the end of the 12th, this type of church spread throughout southern Europe. In

Fig. 8. In the early Armenian churches is the germ of the Gothic spirit which passed westwards with the Crusades

the Holy Land itself, even the cathedrals—such as that at Nazareth—adhered rigidly to the plan, the basis of which is a vaulted basilica with its arcades supported upon compound piers and with an octagonal lantern lighting the eastern bay. In view of their distribution it would seem not unreasonable to describe such churches as 'Crusader' churches.

The universal feature of the Crusader churches is the eastern apse flanked by smaller ones terminating the aisles (Plates 26 and 40). That these are copied from those of the Syrian churches is demonstrated by the fact that even the external columnar ornament of the latter (Plate 25) has been imitated by the western builders by slender half-shafts applied to the walling with string-courses added in imitation of the Classical entablatures (Plate 26). Within (Plate 30) pointed arches rising above compound piers indicate an affinity with churches such as those of Armenia (Fig. 8).

Although the Crusader churches follow the Roman type of plan rather than the Byzantine, the great difference between them and the early type of basilica lies in the fact that the former are covered with vaulted ceilings carried upon sturdy piers. A region which adopted this type of construction and developed it upon a considerable scale was Burgundy, a country well supplied with building stone and occupying a geographical position which enabled its architects to improve upon their designs by absorbing as their fancy led them from the various influences by which they were surrounded. In 1018, for example, they began the largest of the octagonal churches, that of St Bénigne at Dijon, with its double perimeter of galleried aisles. During the era of the great naves they were covering these with barrel-vaults at a time when their Rhenish neighbours were still lacking such amenities. With their cousins of the Auvergne they utilized the spacious days of the 12th century by covering the countryside with well-planned churches, including in the design such monumental features as the chevet with its ring of apsidioles, the central tower—sometimes flanked, after the manner of the German western features, by lofty transepts—and the elaborate porch or narthex covering the principal entrance at the end of a long nave.

The monastic reformation inaugurated at Citeaux in 1098 introduced a note of austerity in Burgundian architecture which was to spread throughout the sphere of the Latin church. The Cistercians eschewed all purely monumental features, such as towers and elaborate porches, but more than made up for this deprivation by instituting a new style of architecture which was perhaps more standardized than had as yet been seen. The plan was that of the normal Frankish great church with its nave, transepts, and presbytery; the latter, however, shorn of its traditional apsidal termination. The Cistercian churches were of no great height and were never galleried. Sturdy compound piers supported the main arcades the arches of which were almost invariably pointed. Ignorant speculation has resulted in the publication of an extraordinary amount of nonsense concerning the 'origins' of the pointed arch: a far more stable spanning device requiring far less abutment than the simple half-round arch, it appears in Armenia during the 7th century and reaches western Europe during the Crusades (Plate 30).

During the 12th century these pointed-arched Cistercian churches with their fine long vaulted naves—for the accommodation of the lay-brothers who worked upon the sheep-runs—rose in their scores throughout the countryside of Europe, affecting the architecture of England, Scandinavia, Poland, Germany, France and Spain.

The addition of a large complement of lay-brothers to the monastic community necessitated the construction of a large house to accommodate them. It became Cistercian practice to erect the long house of the lay-brothers along the western side of the cloister garth, parallel to the house of the professed monks which adjoined the transept of the church. The long west wall of the lay-brothers' house being approximately in alignment with the west front we find the germ of an imposing façade extending from and including the simple but imposing frontispiece of the church. From this elevational arrangement was later developed the fine monastic façades of the European Renaissance.

Most of the Crusader-type churches illustrate the architectural standardization, introduced by the Cistercians, which brought to coherence all the most fundamental of the planning and structural factors which for the last two centuries had been surging to and fro in Western Europe. Even in such Sicilian churches as the cathedral at Monreale, where the architect has obstinately adhered to the Roman ordnance of light columned arcades supporting open timber roofs, the effect is far removed from that experienced in one of the early basilicas. All the old fumbling clumsiness of manner has disappeared;

there is an aspiring graciousness which indicates that the basilican style has here attained its zenith.

It is inadvisable to underestimate the effect of the Crusades of the 12th century upon contemporary European architecture. The centuries had not effaced all traces of the glorious building tradition of the Hellenistic regions; still more important was the existence nearby of a masonry style—that of the Armenian church-builders—in every way capable of carrying on the tradition. The Armenians had in fact succeeded in developing an independent architectural history, deriving from pagan Hellenism and its temples, passing through the Early Christian 'basilican' era, and by the end of the millennium achieving an ecclesiastical architecture which was producing buildings far more efficient in planning and design—though, it is true, on a smaller scale —than those of the western builders.

The Armenian churches were developed directly from the Byzantine 'four-poster' type of structure. The western part of the surrounding aisle was expanded to form a 'west nave' two bays long; the eastern part was similarly prolonged as a presbytery of one bay. The narrow flanking aisles ended eastwards in small apses which, with the principal apse, were enclosed within a rectangular outer wall above which the roofs of the main building rose to display its cruciform massing. At the centre of the cross the Byzantine dome, capping its octagonal lantern, formed the culminating feature of the design. The whole building was barrel-vaulted, the supports being compound piers of a slenderness unequalled in western architecture; by the end of the 10th century the pointed arch had come into general use (Fig. 8).

There is comparatively little difference between the standard Crusader church and its Armenian contemporary. The long basilican nave—four bays or so instead of two—with its wider aisles indicate the Roman influence unknown to Orthodox Armenia. The groined vault makes the Crusader building lighter than its oriental cousin but there is less efficiency displayed by the former in its exterior ordinance. Both, however, subscribe to the octagonal lantern; the Byzantine supported upon its traditional pendentives, the Crusader upon the less sophisticated squinch arches.

It is in truth the octagonal *cimborio* which forms the key feature

67. Chambord, the last and greatest of the mediæval châteaux

68. A range of lodgings added to a château about the year 1500

of 12th-century ecclesiastical architecture and illustrates the final merging of the two great ecclesiastical styles. The Spaniards, pioneers of the Crusader church-plan, created beautiful specimens of the lantern tower over the crossing; that at Toro is a truly magnificent example, its ordinal faces augmented by the addition of circular turrets (Plate 46). The Germans also adopted the feature with enthusiasm; in southern France it was often raised and elaborated to form a lofty central tower.

One important result of the Crusades was the introduction into the Lombardic architectural sphere of the ancient 'triconch' type of chevet which terminated the axis of the church of the Nativity at Bethlehem. Not only the Lombardic churches, but those of the Germans as well, began to adopt this form of eastern termination, which is well seen in some of the 12th-century churches at Cologne. Thus while the French churches were concentrating upon the expansion of the presbytery and the embellishment of its great apse by means of the ambulatory and its apsidioles the Lombard regions were directing emphasis upon the crowning central feature of the exterior. The importance of this tendency will appear later.

Twelfth-century Canterbury notwithstanding, the octagonal cimborium found little favour in England, where the Frankish type of lantern tower reigned supreme. During the century, however, the influence of the Crusader type of church is noticed in the emergence of a series of small churches designed on cruciform lines with a central tower. The humblest class is the 'axial' type of church which has a central tower but no transepts; this type of building is found all over western Europe, especially in England, Flanders and northwestern France.

The 12th century is the first great age of parish churches. The monastic era had passed; the vast churches of the monks had been completed and their treasuries emptied. The mason trained upon the abbey churches had become available for work upon the parish church of his own village. Thus the village church became a building of some architectural note. Its nave perhaps, became aisled; an entrance doorway or chancel arch came in for elaborate embellishment executed by carvers whose monastic contracts had ceased. The western tower, a Frankish innovation in ecclesiastical architecture, appears in connection with parish churches during the 11th century as a means of carrying the church bell.

In north-western Europe the bell-tower was frequently a large structure forming a vertical prolongation of some major part of the church itself. In the Mediterranean lands, however, less affected by Western Byzantine tradition emanating from Ottonian sources, bell-towers were built free-standing instead of perched upon piers. They could thus with safety be raised much higher, being often set out story by story in arcaded stages (Plate 48).

During the 12th century European architecture was becoming less of the ecclesiastical prerogative it had been since its development under the early Frankish emperors. It is true that the tradition of Byzantine palace-building had reached the western lands; such structures, however, were not representative of the ordinary domestic architecture of the period. But at the close of the first millennium the timber houses of western Europe had attained a dignity which unfortunately is today only indicated by contemporary descriptions. Three stories in height, including the attics in the roof, their principal architectural feature was apparently the loggia, provided to protect the wooden walls from the elements.

The residence of Byzantine days was a tall structure having a principal block containing the main living-room on the first floor. This block was often flanked by a lesser one, having its own roof; the two together formed a roughly cubical mass resembling a broad squat tower. Large western houses seem to have resembled these sufficiently for 12th-century writers to describe them as 'wooden towers'; the division into two portions is also noted.

It will be observed that the Frankish private house was already taking on a form more nearly approaching that of the modern house than had hitherto been seen. The classical type of house with its sprawling ranges of single-storied buildings had become a thing of the past. The times were far less peaceful and urban sites were becoming restricted through the development of the fortified perimeter. This cramping of building sites coupled with civic prosperity always creates a tendency towards the erection of multi-storied houses which make up in height for their lack of ground space; the modern American skyscraper is a typical example of this factor in operation.

The arcaded ground-floor loggia or portico became the keynote of the greater domestic architecture of the Middle Ages. By the 12th century, various masonry variations of it began to appear in buildings, usually three-storied, scattered throughout western Europe. In the Lombardic regions, the arcades were generally of the dainty 'multi-fora' type having a range of small arches supported upon slender shafts; the imperial palaces of Gelnhausen and Wartburg have buildings in which the timber loggia of earlier days is represented by an arcaded passage passing along the front of the structure.

Feudal Europe was governed from the palaces of the kings. But in some regions such as northern Italy, where the rule of Emperors lay lightly upon the citizens of powerful trading cities, the government was carried on by a representative council whose headquarters was a civic palace imitating in its design the contemporary royal residence. At Cremona and Como are examples of 12th-century municipal palaces; in each the ground-floor loggia is much in evidence. The warehouses of the merchant princes of Venice were the loggia-fronted ground floors of their *palazzi*.

The 12th century produced an innovation in monastic planning, the cloister arcade. Originally the claustral element had been represented by enclosure within a precinct wall. The development of a standard plan in which the principal buildings had been disposed around a square yard had diverted the use of the term to designate this. The paved path passing round the cloister garth, and connecting the various buildings by which it was surrounded, was covered with a lean-to roof provided to protect the monks from rainwater falling from the roofs. During the 12th century the timber posts supporting the roofing were replaced by a masonry structure consisting of ranges of small arches of the type described above; cloister arcades of this description were added to monasteries throughout the whole of Latin Europe, contributing many delightful architectural compositions to the monasteries they adorn (Plate 49).

The original timber loggias of the Frankish buildings were presumably provided to protect their boarded walling but proved useful shelters to persons wishing to avoid rain or the heat of the sun. Such structures become architecturally comparable with the stoas of Hellenistic times, especially when the rows of timber posts supporting their eaves are replaced by the enchanting little arcaded features of masonry which appear during the 12th century. Thereafter the arcaded loggia attached to the outside of a building becomes a common feature of southern Europe; in Spain a popular site for one is flanking the south side of a church.

A class of 12th-century structure almost entirely limited to England and the neighbouring continental littoral is the fortified house or keep. This is a two- or three-storied building with outer walls of immense thickness: it was provided to replace the inflammable timber house originally constructed within the light defences of the primitive castle. In common with all contemporary domestic structures, it has a *piano nobile* raised above a storage basement (the same arrangement may be met with in the case of the numerous little unfortified houses of 12th-century date which cover the surrounding countryside).

The plans of these tower houses indicate a descent—presumably through Frankish timber-built intermediaries—from the normal Byzantine house with its main block containing the first-floor megaron flanked by a lesser portion occupied by smaller apartments. The architectural appearance of the structures appears to derive from that of the Islamic palace towers of Tunisia built early in the 10th century; the Normans of Sicily were in close contact with this region and during the second half of the 12th century actually succeeded in colonizing it. Soon after the beginning of the next century the Arab fortified house or *qasr* becomes adopted by the Italians—the great *casa*, later to adopt the Frankish designation of *palazzo*.

The century of the Crusades was perhaps the most significant in the history of European architecture. The last outlying districts had been gathered into the fold of Christianity; the tremendous yet tentative essays in building great churches were being crystallized into standard types each of which was to develop into a magnificent architectural style. Western domestic architecture had been founded upon a solid basis of masonry. Western scientific thought was turning its attention to engineering problems such as bridging, windmills, and various forms of machinery hitherto unknown. In the second half of the century, new military engines forced architects to surround their fortified sites with high curtain walls, protected at intervals by towers from which a watch could be kept upon mining operations upon the enceinte. The loss of the angles of towers through mining resulted in the adoption of the circular tower in military architecture.

Above all, the new engineering knowledge encouraged architects to prosecute their experiments in the science of building statics; devoted craftsmen who converted the results of their calculations into terms of stone and lime laid the foundations of the soaring Gothic cathedrals of the 13th century.

In architectural ornament the 12th century saw considerable progress. There had been little enough in the great Frankish churches and this had been of a primitive nature. But a partial rediscovery of the vestiges of Roman culture resulted in the introduction of some of the ancient features which had played such an important part in Classical architecture. Chief of these was that which has throughout all ages been the hall-mark of culture, the Corinthian column. The day of the monolithic column was over; no machinery existed which could turn out the mighty shafts of ancient days. Thus the Corinthian column of the 12th century was usually a drum-built pillar, a somewhat clumsy copy of its classical progenitor, which was nevertheless popular enough in certain regions, especially in Burgundy and in the Ile de France, which proved to be the birthplace of a fine Gothic style. In western England the Byzantine cushion capital, bred of the Doric Order, became, by a sort of scalloped treatment, tentatively Corinthianized.

As early as the 10th century, western European masons had adapted the lathes of their colleagues the carpenters to turn out small copies of the classical column in freestone. It was these slender shafts, crowned by lovely and varied imitations of the Corinthian capitals, which form the principal ornamental features of 12th-century architecture. Their most important use was for the purpose of widening openings in walling, especially for windows. The 'trifora' which carries the inner facing of the wall over the wide internal splay of a clerestory window gave its name to the inspection passage at this point. Windows themselves were also widened by means of intermediate shafts which were in fact the precursors of mullions; the bifora is the best-known type in England, but on the Continent the openings were often multiplied many times.

From such experiments in supporting the wall-face over wide openings developed the arcaded treatments seen in loggias and cloisters; here the shafts are usually doubled, one to each face of the wall. In the Lombardic regions the Byzantine tradition groups these features in short lengths of arcading punctuated by piers. In southern Europe, however, where no such restrictions were accepted, we find lovely cloister arcades sweeping round their garths; even the tall traceried treatments of the Gothic Age cannot compete with the daintiness of these gay little architectural compositions (Plate 49).

As early as the 9th century we find a row of small open arches appearing in the walling of Lombardic apses to fill the gap between the springing of the semi-dome and the eaves of the roof covering this. This treatment spread throughout the western world until by the 12th century we find the high arcade below the eaves a feature of most of the Lombardic great churches, particularly in the vaulted churches of Germany. Church-builders who abandoned the gallery employed the open arcade as an ornamental feature to cover the blank space of walling against which abutted the aisle-vault. Blind arcades also, such as had been used for some time as dadoes on both faces of external walling, were by the 12th century being used as bands of decoration at various levels; indicating that the architects were now considering the horizontal, as well as the vertical, punctuation of the elevations of their buildings.

It may have been to the development of the wall-arcade that we owe the 12th-century introduction of figure sculpture into architecture. Each little arcaded opening formed a frame or niche for a statue; here was too great a temptation to be missed by the early sculptor. The principal site for carved ornament during the 12th century was due however to Frankish development of the principle of the ordered arch. Originally the orders had expanded from the centre of the wall; in external doorways the inner order was turned in line with the internal face of the walling so that all the remaining orders rose up externally to meet its outer face which was sometimes even deliberately projected from the main wall-face so as to increase the number of concentric orders.

It was upon these dramatic portals, with their expanding sweeps of alternate light and shade rising above close ranks of slender shafts, that the carvers of the 12th century turned the full force of their art. Nowhere in all Latin Christendom can one escape these brilliant memorials of the days of the Crusades. The craftsmen who had ornamented the wooden buildings of the sunset lands pitted their writhing monsters against the stately fronds of the Corinthian carver, while the new device of architectural statuary began to display itself upon the semicircular tympanum and the shafted flanks beneath it. And in the more rustic regions that knew no sculptors, the humble chip-carvers hewed their notches and bobbins, turning out a wealth of chevron and scalloping in their efforts to impart the utmost ornamentation to the portals of their day.

The 12th century was the crucible from which emerged the architecture of Europe. The most vigorous element was the Frankish, a people of a sort not yet known to the world of culture and indeed hardly across the threshold of civilization as represented by the decaying empire of Byzantium. Under the spiritual leadership of a ghostly Rome, the Crusaders explored the mysteries of its Holy Land while struggling against the strongest power known to the world of their day—the empire of Islam.

But not only in distant Syria did the two great forces meet. For along the southern shores of the Mediterranean a highly cultured people, the latest heirs of the ancients, had attained a degree of civilization unknown to their Christian rivals. The effect was bound to be a stealthy emulation of Islamic ways—especially in the arts which subscribe to the comfort of the home—by the peoples dwelling along the European littoral. Thenceforth in these regions we begin to find intrusive elements in their domestic architecture. The flat mud-concrete roofs of Babylonia begin to cover, where spans permit, the houses of the southern Europeans; the beamed ceiling becomes a notable feature of the domestic interior. A corner stone of the Renaissance house is in process of being laid.

69. The cathedral of Granada

70. The municipal headquarters of a wealthy trading city built towards the end of the mediæval era (Middelburg)

in the midst of an arcade of lower ones. Even the collapse of their central lantern towers one after the other from this cause left them in complete ignorance of the cause of these disasters. But by the middle of the 12th century they had learnt two very important facts which were to transform their architecture. One was that artificial abutment could always be provided at the sides of an arch; thus they devised the external buttress. A more important discovery was that top weight upon the abutments of an arch would also help to counteract its thrust. This was an epoch-making discovery for from the belfries they superimposed upon their tottering lantern towers sprang the soaring central features which will always remain the great glories of the Gothic era (Plate 61).

The buttress alone was a revolutionary discovery. Hitherto the ranges of arches supporting the roofs of their great buildings had been able to survive only by reason of the solidity of the supports from which they sprang. The introduction of buttresses enabled these supports to be lightened with a corresponding reduction in the obstruction of the interior of the building. By the same token these supports could also be heightened, thus achieving yet another step towards the ultimate aim in all true monumental architecture, concentration on the vertical factor. Such discoveries came at an opportune moment, for amongst the Byzantine architectural effects admired by the Franks was their invariable custom of ceiling their churches with stone, a far tidier arrangement than the untidy tangle of roofing timbers by which the western churches were covered. Stone vaulting was already known to the Franks, but only as a means of supporting an upper floor. But by the beginning of the 12th century they had completed the structural achievement of covering the main spans of their churches with stone vaulting used as a ceiling, another feature which, aided by the new scientific knowledge, was to revolutionize the architecture of the west.

During the 12th century the cultural centre of Frankish Europe was shifting. As Byzantinism declined, its western offshoot declined with it; thus Lombardy, Burgundy, the Rhineland and the Low Countries surrendered their old lead in matters spiritual. The opportunity for which the Roman Church had long been waiting had now arrived. For centuries its missionaries had been infiltrating into France and

England, waiting their turn to establish a culture which would replace westernized Byzantinism by something more truly 'Romanesque'. The Crusades, which had brought scientific methods of construction to the west, had at the same time helped to introduce the æsthetic taste of southern Europe into countries avid to receive it. The combination of refinement aided by science brought about the new architectural era known as the Gothic.

In the middle of the 12th century France was a new land which was just beginning to shake itself free from political strife with its surrounding duchies and piratical England. As a spiritual force the Holy Roman Empire was in the doldrums; thus it was Paris and the Ile de France that became the seat of the new architecture. It was a style which owed but little to Byzantinism; the massive pomp of the old days was giving place to delicacy and a soaring grace such as the world had never seen before.

The series of magnificent churches erected in the Ile de France during the second half of the 12th century exhibits a novel arrangement, that of the cruciform church lacking a central motif. It is as if the four arms of the cross have been raised to such a height as to engulf completely the familiar lantern tower or *cimborio*. Fortunately the acutely-pointed arches of the arcades abutting upon the crossing exerted far less lateral thrust than those of the older churches so that the need for weighting the crossing piers was now reduced. Thus instead of a lofty tower we find a whole church towering above the countryside (Plate 51).

The planning of these early Gothic cathedrals of France indicates development from the Frankish great church. Another indication of this origin is the presence of the galleries over the aisles. The architectural style is, however, entirely different from those of the Frankish churches of the region, being derived from the Crusader style of Spain and southern France with its pointed arches and lofty shafted supports. Unfortunately the French architects were so foolish as to reject the efficiently-planned Byzantine pier in favour of the Classical column with its Corinthianesque capital.

It was the new scientific knowledge which enabled the engineers of the day to raise these huge churches, so much loftier than anything hitherto experienced in architecture. Stability was achieved by means of a complicated system of abutment by which the thrusts of the high arches were countered by masses of masonry forming no part of the walling of the building but provided solely as constructional expedients. The principle adopted was that of the timber strut known as a 'raking shore' which, anchored to the ground at its lower end, slopes obliquely upwards to prop up a wall which is tending to lean over towards it. In masonry the timber strut was replaced by a flat arch known as a 'flying buttress' the foot of which was anchored by a heavy mass of masonry provided for the purpose.

By the end of the century it was found possible to convey the thrust of a high vault over the roof of an adjoining aisle by a flying buttress anchored to one of the buttresses forming part of the aisle wall. In the case of very tall structures there might be a series of flying buttresses, one above the other, engaged in containing the thrust of the main vault. Realizing the importance of loading the anchorage to counteract lateral thrust the engineers developed the fashion of carrying up buttresses in the form of heavy pinnacles, thus introducing what was soon to prove an important decorative feature in Gothic architecture.

In order to give full credit to the genius of the Gothic engineers it is necessary to appreciate the fact that they were quite uneducated men. Lacking the Arabic numerals, they were totally ignorant of even the simplest forms of mathematics; even ordinary addition had to be performed with the aid of the exchequer board. Thus their engineering feats were inspired by the breath of genius alone and frequently had perforce to be checked by the system of trial and error. There was no factor of safety, which makes their tremendous creations all the more amazing. In those days it must have been an anxious time for all when the centering was being struck.

The most remarkable feature of all is the problem as to how the erection of these great buildings was directed. To build a cathedral today requires an architectural staff equipped with paper and efficient drawing instruments—none of which existed in mediæval days—who will work for years turning out hundreds of drawings. There cannot have been anything like this sophisticated organization during the Middle Ages. Yet, slowly but irresistibly, the great churches rose towards the clouds.

Research into the principles of abutment forced the Gothic planners to realize that a new use was being made of masonry walling. Hitherto it had been employed solely for enclosing a building and supporting its roof; now it was being introduced as an engineering device. Moreover these abutment walls were set at right angles to the walls they were supporting, thus introducing an intrusive element into the plan. It was of course found that buttresses fitted perfectly into the ordinance of bay design already introduced for assistance in planning and now emphasized owing to the invention of the vaulted ceiling. Thus we find the architectural bay assuming a structural responsibility instead of being a convenient planning device. Henceforth the history of Gothic architecture is closely linked with the development of a transverse abutment system. The pillar which once merely served to support a wall is now part of a complicated structural frame crossing the building; such frames, set at a suitable distance apart, give an entirely new significance to the principle of bay design in buildings.

These experiments in engineering were conducted with one sole object in view, emphasis upon the monumental factor of height. This in itself provides an assurance that Gothic architecture had achieved its place among the great building styles. The early Frankish buildings, vast thought they were, represented the struggles of primitive builders to cover large areas; it is only when excessive height is aimed at that the architects are seen to be raising their eyes towards the stars. The 12th-century French church-builders excelled themselves. No pains were spared; even the obsolete two-storied aisles were retained in order that the greatest possible height might be achieved.

The primary defect in these early Gothic churches is due to the obstinacy with which their builders retained the pseudo-classical pillar with which they had replaced the far more useful Byzantine pier. Thus all the carefully contrived members of the vaulting system and its abutments came to an ignominious end upon the Corinthianesque capitals of these anachronisms, relics of a determination to Romanize architectural design. Towards the end of the century the principal vaulting shaft was brought down the side of the pillar in imitation of the punctuation device often employed in the Frankish churches; when the pillar became flanked by four of these shafts the route was becoming clearly marked towards the compound pillar which became the ultimate form of support in the perfected Gothic structure of the 13th century and after (Plate 52).

As the Benedictine monks had laboured to spread the Frankish style of church building throughout western Europe so did the Cistercians carry the Gothic style to all those regions not already firmly colonized by Byzantium. As far afield as Spain and Poland the simple masonry buildings with their sturdy pillars, pointed arches, and sweeping vaults rose, not only in the towns, as in past centuries, but in the sylvan recesses of the countryside. One of the most receptive countries was England, the south-western regions of which had already been drawn into the sphere of French influence. Glastonbury was the centre of this area of late-12th-century architectural development. An early creation was the cathedral of Wells, of which the clustered pillars show how efficiently and beautifully the English masons had refined the Frankish compound pier until it seemed to be an integral part of the system of deeply moulded arches and vaulting ribs springing from it. From such confident beginnings was born the English style of Gothic which, although never aspiring to the monumental scale of its French counterpart, is perhaps the most beautiful style of architecture the world has ever seen.

The two styles developed along different lines. The great French churches were built each as an architectural entity. The English churches grew through the replacement of the short Frankish eastern arm by a long structure which was in fact a complete church in itself. The continental church plan retained the choir west of the crossing of the transept; in England it was removed entirely east of this point so that the great transept and central lantern provided a terminal feature to the nave. The new eastern arm was planned with its own transept, west of which were the choir stalls returned against a screen filling the eastern arch of the great crossing. St Hugh's choir at Lincoln, begun in 1192, illustrates the system, while Salisbury, begun in 1220, is a complete cathedral planned in accordance with the new fashion.

It is noticeable that the austerities of the Cistercian planning are reflected in English Gothic to an extent that the apse is omitted altogether; thus a feature which since the beginnings of Christianity had been accepted as the standard termination of a church suddenly disappears from the architecture of a country. This is but one instance of the effect of the political insularity of England which enabled it to maintain its independence even in architectural style. Despite Cistercian strictures, no major continental country has ever dared to abandon the apse. A notable exception is Scandinavia, which seems to have readily adopted the English style of Gothic. It seems probable that the tradition of timber-building common to both countries may have played an important part in bringing this to pass. The apse is, of course, essentially a masonry structure.

By the last decade of the 12th century the French engineers and masons had perfected their magnificent style. They had carried out an architectural revolution. In a generation or so the old primitive technique of roof supported upon wall had given place to a system employing an elaborate structural framework from which the wall as such had been practically eliminated. It was a system of isolated supports between which the walling was little more than a series of screens.

Among the many scientific discoveries of the 12th century was the Byzantine method of filling large window openings with glazing; thus the new structural technique suggested the possibility of improved fenestration to suit the vast scale of the new buildings. The method was to transform the standard 'bifora' with its central shaft by converting this into a 'mullion' grooved to take sheets of leaded glazing secured to iron stanchions and saddle-bars. The head of the bifora was pierced by a foliated opening, thus inaugurating the system of 'tracery' which was to become such an important feature in later Gothic styles. The elongated bifora became the standard form of fenestration employed in the high Gothic churches of France, being set not only in the walls of the aisles but in those of the clerestory. So complete was the confidence felt by the engineers of the day in their new powers that they displayed no hesitation in raising the clerestory to an amazing elevation in order to fill it with rows of tall windows, between which the flying buttresses carried the thrusts of the high vaults down to the ground far below.

It seems probable that it was during the development of the apsidal east end of their churches that the French engineers first learnt the principles of abutment. The surrounding of this with an aisle was an important step as the semi-circular arcade beneath the apse had to be supported to prevent its bursting. The ring of chapels provided the solution; the vaulted ceiling of the ambulatory acting as a flying buttress carrying the thrust from the main wall over to the abutment which they provided. It may have been for this reason that the French not only remained loyal to the elaborate 'chevet' but even expanded it to greater elaboration. As the height of the building rose the abutment had to be still further extended until the ambulatory within the ring of chapels became doubled. From the chevet the double aisles began to reach westwards along the flanks of the short presbytery until by the end of the first quarter of the 13th century the whole church had become five-aisled.

To this factor of excessive height countered by a corresponding outward expansion of the base of the structure we owe the ultimate form of the High Gothic cathedral as seen at Beauvais, begun in 1225. The main span of the building is nearly 160 feet high internally but in the aisles drops suddenly to less than half this, leaving an immense cliff of clerestory walling supported only by the graceful but entirely adequate flying buttresses between which the chapels of the chevet are extended to form an outer aisle of no great elevation. The cruciform plan is retained by the introduction of a transept but the great height of the building results in what might be described as the absorption of the central lantern within it; the efficiency of the abutment system renders the retention of the aisle gallery unnecessary and thus greatly increases the lighting areas. In most Gothic regions the site of the gallery is indicated by an arcade passing along the wall between the tops of the main arches and the sills of the clerestory windows, a feature which also helps to relieve the bareness of this part of the walling covering the rise of the aisle roof (Plate 52).

During the century following the year 1150 the architects of England and northern France drew ahead of their contemporaries in other parts of Europe at a truly amazing rate. The firmly established late-Frankish architecture of the Rhineland held its own throughout the 12th century but by the beginning of the next the 'Ile-de-France Gothic' is found at Limburg-a-d-Lahn cathedral and by the middle of the century is at St Sebald, Nuremberg. The High Gothic follows slightly more rapidly, appearing in humble fashion at the Liebfrauenkirche at Trier in 1227 and in the grand manner at Cologne in 1248. But by this time the over-aspiring extravagances of the style were already losing favour and thenceforth German Gothic churches fall into line with those of the remainder of western Europe.

The Crusader architecture of 12th-century Spain, with its well-planned churches displaying the pointed arch rising from sturdy compound piers, had by the second quarter of the century already introduced itself into the realm of Gothic. Yet the Spanish architects were never to achieve the same *vertical* scale attained by their colleagues across the Pyrenees. The reason for this is one fundamental in Spanish architecture—the far heavier nature of their vault construction. The western European high vault is merely a ceiling above which lifts the pointed roof; the Spanish vault is itself a solid roof upon which rest the roof-tiles.

Thus the Spanish type of Gothic had to develop along different lines from that of France. By the beginning of the 13th century the Spaniards were already producing a sort of sturdy version of the Ile-de-France Gothic. Fortunately, however, Spanish Gothic from the start refused to encumber itself with the restrictions imposed by the Classical type of pillar. Lerida cathedral is an early example in which one can already detect the sturdiness which was to become the keynote of Spanish Gothic and replace in this magnificent southern style the soaring grace which characterizes the daring achievements of the French engineers. For it was the latter which was in the end to prove ephemeral. Before the turn of the 13th century it was clear that the day of such extravagances was passing. With Beauvais the zenith of the monumental factor had been achieved, nothing was left but to abandon henceforth such wasteful architecture and permit its achievements to remain for ever as a proud *nunc dimittis* for the glories of the High Gothic of 13th-century France (Plate 51).

Leadership in church-building passed southwards into the Peninsula. Here the theme was spaciousness. The five-aisled French plan was gladly adopted; Toledo cathedral, begun in 1227, nobly illustrates the Spanish ambition. But extravagant height was eschewed. One of the reasons may have been a wish to retain the *cimborio*, climax of the elevational aspect—internal as well as external—which had been abandoned by the French. Thus the Spanish cathedrals

71. A Spanish alcazar
(Toledo)

72. The walls of a mediæval town
(Aigues-Mortes)

march with those of England in remaining true to this last vestige of Byzantinism in ecclesiastical architecture. For height the Spaniards substituted area; their plans moreover show a tendency towards a better understanding of the principles of enclosing an area to be roofed. The early Gothic cathedral had been a struggling series of narrow buildings stuck together; the English cathedrals, in which dignity had been sought by extension to an extravagant length, being the chief offenders in this respect. Such buildings are of course singularly inconvenient for any practical purpose as only those persons immediately adjacent to any function which may be in progress are able to see or hear it.

The ideal church was still the Hagia Sophia at Constantinople —a rectangle of which the length was about twice the span—in which a concentrated plan had been combined with just sufficient of an axis to provide a sense of orientation. The planners of five-aisled Chartres and Bourges, in their efforts to provide abutment for their soaring vaults, had already tentatively indicated the route towards the perfect plan; the builders of Toledo adopted the same principle and freed it from some of the obstructive internal features attendant upon the need for excessive abutment. Even the reduction in height, however, could not free the structure entirely from the massiveness which characterizes Spanish Gothic and provides such a sharp contrast to the French. The comparative lowness of the Spanish interiors and the less generous fenestration suited to the latitude produces a cavernous aspect entirely missing from contemporary French and English buildings.

One of the most arresting features connected with the history of the magnificent Gothic of western Europe is the poor impression it made upon the country whence it derived its spiritual impulses. That it should have been laggard in spreading eastwards into such primitive countries as Poland or Hungary is understandable, but it was not until the end of the first quarter of the 13th century that the Cistercians had succeeded in introducing a sort of modified Ile-de-France Gothic into Italy of which the abbey church at San Galgano by Sienna is an example. But the soil of Italy seemed from the first unsuited to the soaring Gothic of the west with its pointed roofs and forests of pinnacles. It must of course be remembered that the Gothic is not really a masonry style. While its engineering achievements were due to an advanced knowledge of masonry construction its æsthetic forms are certainly evolved from timber building and the forest glade. For every masonry building we see today there were hundreds of structures cunningly constructed with a framework of posts, beams, and curved braces—true Gothic architecture of which the elements have swept most traces away. It is a fanciful—perhaps, after all, a barbaric—style; possibly its sometimes almost flippant vagaries were too much for such an ancient land as Italy to accept. At any rate, while England, Northern France and Spain were busily experimenting, Italy and Southern France were emulating Germany in remaining aloof from their neighbours' activities.

Thus central Italy made no attempt to investigate the problems of abutment and ignored even the simplest form of buttress. Its ecclesiastical architects held obstinately to the simple arcade with no properly-devised bay design; content with timber roofs, the ribbed vault seems to have made no impression upon them. They seem not to have advanced at all from the days of Constantine. Italy seems to have continued in this state of doldrums for centuries, as if unable to recover from the collapse of the Roman Empire. There is no trace of that western ebullience which produced first the great Frankish churches and then the marvels of the Gothic. It was as if the poverty-stricken land of the Popes had no material gifts to offer to the Church of which it was the spiritual home.

Yet by this time most of the parish churches of Europe conformed to the Roman model. Byzantinism had been defeated all along the line. Every church now possessed a nave, of a length which accorded with the means of its builders and aisled or not to suit the requirements of its span. The simple apse had in most cases given place to a rectangular chancel—sometimes, it is true, apsidal—providing more for ritual and the dignity of seclusion to the altar. Only through the influence of the Crusades did the Byzantine element still survive in the shape of a central lantern tower, with or without a transept.

A feature which had become inseparable from all but the smallest churches was the bell-tower. The Italians clung tenaciously to their slender *campanili*, either free-standing or attached to the church wherever fancy dictated. Frankish practice had adopted the western tower;

in parish churches this remained the normal position for the bell-tower throughout the mediæval period. The early Frankish cathedral and abbey churches were each provided with a single western tower; many of the narrower Gothic churches of Germany remained so equipped throughout the Middle Ages. The great churches of France and England preferred a pair of towers, an arrangement which not only proved less obstructive but actually converted the west end of the building into an elevational feature of great breadth and dignity. From this pair of towers framing a cavernous portal was developed the west front, the first attempt since Classical times to produce something approaching a façade or frontispiece to a building. Yet despite the popularity—everywhere except in High Gothic France—of the *cimborio* or lantern—the only central feature of any altitude was due to the introduction, for reasons of safety, of a belfry weighting the lantern story.

The Gothic age was surely one of towers. 12th-century developments in military engineering had produced formidable types of siege-artillery hitherto unknown and forced military architects to build lofty curtain walls round the sites they wished to protect. The considerable areas of dead ground lying at the foot of the curtain had to be covered by introducing numbers of towers projecting from the wall or rising above it (Plate 55). Thus the tower began to assume a primary importance in military architecture. During the 13th century large numbers of lofty towers were built as fortresses or watch towers; Germany and Italy especially producing a crop of these striking examples of military architecture in which the height factor is sometimes increased to such an extent as to introduce the monumental element, employed in this case not for religious expression but in order to advertise the social and military status of a civil owner (Plate 66).

In the Frankish regions, including England, the principal domestic building was the feudal hall, a simple structure rather like a barn, a class of building from which it was in fact descended. In the event of the span being too great for a simple roof it was divided by rows of timber posts supporting purlins or stone arcades as in a church (Plate 56). In considering the nature of Gothic architecture it is as well not to underestimate the importance still enjoyed by the timber architecture of the period. The principal factors involved are the post, the horizontal beam, plate or purlin, and the curved braces sweeping from post to beam and stiffening the whole structure. It is from the lines of these last features that the unique form of Gothic architecture is derived; thus arch and vaulting rib are not merely carried upon the support, as in a purely masonry style, but are made to appear as if *growing* from it.

The large ground-floor apartment or hall finds its way into most classes of Gothic architecture. The domestic variety has already been dealt with. Refectories, chapter halls, and infirmary halls have a place in monastic plans. There is the great hall of the castle and the hall of the tradesman's guild; the moot hall or council room is the origin of the complex structure of today known as the Town Hall. In the wealthy cities of Flanders and Lombardy one finds market halls and warehouses for the storage of goods.

The Gothic house is simply a copy of the type developed by the Byzantines. The governing factor is the placing of the principal rooms upon the first floor or *piano nobile*. In town houses the entrance is at ground level; in Italy it is often covered by a loggia or portico. In country districts the doorway is set for safety in the upper story and is reached by a stair, usually of wood. This stair is an important innovation in architecture; from it is developed the grand stair of later centuries. Internal stairways leading from floor to floor or to the tops of towers are spirals of stone, each enclosed in its own slender turret.

Verticality being one of the fundamental factors in Gothic design, the architects of the day made great play with turrets; during the 12th century their pyramidal roofs were being replaced with stone caps and during the next century towers themselves were being covered with high stone spires.

The Gothic architects were forever at pains to emphasize the soaring effect of their buildings. Vertical prolongation was exaggerated wherever possible; turret-tops and the weighting pinnacles of buttresses were brought into use for this purpose. Ornament was concentrated as high up as possible so as to lead the eye upwards; hence the lavish efforts expended upon pinnacles. The introduction of parapets necessitated by the use of lead for covering roofs provided

74. A late-Gothic façade above a Venetian canal

73. The graceful façade of a fifteenth-century Venetian palace

75. The Palazzo Rucellai at Florence

76. Above the façade of the early-Renaissance palace rises Brunelleschi's dome
(Florence)

77. The dome of St. Peter's at Rome

another field for the display of ornament; thus arcading or crenellation was introduced to attract the eye to this feature. Arcading was also employed to great effect in connection with the new façades which were being applied to the west ends of great churches; mediæval figure sculpture reached a high level in the statues filling the niches of the arcading.

Architectural ornament, as opposed to pure sculpture, was mainly confined to the capitals of pillars and shafts. The model seems to have been Corinthian in origin. The angle volutes are repeated in the Gothic copies in various forms, often translated into terms of western botany; the acanthus covering the bell is similarly converted to forms which the carvers knew. Nothing could more perfectly illustrate the complete independence of the Gothic craftsman than his utter disregard of the long-established Classical patterns. It is this wealth of free carving, applied to the most skilful products of engineering the world had ever seen, which helps to make the High Gothic of Western Europe the most beautiful style known to the history of architecture.

Yet its effect upon the history of architecture is but small. For almost the whole of the skill of Gothic architects and builders was devoted to the erection of enormous churches, and when these were no longer required the Gothic style withered and died. For it had made too little contribution to the design of secular buildings (as attempts to revive it have shown) and architecture cannot live by monumentalism alone.

But side by side with the great stone buildings of the Middle Ages were the homes of those who raised them. The timber frames upon which these were constructed have long ago perished, yet it was this impermanent form of building technique which was to lay the foundations of future architectural style. Thus the enchanting arches of romantic Gothic were forced to give place to the uninspiring wooden beams of contemporary domestic buildings until in the end it was masonry construction which had to adjust itself to suit the horizontality of what had become a trabeated style.

Chapter XIII

MEDIÆVAL EUROPE

During the three centuries or so which preceded the close of the 11th, western Europe had been principally concerned with the struggle to emerge from the turbulence of the Dark Ages and the establishment within still restricted borders of a culture which could hold its own in the world of its day. Benedictine colonists helped with the work; their successors the Cistercians carried the task yet another stage forward. Through the medium of the ebb and flow of Crusading hordes the sunset lands acquired something of the wisdom of the ancients and at the same time encountered a highly advanced civilization, that of Islam. The west was avid to absorb knowledge and during the great days of the 12th century founded universities for the purpose. The earliest, that of Paris, helped to bring about the architectural lead of that region in the second half of the century. The foundation of Oxford University in 1167 may have played no small part in encouraging the development of the English Gothic style.

Thus by the beginning of the 13th century the culture of western Europe had emerged from the primæval fog of superstition, passed through a period of experiment, and now stood firmly upon a sound foundation—that of knowledge. A new factor had come to the assistance of western Christendom: the establishment of the Mendicant Orders. The golden age of monasticism was ended; the bustling world of the 13th century held no place for men who shut themselves away from it. But the friars were of different calibre; as men of learning and worldly understanding they ranged the European world and taught wisdom to men searching for knowledge. The great monasteries had long ruled the roost; the glorious Gothic choirs of the early 13th century remain as memorials of the wealth and power of the abbots. But the friars aspired to no such extravagant displays. When they built it was to provide commodious naves in which men might gather and learn. The friars' contribution to the history of architecture was a notable one. It took two forms: the modification of the existing Gothic and the creation of an entirely new style which was to carry on architectural tradition to the end of the mediæval period.

At the turn of the 13th century western Gothic was almost static. French leadership collapsed while their architects wore themselves out struggling to nurture to maturity the towering white elephants they had reared. English Gothic, still a vigorous style, was nevertheless making little practical headway. Losing much of the grace which had enshrined their earlier creations the English architects were trying to make up the loss by enlisting armies of carvers to cover the masonry with a wealth of ornament, without which 14th-century English Gothic would simply have become a slightly coarser variation on that of the century before.

It was left to the frontiersmen of eastern Germany to supply the necessary fillip to Gothic architecture. Working in a region devoid of building stone its architects turned their attention to the possibilities of brickwork. There are great advantages in this material. It is easy to make, transport, and work into walling, can be moulded or carved into any form desired, and has a colour and texture even more interesting than freestone. But structurally it has serious defects which make it necessary to restrict the uses to which it is put.

The stability of masonry is dependent upon the weight of each individual stone, acting either vertically or, as in an arch, transferred to a neighbouring stone through a carefully-designed joint or bed. Mortar is employed as a convenient means of filling up interstices, especially those found in rubble masonry; it plays no part in the structural design. Brickwork, however, is a material of quite another character, being a sort of concrete having the individual bricks as its aggregate. It is a far weaker form of construction than masonry and is not capable of being used for engineering feats such as those of early Gothic days; thus a masonry arch will settle and adjust itself under stresses which would break up a brick one. Yet despite the small size of the brick compared with the block of freestone it is the latter which can be used to create the most delicate constructional design.

are excellent in piers and again in simple abutment; but they cannot be employed in flying buttresses, a fact which is largely responsible for the architectural character of northern Europe.

Again it was the Crusades which brought to western Europe the knowledge of brickmaking. By the end of the 12th century most regions, such as eastern England, having an inadequate supply of building stone were turning to bricks. They formed a convenient ballast for returning trade-ships; another fact which helped to spread their use. During the 13th century the Teutonic Knights created in Prussia a brick architecture which was to develop into one of the most elaborate of the mediæval styles (Plates 59 and 60). The brick-builders of Prussia colonized Poland and brought Gothic architecture into touch with the partly Byzantinized Russians.

German brick architecture is characterized by a simplification of the abutment system in order to avoid the intricate extravaganzas of contemporary French examples. Brickwork is excellent for vaulting systems, especially if enough freestone can be found for the ribs; thus the humblest mediæval churches of the lower Baltic regions are often vaulted throughout. Yet the height of the building need present no problem as the thrust of the vaulting can be met by simple buttresses of massive brickwork. Low aisles on the other hand create the problem of transferring the thrust of the central vault over them without the use of flying buttresses, a fact which as early as the second quarter of the 13th century had begun to set the fashion for building churches with all three divisions of equal height.

At first the aisles were far narrower than the nave—as at Marburg —in conformity with standard mediæval tradition, but it was soon realized that the simplified abutment system now made it possible to increase the width of the aisles to anything desired. Hence the 'hall church' with its three identical aisles which during the 14th century became the standard form for Germany and the Low Countries (Plates 63 and 64). In eastern Germany and Poland, however, where the height factor was still very much to be desired, width was sacrificed to this end so that we find a series of lofty aisle-less churches surrounded by simple well-designed buttresses. To the north-west are the great hall churches, in both brick and stone, of the wealthy peoples trading across the North Sea and the lower Baltic (Plate 60).

78. An example of the 'giant order' of columns passing through two stories
(Vicenza)

79. The type of bay-design used by the Vicenzan architect Palladio

It is interesting to note that the novel design of their churches does not prevent the Dutch and Flemish architects from remaining almost entirely constant to the pseudo-classical pillar of the early Gothic builders.

A notable exception to the style is Antwerp cathedral, begun in 1352 in the normal fashion with a high nave flanked by aisles of a lower altitude. There are, however, no less than three of these on each side, presenting a roofing problem hitherto unencountered. Each bay of the aisles is covered by a separate roof set at right angles to the axis of the building, an innovation which is found repeated in many of the churches of Germany and which seems to be the origin of the dormer window. The subsidiary roofs at Antwerp are hipped back at their inner ends so as to offer no obstruction to exceptionally huge clerestory windows.

This device is yet another example of the concentration of the 14th-century architect upon bay design and the transverse element in planning. Attenuation is no longer a factor sought by the church-builder; lateral spaciousness is now the keynote. Excessive height having been also abandoned it was now possible to utilize engineering knowledge for the purpose of spreading the weight of the vault over as large a span as possible. It was the Spaniards who throughout the 13th century had been concentrating on this problem; a series of huge cathedrals, structurally and decoratively far more magnificent than anything to be found elsewhere, proudly illustrate what the architects of this wealthy and highly-cultured country could achieve with the aid of its invaluable freestone.

By the beginning of the 14th century a new trend is discoverable in Spanish planning. This is the obvious desire of the architects to destroy the last relic of axial planning, the rhythm of the bay-system so insistently forced upon the interior elevations through the recurring arches of the main arcades. By widening each bay and reducing the number of piers in the arcades they also were able to increase the effect of spaciousness by removing obstructive features.

At last the whole historic plot of mediæval church-building stands revealed before us. We have watched the long lines of sprawling extremities gathered in to heap themselves in one soaring mass towards the firmament as barbaric chaos resolves itself into monumentalism.

And now reason has taken command and the pile sinks once more to spread in gracious hospitality as though anxious to gather the humblest beneath the shelter of one vast roof.

Fig. 9. The vast nave vault of Gerona cathedral equals in span those of the choir and its aisle together

There was yet one task to be completed: the freeing of this new spaciousness from its last obstructions. We have seen how from earliest times internal width has been achieved only by the introduction of supports to divide the span. But the science of abutment, first employed to achieve height, was now to be utilized in order to gain width. Witness the nave of Gerona cathedral, begun early in the 15th century, where the mighty vault sweeps across a clear span of over seventy feet (Fig. 9). The mediæval engineer could do no more.

The abutments of this magnificent Spanish vault consist of ordinary buttresses, of considerable projection from the wall-face, but producing a very different effect from those of earlier buildings owing to the distance they stand apart. There is nothing suggestive of the narrow bays found in the original Gothic cathedrals; the Gerona bays are more than forty feet in width. In this we see once more reflected the new conception of the bay as a building unit. The Gothic bay originated as a transverse strip confined between two constructional frames spanning the structure and the plan was assembled as a string of such strips. Now we find such sub-divisions of the plan as may be needed for constructional reasons consist, not of strips, but of areas.

This new type of building bay, so vitally important as a step towards the rationalization of planning, produced an even more striking effect upon the elevational aspect of the building. The huddle of mediæval buttresses begins to spread out as each takes up a position of massive isolation, while ranks of narrow windows are thinned out and replaced by spacious sheets of glazing stiffened by complicated systems of traceried masonry. The primitive sense of mystery is dispelled, giving place to an air of invitation as, within and without, the trees of the old Gothic forest are felled and cleared away.

The parish churches of the late-mediæval era reflect the same desire for space and lightness. Everywhere supports are reduced in number as the building-bays expand while the soaring Gothic arches begin to sink resignedly into strange debased attitudes as they are forced to stretch themselves across the ever-widening gaps separating their pillars. Grace, as well as mystery, was being abandoned in the struggle for spaciousness. But an ancient craft was brought into the field as the carpenters who had for so long been watching their achievements callously concealed behind stone ceilings were now being called upon to invent new methods of framing the trusses of their roofs so that these could form visible features of the architecture of the building. The response of the carpenters to this challenge is one of the most notable incidents in the history of architecture. The science of abut-ment had helped the masons to prop up their mighty vaults; now brilliant adventures in the craft of joinery enabled the carpenter to devise complicated roofing systems which would bridge the widest span without subsiding.

What the stone vault was to the great church, the traceried oaken roof was to the parish church. The latter also formed the crowning feature to the banqueting hall of the later mediæval period, successor to the more primitive barn-like hall of feudal days. Such was the simplicity of mediæval constructional principles that there could be little difference between the nave of a church and the hall of a noble-man. The hall still formed the principal apartment in the complex of structures which made up the great house of mediæval days. In company with it were various two-storied houses, each with its private chamber on the upper floor for residential purposes, while a medley of kitchens, store-rooms, stabling, barns, and so forth added to the confusion of the site.

The establishment of the Gothic form of castle, however, having its perimeter furnished with lofty curtain walls and an assortment of projecting wall-towers, encouraged the castle planners to set out their buildings along the inner face of the walls, thus economizing in masonry and clearing the interior of the place to form an unobstructed yard. It being difficult to set out large buildings along a curved wall, the fashion for rectangular plans eventually superseded the old oval form. By the last quarter of the 13th century the castle had become a towered rectangle having the buildings within set against the inside of the walls and opening on a central courtyard.

The courtyard is not an indigenous feature in western European planning. The monastic cloister, which often lacked its western range, developed as the simplest way of assembling a group of three large buildings: church, house, and hall. The cloister walk, arcade, and alley, are likewise developments upon a primitive theme. The courtyard was, however, a universal feature of oriental planning. It is as well to remember that throughout the mediæval period the culture of Islam was vastly more advanced than that of Christendom. While the latter was struggling to emerge from the night of barbarism, Islam was still basking in the sunshine of its mighty dynasties and enjoying the fruits of their labours in the courts of lovely palaces undreamed of by the Franks and their heirs. The courtyard with its graceful shafted loggia was a commonplace in Islam.

In mediæval days the Islamic *kasr,* or great house, was a square of apartments, several stories in height, set around a cloistered court and presenting to the outer world a high wall of stern, almost military, appearance. Towards the end of the 13th century, when the Gothic castle plan was beginning to develop along similar, if humbler, lines, the Teutonic knights were beginning to introduce into eastern Prussia a type of castle which seems to have modelled its planning on the oriental *kasr* (Fig. 10). In the design of such castles as Marienburg or Marienwerder we find a new sophistication, a stern orderliness quite different from the muddle of the Gothic and already suggestive of the Renaissance palace lay-out with its *cortile* and towering façades.

In such buildings as these we can detect a new note in domestic architecture: an attempt to take account of elevational aspect. This is understandable, for with an assortment of architecturally unrelated structures there can be small chance of treating any single building, let alone the whole complex, as an elevational essay. But the organizing of the separate items so that each fitted into a pre-conceived plan revolutionized not only domestic planning but the whole course of domestic architecture. A great house was now really a house and not a small village.

Much has been written upon the skill with which the Gothic architects set out their elevational treatments. The fact is, however, that it was the *section* of the structure which governed the design. Plan was merely the addition of bay to bay and was principally influenced by the means available; by the same token the lateral elevations were invariably entirely fortuitous. Section, however, entirely governed the principal elevation, the end of the building in which—in the case of a church—was situated its principal doorway. Thus we have here the makings of a frontispiece, in which the doorway, set centrally, provided a focus.

Nowhere is the ingenuousness of the Gothic architect more clearly exhibited than in the design of these façades. The splitting-up of the Frankish western tower into two at once provided a pair of terminal features which could be utilized in a scheme for a grand frontispiece.

The obvious course was to make them similar, yet even this simple elevational device was often ignored, thus depriving the mediæval architect of his only chance of designing an orderly façade. It is indeed

Fig. 10. The courtyard of the mediæval Schloss reflects that of the Islamic great house

clear that the Gothic architect had little or no appreciation of how to design elevations. His aim was monumentalism as expressed by height; to him an elevation was merely a wall—which might or might not be covered with architectural or carved ornament.

It is in the search for height that the Gothic builders achieved their apotheosis. In all architectural history there is nothing to equal their glorious towers. They cared not for the symmetry of façades; if a tower was to be raised they raised it. The architect of Beauvais would have counted his labour lost if he could have seen the marvels of Lincoln (Plate 61), Canterbury, or Ghent lifting fearlessly into the sky. Raised stone upon heavy stone by generations of men climbing wearily through a forest of scaffolding, these towers can gaze down from the summit of all architectural achievement upon the sky-scrapers of New York.

One might not have supposed that the early development of the façade in elevational treatment was due to the military architects. It is yet another example of the practical origins of most architectural devices. The west doorway of a church was merely an entrance into a religious building; the outer gate of a castle, however, was a feature upon which the whole safety of the occupants depended. Such indeed was the dire necessity for providing the utmost protection to this, the weakest spot in the castle defences, that it came to be sited between two wall-towers from which fire could be concentrated before it. Towards the end of the 13th century the twin-towered gatehouse became the normal entrance feature, entirely replacing the keep as the outward symbol of military might. Being of practical origin and unaffected by the need for undue height its two towers remained of equal height and indeed eventually became, with the entrance passage between them, a single building of standardized form.

The combination of the twin-towered gatehouse with the plan of the courtyard castle suggested the siting of the former in the centre of one side of the latter, midway between two of the corner towers of the rectangle. Thus we have at last not only a symmetrical façade but one of considerable extent and displaying moreover several features of architectural significance. One has only to glance at the late-13th-century façade of Harlech castle to appreciate the dignity of the design; it is difficult to appreciate that three centuries were to elapse before the principle underlying it was to penetrate into the ordinary domestic architecture of this country. The builders of Harlech were able to attempt symmetry merely because the simple lay-out of the enceinte imposed no restriction upon them. But architects had first to collect the jumble of apartments forming the mediæval great house into a coherent group and gather them together under one roof before façades could be considered at all; even then there was a long distance to travel before the skill needed to force them behind a symmetrically designed elevation could be acquired.

Thus to the mediæval architect symmetry was a device only to be employed on a large scale. The fortified town surrounded by lofty towered walls was a feature of the landscape of western Europe during the late 13th and 14th centuries. A number of new towns, such as Aigues Mortes (Plate 72), were laid out; where level sites existed they were planned on a grid pattern for the convenience of enclosing them within a rectangular perimeter. The town gates were of the normal twin-towered type and were made the principal features of the elevational aspect of the fortifications. Thus we find a monumental factor creeping into the planning schemes of the western world and replacing the mediæval muddle which had existed since the end of the Roman occupation.

Throughout the history of mediæval architecture one can detect a striving towards the tidying up of the Gothic muddle which passed for planning. Thus by the end of the 13th century the monastic plan had been stabilized in a form which brought it into line with the advanced *kasr* type of layout which had already been accepted by the military architects of Prussia. Hitherto the principal buildings—church, house, and hall—had sited on three sides of a yard or court, eventually closed by a fourth range containing lodgings and offices. The provision of covered ways surrounding this claustral court had by the 13th century produced permanent cloisters with their outer walling pierced by the usual traceried openings and in the finest examples ceiled with stone vaulting. It had now become the fashion to set out this cloister first, aligning the buildings of the monastery along the sides of the nucleus thus created. Thenceforth the cloister became a very beautiful feature. In the Mediterranean countries it was often two-storied so as to provide access between first-floor rooms in addition to those at ground level; the Spanish architects in particular made much of these beautiful features, enriching walls and vault until they rivalled those of the church itself, for to their neighbouring

80. In Michelangelo's façade to the Capitol at Rome can be seen an early use of the 'giant order'

81. The Farnese Palace at Rome

Moslem colleagues the court with its loggias was the principal architectural feature of the domestic *kasr*.

While the courtyard surrounded by loggias represents Islam's most important contribution to the plan of the Gothic palace it is also important to remember that the Moslem architects were indirectly responsible for the first steps in elevational architecture undertaken by the Gothic builders. We have spoken of the external loggias or porticoes which form such charming features of the Islamic housefront; graceful compositions which in Gothic hands were translated into terms of sturdy pillar and pointed arch. As arcades of this description could be made to carry heavy masonry walling the loggias could be incorporated within the ground story of the main building with the upper part of the façade supported upon the open arcade. This carrying of an *external* wall upon an arcade introduced an innovation which revolutionized the appearance of building frontages by forcing upon them a regular system of punctuation by bays; thus from the end of the Crusading era we find attempts at planned elevations being undertaken by the Gothic engineers.

The culminating glory of the mediæval cloister or loggia is its vault. Ever since the day when they had first succeeded in raising a vast stone ceiling above the lofty interior of a church the Gothic masons seem to have been fascinated by the wonder of the architectural firmament they had thereby created. It was as if they had spread above their heads a mysterious canvas of stone which invited them to try their skill upon its embellishment. As true craftsmen they began their self-appointed task in practical fashion by seeing how they could make the vault easier to construct. The introduction of intermediate ribs to reduce the individual areas of vaulting was the first step; this was followed by the insertion of short ribs which began to make a pattern upon the vault. Rib-intersections were masked by 'bosses' upon which the carvers were allowed to play (Plate 62). After this stage had been reached the mason's enthusiasm did the rest; from Germany to Spain the most elaborate systems of vaulting design spread throughout the western world to achieve perfection in the incredible 'fan-vaulting' of 15th-century England.

The late mediæval period is one of elaboration. The spacious windows which filled the new wide building bays were divided up by mullions which rose into a complicated maze of tracery contorted into a variety of designs, many of them clearly derived from Islamic sources. The windows of the aisle-less churches of eastern Germany soared to the full height of their lofty narrow bays, helping with the aid of the adjoining buttresses to lift the building, in true Gothic fashion, towards the clouds. Vast circular 'rose' windows, writhing with tracery, filled the gable elevations.

Everywhere the carving spread. Wall-faces became covered with oriental-looking diaper; the bells of Corinthianesque capitals found their pseudo-volutes smothered by a burgeoning of naturalistic foliage which soon swarmed along the mouldings of the arches. German brickworkers, not to be outdone, carved and wrought their soft material into ornamental forms rivalling those of the stonecarvers. The crenellated parapets of the castle-builders were transplanted to the churches and there forced to join in the riot of ornament; even the lowering 'machicolations' which carried the parapet out beyond the wall-face in order that the base of the curtain might be surveyed by its defender (Plate 66) were modified and employed as a decorative feature in non-military architecture.

The brickworkers added their own special contribution, beloved throughout the centuries by all who have worked in their material. The top of a stone wall is protected by a stone coping the use of which is denied to those who have only brick at their disposal; thus the rain may seep down into the open joints of a brick wall, freeze there, and begin to destroy it. The method of preventing this is to lay the upper-most bricks so that each covers the joint separating the pair below it. By continuing this arrangement for several courses below the wall-top this is given the zigzag silhouette so often illustrated in the bas-reliefs of ancient Assyria. In north-eastern Germany and the Low Countries, where the brickbuilders reigned supreme amongst building craftsmen, the battlemented parapet became a standard feature in buildings of all classes. By the 14th century the invention of brick 'tumbling', that is to say bricks laid sloping, enabled a form of coping to be constructed which could be used horizontally but would not pass up gable ends; hence the familiar 'corbie-steps' always found on brick gables of the mediæval period.

The brickbuilders *par excellence* had always been the orientals.

From the ancient lands of the east the Moslems had carried their art into southern Spain whence they were now slowly being driven by the ever-growing power of Christian kings. The victors made full use of the craftsmen—the *mudejares*—who chose to stay behind in the regions lost to their religion and with their aid created yet another elaborate style of ornamental brickwork. It was in the design of bell-towers to replace the now-vanished minarets that the *mudejares* were chiefly employed; during the 15th century in particular a great many of these fine towers were built in the conquered regions.

Another region in which brick played an important part was Lombardy, where the long-established use of roofing tiles, coupled with a temperate climate that produced no heavy falls of snow to tax the strength of roofing, kept the roof-pitch unassuming and gave no encouragement to architects to attempt the towering compositions of western Europe. Thus the High Gothic, save for a few essays by Cistercian colonists and the one magnificent outburst at Milan, never crossed the Alps into Italy. That ancient land was too conservative and perhaps too poor, to interest itself in such extravagances. Thus when Gothic influences began to penetrate, they were gently absorbed and never allowed to revolutionize the old architecture of the country.

Venice, the brick city rising from the sea, was the architectural capital of Italy during the era which saw the High Gothic of the west. But as early as the second quarter of the 13th century the orders of friars had set their sign-manual upon the ecclesiastical architecture of the island republic. No elaborate Gothic choirs were to appear in the city; the national 'basilican' nave with a simple apse at its eastern end was still to form the church plan. It was the nave, employed as an auditorium for preaching, which interested the friars; thus Italian Gothic was concerned from the beginning with this only.

In 1333, the Dominican fathers were beginning SS. Giovanni e Paolo, the civic church of the powerful Doges of one of the wealthiest cities in Europe, in a style of such austere dignity that it seems to shame the wild extravagances of the west. The cruciform plan, with choir and transepts of restrained projection, are a concession to the now long-established Frankish convention, as is the fine vaulted ceiling hiding the timber roof. Yet it appears in reality little more than a magnified version of the old 'basilican' building with the two ranks of columns dividing nave from aisles. The columns have become lofty pillars with floriated Corinthianesque capitals from which vaulting shafts rise untidily to an insignificant clerestory; externally, primitive punctuation features have been but slightly expanded to provide some kind of abutment. But there are only five wide bays in the great nave; an achievement in spaciousness far in advance of anything found in the west. This great republican church was modelled upon that of the Franciscans (Plate 65) begun three years earlier.

There is something startling in the realization of the utter lack of similarity between the churches of the feudal countries and those of contemporary Italian republics. There is a freedom of spirit discernible in the latter which contrasts strikingly with the fever of the Gothic. The Italian churches are not awe-inspiring, but they dispense an atmosphere of tranquillity absent from the glorious creations of the barbaric west. Setting a feudal cathedral beside a republican friary church of contemporary foundation reveals instantly the reason for the Italian Renaissance.

In 1294 the Florentines had begun the huge church of S. Croce, an aisled hall far too wide to carry a vault, and with the bays of its graceful arcades themselves so spacious that the architect introduced a horizontal cornice above the tops of the arches in order to tie the composition together. Something of the sort also appears in western churches, generally indicating a level such as a line of window sills or the floor of a gallery; at Florence, however, the cornice appears as a vigorous æsthetic device deliberately introduced to steady the design.

Towards the middle of the 14th century Florence cathedral was being replaced. The republican style had reached maturity and the task was approached with confidence, as the four great bays of the nave illustrate to this day. One cannot but be impressed by the dignity of this fine structure, of the same era as the nave of York and yet infinitely more sober and sophisticated. In all three dimensions the Tuscan nave has the advantage of its English contemporary; yet the former has but four bays to the latter's eight. It comes as a shock to realize that, notwithstanding all the raptures of the Gothic era in the west, it was the ugly Italian duckling that turned out after all to be the swan. It should moreover be observed that at Florence it was the cathedral nave, not the bishop's choir, which was first erected; yet another sign of the new enlightenment. Fifty years later the great nave of S. Petronia at Bologna was built; even today it lacks its choir.

A feature peculiar to Italian ecclesiastical architecture is the manner in which refinement is achieved not by detail but by the absence of this. The great dignity of the republican naves is due to the elimination of all features that are not absolutely essential for structural or æsthetic reasons. Externally this same austerity is carried still further so that even the projection of a buttress is restrained to a degree that reduces it to a mere note of punctuation. Openings through the light, well-constructed, masonry walls are innocent of the elaborately moulded soffits inseparable from Gothic architecture while ornament is practically limited to the Corinthianesque capitals of the principal supporting members. Italian sunshine can penetrate the interiors of buildings with an ease which renders unnecessary the vast traceried windows of the west; even the mullion is seldom introduced to replace the slender shaft of the traditional *bifora* which, elongated somewhat to suit the height of the building in which it now finds itself, continues to represent the highest form of Italian fenestration.

The fact is that Italy's lack of a Gothic phase in her architectural education caused her mediæval builders to be very unenterprising in that branch of elevational art which deals with the design of features. All her architects had to go upon were the remains of Classical structures having their openings treated in an archaic fashion quite unsuited to the general style of the period. Nevertheless the mediæval Italians were forced to employ the ædicule with its pediment supported by the pair of flanking pilasters; even their grim Crusader castles were provided with portals of this design. In such fashion did the thirteenth-century Italian architects keep the feeble embers of the old Roman fire glowing until such time as it should be required to kindle the mighty conflagration of the Renaissance.

Chapter XIV

DOMESTIC
DEVELOPMENTS

During the mediæval era the Church was paramount and architecture the prerogative of the ecclesiastic. From its beginnings under Benedictine auspices we have seen it carried throughout western Europe by the Cistercians and developing, under the culminating influence of the Crusades, into the Gothic style which became essentially its own. Its zenith attained in 13th-century France, we find ecclesiastical architecture settling down into a rationalized Gothic shorn of its inspiration and beginning to show signs of mediocrity. With the 13th century ended the era of the great churches—though bishops and even abbots were continually completing or adding to their buildings. Such additions were in the nature of refashioning obsolete portions of the structure and bore no comparison with the noble ventures of the past.

The 14th century was a period of great civic churches, products of trade and advertisement of the wealth of cities. Attached to no monastery, the late-Gothic city church might be served by a college of secular clergy; more often its long presbytery was but a relic of the days of crowded choirs now emptied of their monks but still provided as part of the established plan of a mediæval church. Even the elaboration of their ornament, produced by armies of craftsmen paid out of the profits of inter-urban trade, fails to compensate for the lack of inspiration so noticeable in the design of these buildings, laid out along inevitable lines by men deprived of a spur to architectural enterprise. Yet out of all this mediocrity one feature emerges to sustain the honour of the fast-dying race of mediæval architects as their era closes to the sound of music from a glorious company of bell towers—noblest achievements of any architectural age (Plate 57).

One European country escaped from the slough of architectural dullness in which its neighbours had become engulfed. In Spain the spirit of the Crusades had never flagged. Century by century the magnificent but failing power of Islam retreated before the more virile forces of its ancient enemy. In each conquered province the Christians erected mighty churches as monuments of their victory. The 15th century opened with the foundation of the largest church in the world at the old Islamic city of Seville (Plate 53); a century and a quarter later the establishment of the cathedral of Granada (Plate 69) showed the Spanish architects to be still at the top of their form. The spirit of the frontiersman seems to be as strong as ever before; during the 15th century the Spaniards covered their buildings with architectural and sculptured ornament which is not only quivering with vitality but enthusiastically displaying excerpts from the best of both worlds, Islamic as well as Christian.

A feature of late-mediæval architecture common to two very diverse regions, Spain and England, is the reduction in pitch of the Gothic arch to its four- or three-centred outline. In the latter country this is due to the presence of an ample supply of lead ore and the consequent use of lead for roofing. The waterproofing value of this material is so high that the roof pitch can be reduced to practically nothing; moreover lead laid on a steep pitch is apt to creep downwards through its own weight. In Spain, where interlocking tiling set upon a stone vault has from early times been the standard method of roofing, the acute Gothic roof was never employed; thus the Spaniards made great use of the low-pitched arch, often in its ogee silhouette, a fact which contributes greatly to the richness of Spanish architectural ornament. At the end of the mediæval period the Spanish three-centred arch had spread throughout western Europe to replace the archaic Gothic form with a silhouette more suited to the ordering of an elevation and, in particular, the insertion of door and window frames.

Spain excepted, architectural prerogative passed out of ecclesiastical hands at the close of the 13th century. The power of the Church was waning while trade was pouring wealth into lay coffers; thus, building, still the most popular form of expression, began to flow along domestic channels. At this time domestic architecture was still at a very primitive stage, the only structures of note being the great hall and the two-storied house with its chamber floor raised above a storage basement. There were, of course, the usual minor offices, kitchens, store-rooms, buildings for baking and brewing, barns and stabling, and such like, but hall and chamber formed the principal apartments. The constructional principle employed was that of the roof supported by two parallel walls and closed at each end by a gable wall; improved knowledge of abutment principles and joinery methods was now making it possible to increase span without resorting to internal arcades.

The hall was the place for assembly and meals; the chamber was the home of a wealthy family. The chamber might be divided up by hangings or timber partitions into separate apartments but such division was arbitrary and haphazard: in the nature of furnishing rather than architectural design or planning. By the 14th century it was becoming apparent that such a primitive arrangement, little better in fact than that found in a large tent, made no provision at all for the accommodation of the occasional visitor who—in primitive households doubtless a rarity—now formed a factor in the social economy of the age.

A person of consequence travelling about the country could find accommodation in monasteries. At first his chamber might be situated in the western range of the claustral buildings; it might even be that of the abbot himself. It may have been due to this inconvenience that it became the practice to construct a guest house set in the outer court, a building which appears as an addition to the types of mediæval structures so far encountered in that it is designed solely for the purpose of providing lodgings for visitors. It would seem reasonable to make the plan permanent by building the internal partitions in stone; thus we get a new feature in architecture.

The height to which the curtain walls of castles had risen by the end of the 13th century made it possible to build such lodging-houses against their inner faces and raise them to include several stories of apartments; thus we reach a stage at which domestic architecture has become multi-storied. Thenceforth the multi-storied range of lodgings becomes the principal building of the late mediæval period in western Europe. From the planning point of view it is

82. Seventeenth-century town walls designed to withstand cannon and concentrate maximum enfilade fire upon storming parties
(Floriana)

83. It was upon the vast stages of the Renaissance theatres that architects experimented with pasteboard architecture (Vicenza).

simply a single-span structure divided by cross-walls into a number of separate apartments. Constructional problems being eliminated by the presence of internal supports there is no need for any additional architectural features such as buttresses; thus the walls of the structure can be quite plain and simple. Such walls, on the other hand, provide scope for elevational design never before experienced in mediæval architecture. All the factors suggesting punctuation—bays for each apartment, stories for each floor—are already present and waiting for architectural acknowledgement. In ecclesiastical architecture the long elevation had to be kept subservient to a western façade too constricted to give the architect a chance to spread himself; now at last he had the whole length of a building presented as a canvas upon which he could exhibit his skill at elevational design (Plate 68).

It was the multitude of windows which provided the architect with his raw material. Already lying in horizontal layers along their several stories, by aligning them vertically in bays he was able at once to produce the nucleus of an elevational treatment new to mediæval architecture. From the 14th century onwards many a harassed architect who had for so long been plagued with tiresome constructional problems could now relax a little from such material worries and spread himself happily in the new pastime of façade-making. Mullioned windows were themselves delightful features capable of almost unlimited variation in the proportions of their lights; introduction of the horizontal transom, separating fixed from opening portion, served to augment still further the brilliance of fenestration so characteristic of late-mediæval elevational treatments. The eventual abandoning of the arched window head in no way detracts from the atmosphere of gaiety and lightness which seems to permeate domestic architecture as windows gather still more thickly in the façades of the great houses.

The most striking feature of western European architecture has always been the high-pitched Gothic roof which gives no lodgment for the winter snows. It is indeed the roof which is the primary necessity; walls inserted beneath it only serve to increase headroom at the sides of the building or, in monumental architecture, to emphasize the height factor in elevation. In mediæval Germany the domestic roof completely overwhelmed with its vast mass the lower part of the structure; in civic buildings especially we find enormous roofs of a scale encountered in no other architectural style.

In mediæval times a good deal of the sleeping accommodation was situated within the roof. The development of the range of lodgings and the ordering of its elevations into a bay system suggested that the fenestration should be continued to include the attics; this was effected by carrying up portions of the wall-face in the form of gables enclosing windows. The vast German roofs with their several stories of attics required large gables containing whole systems of windows; from this fact originates the many-gabled style of building popular in the 16th century, a fashion which spread to England and finds its best exposition in the Cotswolds.

From the brick or masonry gable was developed the wooden dormer window built into the roof timbering; France and Germany, in particular, made great play with the dormer, both in its simplest form and as a fine piece of ædicular architecture playing an important part in the fenestration system. Another prominent feature connected with the roof is the chimney stack taking the flues from the wall-fireplaces with which many of the apartments were now being furnished.

The stories of mediæval buildings were connected by spiral stairs usually set in the angles of the structure. In addition to these internal features there had to be a more important stair by which the first floor or *piano nobile* was approached; this might be an external wooden construction or—in the case of important or fortified buildings—might be enclosed within a forebuilding or porch-tower. The introduction of the multi-storied range of lodgings suggested the development of the circular internal stair as a primary architectural feature of the design. At first this was done by merely increasing the diameter; later, in order to omit the narrow inner parts of the steps, the large solid 'newel' was removed and replaced by a ring of pillars surrounding an open 'well'. By the end of the 15th century the grand staircase had become the principal ornament of the range of lodgings, an ascendancy which it maintained until it had achieved a magnificence thereafter unsurpassed by any other internal feature known to architectural history. At first these large circular stairs were accommodated within projecting towers; the old mediæval love for such being still unabated, the stair towers provided excellent opportunities for vertical treatments contrasting with the long ranges of windows linking the façades. The turret window or 'bay' window and its upper-story counterpart, the 'oriel 'window on its projecting bracket, also served to perpetuate the Gothic taste for verticality.

With the development of the modern type of dwelling house, with its complex of rooms for all occasions, the great hall of mediæval days begins to surrender its pride of place in the domestic plan. For some time to come, however, it continues to be the largest of the apartments forming the house, in its new and more sophisticated guise of 'salon'. In public buildings, especially hospital wards, the great hall of the fifteenth century loses nothing of its scale or architectural magnificence.

Military architecture of the 15th century was chiefly concentrated at either end of the western European region. In Spain the frontier with Islam was held by a series of enormous castles over which mighty keep-towers still hovered. Central Europe was similarly sown with castles, on a much smaller scale but also aspiring to monumentalism in the height of their towers and curtains. It is this extravagance in the vertical that characterizes the military architecture of the period (Plate 66). The fashion for lining the inner faces of castle walls with lodgings was no innovation to the Germans as the Teutonic Knights had already introduced a version of the *kasr* plan into Prussia; it was from this source that has developed the great *Schloss* with its four-square plan and angle-towers between which multi-storied ranges of lodgings rose high into the air. During the 16th century the German countryside became covered with these huge structures, ultimate achievements of the military architects of mediæval Europe.

Yet even the impressive magnitude of the palace-fortresses of Germany could not disguise the fact that such buildings were already obsolescent as strongholds. The rows of mullioned windows by which the once-grim curtains are broken clearly indicate that the domestic element has superseded the military. Indeed the very introduction of the range of lodgings proved that European domestic architecture itself was passing out of the mediæval era into that of the Renaissance—the feudal stronghold was being expanded and emancipated to become a new type of structure, the great house.

The end of the Hundred Years' War saw France established as the

principal European power and Paris as the capital of western civilization. Architecture having passed from the patronage of the ecclesiastic
to that of the noble the great buildings of the era were not cathedrals,
but castles. The mediæval fortified house with its lofty curtains lined
with rows of pugnacious towers was now threatened by the new
cannon which made short work of such tempting targets. The loftier
the wall, the greater the ruin it made; the 15th-century noble was
finding that the heyday of his embattled predecessors was long past
and that there was no future in setting up as a bold bad baron.

Castles were now becoming houses; the *château-fort* had become
merely *château*. Fortification of the enceinte was being abandoned in
favour of improving the accommodation within as from the castle
courtyards the grim curtains were swept into oblivion, to be replaced
by ranges of lodgings presenting to the countryside gay façades pierced
by countless windows. Crenellated parapets are seen no more, and
the soaring Gothic roofs, no longer protected by masonry from the
besiegers' missiles, sweep down over the walls in shadowed cornices
and rise steeple-wise above the tower-tops.

Emancipation from military requirements revolutionized domestic
planning. The old muddle of scattered buildings was replaced by an
orderly rectangle with the new ranges of lodgings gathered round its
perimeter. Symmetry of planning, unknown in mediæval days except
in a few isolated castles, now became accepted as standard practice.
Towers—now transformed as 'pavilions'—balanced each other
across the plan, and entrances were strictly centralized in the façades.
Elevational treatment, at first limited to the walls of individual ranges
of lodgings, now became developed so as to include the whole façade,
eventually being extended until the château presented to the surrounding countryside a well-designed elevation upon each front (Plate 89).

The standard treatment of the entrance front was developed from
that of the mediæval castle with its twin-towered gatehouse set in the
centre of a long wall flanked by terminal towers. The first modification was to abandon the military form of gatehouse and replace it by
a single lofty feature framing as well as emphasizing the principal
entrance. The tower was still the principal monumental feature in
architecture; at one period during the 15th century it was the fashion
to construct tall tower-houses in imitation of the great military struc-

tures of the 12th-century Franks but containing warrens of apartments to serve as lodgings. But for the most part the tower became relegated to the position of porter, indicating the entrance and bearing over its arch the blazon of the proprietor. Such was the end of that finest of all mediæval features; by the middle of the 16th century the tower had all but disappeared from architecture, thereby depriving it of a monumental character which it did not regain until the renaissance of the domes. In French domestic architecture the ghosts of bygone towers lingered in the pavilions terminating the long ranges of the château and thrusting their soaring roofs towards the clouds.

The mediæval roof had a ridge terminating upon two gables which, in the case of buildings set within the walls of castles, formed part of these walls so that the gables did not appear externally. Removal of the curtain wall, however, left the terminal gables of each range exposed to view, a factor which interfered with the regularity of the elevational design. It thus became the custom to dispense with these gables and construct the angle so that its roofs met along a sloping ridge called a 'hip'. The introduction of the hipped roof revolutionized western architecture by depriving it of the gabled skyline which had been its most characteristic mediæval feature. By the same token the circular pavilion with its conical steeple-like covering gave place to the square pavilion, with its tall hipped roof, soon to play an impressive part in the greater domestic architecture of western Europe.

Throughout the latter part of the Middle Ages the great house had been developing a comprehensive plan in place of the assortment of structures with which it had begun. The process was, however, a slow one, for the reason that the varying types and sizes of the buildings precluded their being gathered together under one roof; in the case of very large houses it was not even possible to attach all the subsidiary structures as wings to a central mass. Thus the assemblage was inclined to be centripetal, the various elements of the plan being moved to the edges of a courtyard instead of to its centre. The fact that most great houses were surrounded by a fortified enceinte made this no very difficult task. The late-mediæval great house was eventually tidied into a rectangle with its principal buildings set in a range facing another containing the main entrance and having the ends of these two structures joined by lateral ranges containing lesser apartments.

The 16th century saw the plan of the western great house being improved still further by the removal of the whole of the entrance range and the concentration of accommodation within the remaining three ranges (Fig. 11, Plate 94). Thus the enclosed courtyard disappeared and the building became a central mass flanked by two

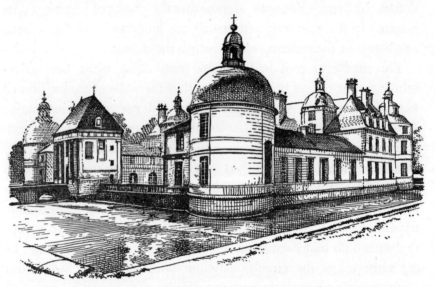

Fig. 11. The fourth side of the courtyard of a sixteenth-century chateau may be occupied only by a gatehouse

wings. The gradual shrinkage of these two wings and the absorption of all accommodation within the central block resulted in the house-plan of the Renaissance and the type of house with which we are familiar today (Plate 96).

The removal of the gatehouse range which had formed the entrance façade of the great house at once concentrated attention upon the now exposed elevation of the principal block. All the principles of elevational design had now to be transferred to the structure which had for so long been concealed by a feature specially provided and designed to be a frontispiece. For the range of lodgings or stables flanked by pavilions and punctuated by a great gatehouse was now substituted the principal front of a multi-storied structure containing apartments of all sizes and varying degrees of dignity. It was this important development in the form of the great house which spurred the Renaissance architects to concentrate on the study of elevational design in order to be able to assemble all the factors making up the building within the scope of homogeneous plans while at the same time assuring themselves that the external result would be pleasing to the eye. To recapitulate: the removal of the fourth side of the mediæval courtyard signalled the birth of modern architectural design.

Elevational symmetry, developed in the façade of the entrance range, was automatically transferred to the front of the house itself. The gatehouse became a large pavilion breaking the long line of the range; often the shortened wings withdrew still further until they had become little more than terminal pavilions. It is the gradual absorption of all subsidiary features within the central mass, in order that this may present properly designed façades on all four faces, which characterizes the subsequent development of the design of the great house in western Europe.

The story of this transformation from *château-fort* to *château* forms a strong contrast to what was happening during the same period in the republics of Italy. The feudal great house had grown out of a rural farmhouse with its scattered assortment of structures. Generations passed before anyone thought it worth while trying to gather all these isolated buildings within the confines of a cohesive plan. In cities, however, constriction within the fortifications of the period began to have the effect of forcing house-builders to plan along less haphazard lines. The Italian republics consisted mainly of densely-packed cities, frequently at enmity with each other; thus rural domestic architecture of the western type is limited to the fortified castle while the great house is generally found occupying an urban building-block.

Thus it was into the confines of such a site that the Italian nobles had to force the great house with its stable yard and outbuildings. At the beginning of the 13th century they were beginning to adopt the Islamic *kasr* type of house with its small internal court surrounded by a loggia. Such structures were suited to the climate of Italy; the loggia, especially, provided welcome shade and under monastic influence became assimilated with the cloister to produce such magnificent compositions as that at Assisi. But it was the courtyard of the *kasr*—in Italian hands the 'casa'—which became the stable-yard of the nobleman's town house. Adjoining it is found an ordinary Gothic house having its great chamber on the *piano nobile*. The constriction of the site necessitated the raising of the house several stories in height; thus the 13th-century Italian *palazzo* is one of the progenitors of the skyscraper. The whole construction was enclosed within a lofty outer wall similar in appearance to that of its prototype the *kasr*. Elevational design was as yet in its infancy and no architect of the day could cope with such a tremendous canvas; thus the façade of the *palazzo* was grim in the extreme and suggested an urban fortress rather than a palace.

Each of the great Italian cities had one such structure within which the great chamber served as the council chamber of the government. Such are true strongholds of urbanism, with their massive outer walls, crowned by tremendous machicolations, towering above the market place. Often the monumental factor was introduced by the construction of an extravagantly lofty tower like a campanile, also formidably crenellated; these Italian towers form excellent examples of architecture employed in a monumental capacity not for religious reasons but as an advertisement of military might. Towards the end of the 13th century town halls begin to adopt a less menacing attitude; many present to the piazza a tall façade displaying attractive windows and rising above a pleasant loggia beneath which the citizens might find shelter from the noonday sun.

With these 13th-century Italian structures is launched a new phase in western architecture, the development of a class of civic buildings. The Italians being, however, at this time still a backward people and their brand of republicanism but a variation upon the old theme of feudalism it was left to the wealthy trading cities of the west to establish a proper system of municipal government. During the 14th century the great commercial centres of Flanders began to house their administrative offices in great buildings modelled upon the Italian town halls. Even the tall tower was included in the design; thrusting high into the sky above the market place and rivalling the highest tower of the cathedral itself, such proud municipal towers as those of Bruges or Ypres indicate as nothing else the growing supremacy of the material over the spiritual (Plate 70).

Nothing like this had hitherto been seen in western architecture.

84. The *cortile* of an Italian palace
(Rome)

85. An elaborate church façade in New Spain
(Tasco)

Architects were called upon to erect vast façades on an unprecedented scale. Obviously the fenestration system of such a building could not be left to arrange itself, as hitherto, entirely without some form of discipline; thus it becomes still clearer that the 14th-century architects found themselves forced to accept the principle that the plan must be regulated to some extent by the dictate of elevational design. The principles adopted for this were indeed simple enough, comprising merely the standardization of openings and the regimentation of these into vertical and horizontal lines represented by the building-bays and stories respectively. The Gothic love of ornament was allowed full play in the enrichment of each unit of the design and a sense of cohesion was often achieved by the grouping of openings within the range of an ornamental arcade.

Many architectural historians might be in a more favourable position from which to analyse the elevations of buildings were they first to instruct themselves in the elementary principles governing the design of these. It is perhaps due to the unfortunate custom of illustrating some buildings by their plans only which forces the student to ignore the essential third dimension.

Elevations are composed by equating the plan of a structure with its *section*. In the case of a multi-storied building the plan of each floor must be projected upon the proposed elevation in order that the windows may be sited clear of internal walls. After experiment with the series of vertical lines thus obtained it is possible to devise a convenient system of building-bays in the centres of which the windows may be decently set. The floor lines of the building must next be introduced in order to fix the levels of window-sills, another important series of horizontal lines to control the ultimate design.

Only when considering the proportions of openings is the architect released from practical exigencies; by this time, however, the main lines of his elevation are already determined for him. Fenestration completed, it remains to punctuate the design by introducing artificial features specially imported for the purpose; lastly comes detailed embellishment by which to emphasize the position and form of openings.

By the 15th century the importance of elevational design was becoming appreciated in Italy. The wealthy trading city of Venice had already erected a municipal palace rivalling the glorious structures of the west. Considered architectural treatment was even being applied to the fortress-like *palazzi* of the Florentines as their primitive *bifora* windows settled down, story by story, into rhythmic ranges. Never having been absorbed within the sphere of Gothic influence the Italians were still unaware of the elevational possibilities of properly-applied bay design, thus their early attempts could scarcely be described as inspired and the effect was dull compared with the productions of the unfettered licence of their earlier days. But western elevational architecture had to be inaugurated somehow and as matters turned out the Italian architects proved that after all they were the men to bring the art to some degree of perfection.

It is to be regretted that the results of their labours should have been subjected to such a spate of hysterical eulogy. The pompous façade of many a Renaissance *palazzo*, deprived of its attendant sculptural effects and bereft of the warm sunlight dispensed by the blue skies of Italy, would then appear as the copyist effort of an amateur designer —not even a mason, but a goldsmith, painter, or sculptor—to arrange a collection of second-hand architectural features in a pattern upon the surface of a building.

Notwithstanding the atmosphere of intense erudition in which these structures were erected, there seems to be no indication that the architects understood the elementary principles governing proportion, the optical devices which stabilize the design, or the methods by which to introduce the all-important factor of contrast without which no elevation can inspire interest.

No one can deny that the architects had created a revolution. Yet is it not unwise to permit the glamour of the Renaissance, with its glories of painting, sculpture, and literature, to scatter its lilies indiscriminately over the often extremely uninspiring elevations of its buildings? For architecture is a serious business, not to be treated as an art unfettered by practical considerations; was it not for that very reason that European elevational architecture, its exponents convinced that they had achieved perfection, withered away and perished for lack of ambition to sustain it?

It is in the arcaded interiors of their courtyards (Plate 84) that we may best appreciate the work of Italian designers. The courtyard of the 15th-century Italian *palazzo* was in effect a deep narrow well surrounded by arcaded loggias and bearing little resemblance to the spacious courtyards of the west. The latter were enclosures surrounded by buildings; the Italian *cortile* an open shaft in the heart of a building block. The two types were combined in the Spanish type of *palazzo* —called by its Islamic name of *el-kasr, alcazar*—four-square structures, lofty and fortress-like (Plate 71), built round spacious *khan*-like courts surrounded by loggias on each story (Plate 86). Such was the strength of Islamic influence in the Peninsula that Spanish architects continued to employ the *patio* as a standard feature of domestic architecture long after even the Italians had abandoned it as a relic of antiquity. Externally the Spanish house remained severe and un-inviting; only to the accredited visitor were its internal glories displayed.

It was in its claustral form that the mediæval courtyard attained its architectural zenith. The loggias of the Mediterranean countries— Moslem and Christian—provided to give shelter from the sun to those passing from building to building, are in less kindly climes interpreted as vaulted walks protected by traceried windows. From the monastic cloister the same treatment was borrowed for use in other communal buildings, such as university hospices or hospitals for the infirm, which consisted of a multitude of small lodgings attached to a common hall and chapel. But by the 16th century the mediæval courtyard had given place to the modern block of apart-ments having internal communication between the rooms, thus depriving western architecture of the principal monumental device known to the planner.

The rectangular cortile or patio is not a feature indigenous to European planning. Of sub-oriental origin, it is found in Classical architecture but disappears during the Byzantine era. The Middle Ages saw it reintroduced into Europe from the Moghreb complete with its characteristic Islamic feature, the fountain. Only in very large structures, however, does it remain as a monumental factor in the plan.

In western Europe an irregularly-shaped court of small area begins to appear in the town-houses or *hôtels* of the 15th-century nobles. These *cours* are merely reduced versions of the castle courtyard of the period and are planned on equally haphazard lines; the principal feature of each is usually a turret containing an elaborate spiral stair. Although lacking the loggias of their Italian counterparts the courts of these *hôtels* are architectural features of the first importance and play a part not only in the history of urban domestic planning but also in the story of the development of the public hostelry which by the end of the 15th century had appeared as yet another novel class of building.

In considering the architecture of mediæval Europe we have so far been concerned only with those regions possessing building stone or the facilities for developing a brickbuilding technique. In such districts even the lesser towns were able to take part in the architectural activities of their day. But parts of central Europe had not yet succeeded in catching up with the times in this respect and were still employing a traditional form of timber construction.

Primitive building in timber is primarily concerned with the provision of a roof; in some cases there may be no walling of any description to raise the feet of the rafters off the ground. It was to the development of roof construction that much of the effect of the Gothic style was due, for no other ancient building style produced the tall spacious roofs of the Frankish lands. In such regions as Bavaria even as late as the 15th century important buildings such as town halls were still mostly roof; several stories of attics provided a large proportion of the accommodation. Even in the following century there were plenty of good masonry structures covered with roofs almost as tall as the walling from which they rose; the result of making the span of the building awkwardly wide. Well into the era of the Renaissance the tall Gothic roof still played an important part in the architecture of the whole of the north-west of Europe.

The development of the range of lodgings, a group of apartments of assorted sizes gathered together under one roof, suggested imitation by humbler house-builders of the new planning principle thus introduced. Thus from the end of the 14th century onwards we find a new type of domestic architecture, the small country house or farmhouse, beginning to appear in western Europe. This, the first middle-class residence outside urban architecture, consisted, simply enough, of a rectangular building containing two or three rooms on the ground

86. The *patio* of a Spanish alcazar
(Toledo)

87. The University of Alcala de Henares

Chapter XII

GOTHIC

During the early part of the second millennium of our era the principal influence upon western European architecture was undoubtedly Byzantine. The so-called 'Romanesque' style pays in fact but little tribute to the architecture of Rome. Under the influence of the primitive Roman axial plan, however, the westerners had developed a style of church-building entirely their own. Although Byzantine detail was employed, the Frankish designers were far behind their mentors in matters of construction; thus the vast extent of their huge sprawling buildings serves only to emphasize the lack of refinement in their architecture. This was inevitable: the Byzantines had been the heirs of antiquity, whereas the distant Franks were but a few centuries removed from obscure barbarism.

As the 12th century wore on, the reverses of the Crusades were gathering still wider regions into the sphere of Islam. The shadows were fast closing in upon the Old World. For Christianity the only hope seemed to lie in the sunset lands of the west. The Franks were equal to the challenge; as the new century opened they asserted both their political supremacy and their contempt for the old regime by turning upon the venerable capital of the Byzantine world and putting it to the sack.

The Crusades had brought the Franks into close contact with the wisdom of the ancients. It had brought them into touch with matters of far greater architectural significance than the method of turning a column or the design of window openings. They began to learn something of the principles of building science. Hitherto they had understood but little of statics; they appreciated in a vague sort of fashion that an arch required abutments but their knowledge was so surprisingly limited that they had no hesitation in inserting a tall arch

88. The Escorial

89. Schloss Aschaffenburg

floor with the same number of bed-chambers above. Only in the building-stone districts would such homes as these be constructed in masonry; for the most part they would be of wood, perhaps with the upper story entirely contained in the roof. One of the most noticeable features of this type of house is the abandoning of the mediæval planning principle of the *piano nobile* by which the principal living-rooms are sited on the upper floor, with the story below used for storage only, in favour of the modern arrangement which brings the living-rooms down to ground level. In the Mediterranean countries the farmhouse is planned as a miniature copy of the *kasr* type of building but without the internal court; these little cubiform farmhouses are generally provided with a *piano nobile*.

The 14th century saw the arrival at maturity of the mediæval civilization of western Europe. Thenceforth the story is one of recession from the old primitive Gothic way of life as European society begins to feel its way tentatively towards the modern era. Mediæval civilization had grown up amongst the fields where the peasants' hovels cowered away from the grim stone walls of the nobleman's private fortress. Culture was the prerogative of the abbot or bishop in his spiritual stronghold of pinnacled masonry; he and the castellan between them shared the profits of the countryside. But here and there amongst the fields and pastures were rising the symbols of a power which was in the end to bring to naught the power of sword and crozier—hugging the havens and straddling the crossways were the ever-growing market towns. Wealth poured into these seats of the new trading power; by the 14th century the town walls of the merchants far outrivalled the private fortifications of the obsolescent barony.

Within these walls there was nothing resembling town planning. The road upon which the first settlement had been founded became the high street and the village green the market square, later to be endowed with a market house or town hall. Cathedral, abbey, or town church expanded in size and magnificence together with the fortunes of the citizens. As the highways lengthened to accommodate new settlements of tradesmen and merchants additional parish churches were built along them until the skyline of the city bristled with towers and spires. From highway to highway passed other routes also lined with the houses of the citizens; beside and behind these a labyrinth of alleys and kennels threaded their devious and uncertain courses.

In this fashion the great mediæval cities prospered and thrust their bustling suburbs into the feudal countryside. But expansion had to end when the municipality decided to enclose the city within lines of fortification. At a blow the whole primitive system of lateral expansion was brought to an end. But within the towered curtains the population still grew, presenting urban architects with the problem of its accommodation upon sites already covered with houses. The solution was obvious: mediæval Europe, hitherto satisfied with two stories and an attic, had to expand upwards.

From earliest times urban building sites have been organized in terms of frontage to a public way. Such frontages had of necessity to be restricted in scope, usually twenty feet was the most that could be allocated to an individual house-builder. In some cases it might be possible to acquire a double or treble plot—a nobleman or merchant prince might even acquire a complete island block for his *hôtel*—but as a general rule urban domestic architecture developed in narrow uniform strips fifteen to twenty feet in width. Thus the town house was as a rule set with its narrow gabled end to the street frontage, a fact which bestows upon the skyline of the mediæval street its characteristic serrated silhouette.

Building in masonry having been originally the privilege of the wealthy, early mediæval town houses were constructed of timber; yet as far back as the 12th century byelaws were being introduced forcing the townsfolk to separate their building plots by fireproof walls of rubble in order to minimize the risk of conflagration sweeping from one end of a street to the other. Such party walls were useful as supports to the joists of upper floors; thus by the end of the century the town house had fallen into line with its rural counterpart and adopted the standard Gothic two-storied arrangement. The mediæval word denoting a joisted floor being some variant of *soller,* the first western-type town houses to be built in the Christian parts of Spain were known as *solares.*

Overcrowding within the late-mediæval walled cities resulted in the raising of the party walls and the provision of additional stories;

during the 15th century especially the town house began to expand vertically to the proportions with which we are familiar today. In the west the result was to give great prominence to the gabled street-fronts; in the Low Countries and Germany the great Teutonic gables began to play an important part in the architecture of the wealthy commercial cities.

This development of the urban house, which may certainly be attributed to the availability of bricks and building timber, was almost entirely limited to western Europe. The Mediterranean countries were still too deeply involved in the mediæval tradition for there to be any masons to spare for private building; in these regions therefore the town house was still two-storied and unimpressive in elevation. The farmhouses of the West were long low structures still based on the mediæval hall while those of Spain and Italy tended more towards the Byzantine turriform house of two stories. The home of the peasant was the merest hovel. With the exception of the new multi-storied town houses of western commercial cities, architectural treatment was still limited to ecclesiastical, civic, and palatial structures.

In Bavaria and the eastern parts of Germany lying beyond the building-stone regions architecture necessarily made slow progress. But the traditional timber technique of these areas was being developed until by the end of the 15th century the science of house-carpentry had achieved a very high standard and large buildings were being erected either entirely of wood or at the best having only the lower story of simple masonry. At first the construction was achieved story by story, each being 'jettied out' over the one below in order that the weight of the framed walling might serve as a counterpoise to the loads on the floor within; by the 16th century technique had improved to such an extent that the whole façade could be framed-up as a structural entity, the pattern of opposed vertical and horizontal timbers providing an excellent framework upon which to develop an elevational design suited to the taste of the day.

In view of the vital part to be played by elevations in the subsequent development of European architecture it is perhaps as well to consider at this stage the principles underlying what might be described as the pictorial side of the building art. Architecture is primarily the solution of planning problems; during the Middle Ages plans were distorted only when dictated by structural necessity. But this latest development placed the planners at the mercy of their elevations, for the time was rapidly approaching when even the layman was beginning to be conscious of the rules of architectural expression.

The design of elevations is primarily concerned with the arrangement of essential architectural features such as openings. These, if kept to standard sizes, fall naturally into horizontal layers representing the internal stories of the building. Horizontal punctuation can be further emphasized by introducing strings of moulding at each floor level, a device already discovered by the Gothic architects. But the most notable contribution of these skilful craftsmen was the development of the building bay and the elevational ackowledgment of this the most vigorous form of vertical punctuation. External division by means of strip pilasters was naturally followed by the centralization of the windows between these. The perfected system, which omitted the artificial divisions but retained the bay arrangement of the windows, proved of the utmost value when these were subsequently enlarged, the continuity through each story of the supporting masonry enabling reductions to be made in this without interfering with the stability of the structure.

Vertical punctuation being thus permanently achieved by setting windows one above the other, the architects were able to concentrate upon the horizontal element. The old Gothic strings and cornices would not stand up to the job; their projection was too slight to allow them to compete with the strong vertical lines produced by the large windows of multi-storied structures. Various forms of bracketed cornice were tried, including certain ingenious modifications of the military machicolation. But in the end the architects adopted the only possible course and returned to the newly-rediscovered cornice of Classical days.

The end of the 15th century saw western Europe passing out of the Middle Ages into that Renaissance era which gave our people their first glimpse of modern times. Religious and political upheavals rocked society and swept away abbey and castle almost as if it were intended that the home should henceforth become uppermost in the minds of architects. A house was in future to be more than four walls

90. The Spanish Plateresque style of ornament applied to the façade of a
municipal building in the Low Countries (Bruges)

91. A Spanish gable in the Cape of Good Hope
(Morgenster)

and a roof; it was to be something in which one might live in ever-increasing comfort. Protection from the elements had now been completely attained by the general use of window-glass; the squaring-up of window openings and their subdivision by horizontal transoms as well as vertical mullions made it possible to maintain ventilation by providing opening casements made of wrought iron. The joisted floor had already suggested the boarded ceiling; from Spanish Islam was being learned how its exiled orientals protected their chambers from the down-draughts lurking in open timber roofs by lining these with ceilings framed in a network of beautifully-wrought carpentry. Ceilings, screenwork, and other forms of draught-excluder provided a new and vast field upon which the carpenters of Europe could display their skill in the embellishment of the dwelling-house.

The course of the 16th century which saw the gradual disappearance of the elaborately-carpentered open roofs of the great halls of western Europe saw great changes taking place in the interior appearance of the principal apartments of the great house. Despite the abandoning of what had been the noblest factor in mediæval domestic planning, the vast *salons* of the new era, low in proportion though they might appear, achieved an air of comfortable opulence by virtue of the coffered, richly-arabesqued network of beams with which they were now ceiled.

An important feature of 16th-century architecture is the appearance of elevational architecture *within* the principal apartments of the domestic structure. In the mediæval era interior decoration had been effected by means of hangings; there had been little attempt to introduce architectural features such as door or window casings within the building. In Italy, however, the persistence of the ancient Roman tradition had perpetuated the Classical device of the ædicule as a method of framing the entrance doorways of important structures; by the end of the 15th century this feature was also being applied to the inner reveal of the opening. To the elaborate ceilings was added the Classical cornice, as a means of joining this æsthetically to the wall-face below. Such architectural devices as these all indicate that elevational architecture had now an internal function to perform.

As the most highly finished products of the mediæval European builder were nearly always of an ecclesiastical nature the private builder had to fall back upon a coat of plaster with which to conceal the irregularities of his rubble walling. Mediæval plasterwork is of good quality and under Byzantine influence was frequently embellished with painted decoration. The introduction of the joisted upper floor, by providing the room below with a ceiling, suggested the covering of this with a skin of plaster. During the 15th century Moslem influence is seen in the introduction of sham architectural features, such as vaulting motifs, within the apartments of the Italian *palazzo;* soon the ubiquitous Classical cornice rediscovers itself in moulded plasterwork.

The modern living-room had in fact arrived. The sunset lands had at last attained to a reasonable state of civilization. Although even now barely on level terms with their ancient enemies—the Moslems from whom everything had been learned—in respect of luxurious living, they were at long last discovering how to be comfortable. Heating, for example, was now regarded as an essential factor in the design for living and the wall-fireplace had become an ubiquitous architectural feature, special attention being paid to those in the more important apartments by the provision of sculptured surrounds and overmantels. Chimneys, once mere appendages, became vital factors in the new buildings, thrusting their way confidently through the tall Gothic roofs as triumphant successors to the serried pinnacles of bygone days.

In this, the twilight of the Middle Ages, we can detect the beginnings of a vernacular architecture such as can be utilized by anyone having the enterprise to build himself a home. He may raise walls of rubble, brick, mud, or timber framing; rough-hewn rafters will carry a roof of thatch or tiles brought down over the walling in spreading eaves. Plain wooden lintels will bridge the openings of doors and windows, while over the fire-hearth a great bressummer supports the chimney. And window casements, divided by smith or joiner into small panes of glazing, supply with their play of light and void an element soon to enliven the elevation of the humblest home as it emerges from the shadows into a new world of architecture.

Chapter XV

RENAISSANCE

L et us consider the stage reached by western European architecture at the middle of the second millennium of our era. The growing-pains of the planners were over; the development of the block of lodgings with its auxiliary features such as stairs and chimneys had made the planning of any domestic or civic building a matter of little difficulty. Great churches with their vaulted ceilings rising into the sky were no longer fashionable but the construction lessons learnt from them could now be brought to bear upon any engineering problem the architects were likely to encounter. Thus most practical difficulties had been overcome and it was left for the architects to experiment with the presentation of their soundly-planned and constructed buildings to the criticism of a more and more sophisticated public. In short, the need was now for novelty in elevational design.

We have seen how the nature of the mediæval church-plan encouraged no experiments on these lines except in so far as the west front of the building was concerned; here the confusion of architectural factors involved suggested no obvious plan to follow in disciplining them to form an elevation. The great house of the Middle Ages was a jumble of assorted structures still to be gathered together to form a homogeneous complex. It was only in the large civic buildings that any attempts were made to produce elevations; thus it was left for wealthy trading cities to indulge in architectural experiments of this nature. The principal mercantile regions of mediæval Europe being Venetia and Flanders it is here that one may expect to discover the beginnings of large-scale elevational experiments. The Cloth Hall at Ypres is an example of the magnitude already attained by the 13th-century civic building. It was, however, Venetia which provided the principal link between the rising culture of central Europe and the long-established civilization represented by the Moslem empire. Christian Spain, struggling against Islam, was at the time incapable of deriving the same benefit from her mighty neighbour as were the traders of more distant Venetia. Thus by the 13th century we find the Doges building for themselves a palace incomparably more magnificent than anything to be found elsewhere in Europe; by the 15th century their architects had combined with those of pan-Islamic southern Italy to produce such glorious buildings as those of Dalmatia, notably the Rector's palace at Dubrovnik.

While in great mercantile cities such as these the architects were quite content to exploit the rich legacy which had been handed down from primitive Gothic days, those of central Italy had no such fund upon which to draw. This situation, coupled with the fact that they alone could see beside them considerable vestiges of a highly developed architectural style, had the result of turning the minds of Italian architects towards the study of the elevational schemes of the ancient Romans. It is this movement which is known as the architectural Renaissance.

Let us examine the canvas upon which the architects were required to exhibit their skill. It was the day of the great house, palace, or château. We have seen that this now followed two main plans; in the west the long central block flanked by short wings and in the Mediterranean countries the square block with the internal court. The former was not yet sufficiently compact to form an ideal subject for elevational treatment; the latter with its short unobstructed façades was practically ideal for this purpose.

Notwithstanding the commercial might of Venice—a city which together with most of Lombardy, lies within the western European or pan-Gothic sphere of influence—the cultural capital of 15th-century Italy was Florence. The year 1451 saw the Florentine architect Alberti designing the first façade—that of the Palazzo Rucellai—upon which punctuation was achieved by application of the Classical Orders, story by story, with the bays separated by pilasters supporting entablatures at each floor level (Plate 75). Thus was reintroduced into Italy the elevational principles employed by the ancient Romans.

The model from which the Renaissance architects drew their inspiration was probably that most imposing and at the same time most ineradicable monument of Ancient Rome, the Colosseum (Plate 15), which still towered above the humble buildings of the eternal but impoverished city. Providing as it did a most perfect example of a well-ordered elevational composition, one can imagine with what ardour the architectural students of the 15th century swarmed over the mighty ruins, gazing, measuring, and sketching, thenceforth to cover the façades of their rising *palazzi* with storied Orders after the ancient manner.

The plan of the Italian *palazzo* had by this time settled down as a building of three stories: basement, *piano nobile,* and an upper story containing lodgings. Towards the end of the century another Florentine architect, Bramante, began to extend his practice to Rome itself, to which he introduced the elevational refinement of confining ornament to the two upper stories and making the basement act as an æsthetic foundation to the composition by incising the jointing of its masonry in the fashion known as 'rustication', a traditional technique well-known in mediæval Italy and already employed in the early Florentine *palazzi* in order to make them look more formidable.

The well-regulated elevations of Gothicized Lombardy were soon being adjusted to fit into the new scheme of things. The stately arcades of the Colosseum were transported with but little modification to the gay façades which looked out over the busy canals of the greatest Lombard city. Each wide arch was almost filled by a huge window displaying a simple form of tracery derived from the traditional *bifora* (Plate 73). Nothing displays more clearly the advantages of a Gothic education than the comparison between the late-15th century palaces of Venice and Rome. The Romans lived in prisons, the Venetians in fairy palaces filled with sunshine from the glorious windows. The Roman wall-decoration is composed of meagre strip pilasters little better than those humble essays in punctuation which had been introduced into the Romanesque churches of nearly a millennium earlier; from the sturdy half-columns of the Lombardic Renaissance the architect Palladio brought back the column itself into its own again (Plate 79).

Meanwhile, in Rome itself, the architects were introducing a new factor into their elevations by abolishing the traditional *bifora* window. First removing the shaft and leaving a large opening with a semi-circular head they next replaced the arch with a lintel in order to steady the whole feature within the lines of the new elevational system—and, incidentally, to bring their windows into line with the fashion already followed by the majority of western domestic architects. Their next discovery was of the utmost significance, being that of the ædicular principle in the ornamentation of openings—again the result of examining the remains of Classical structures. In its simplest form this consisted of flanking the opening with a pair of small pilasters or shafts supporting an entablature of appropriate scale, the whole being set upon a projecting sill and often crowned by a miniature pediment. By association with the semi-circular windows of the past the pediment sometimes becomes segmental in shape, a variation upon standard Classical practice which was to have an important effect on the later Renaissance. The rectangular window with an ædicular frame became the standard form of Renaissance fenestration and eventually replaced all other types of opening to set the seal of the matured style which was to establish itself in all the countries of Europe.

The domestic window of mediæval days had been provided with a wrought-iron casement opening on 'hooks and bands'. The sudden doubling of the window opening by removing the central division made it impossible to provide a casement; this would have been either too heavy or not rigid enough. The remedy was to resort to joinered timber, making a wooden frame to fit inside the opening with a horizontal transom below which a pair of wooden 'French windows' closed against each other. The lead 'calms' of mediæval days were replaced by wooden 'glazing bars'. From this revolutionary method of closing openings was soon developed the wooden door frame which was substituted for the older method of hanging the door on 'hooks and bands'.

The removal of glazing bars and the substitution of large areas of plate glass has done much to spoil the appearance of Renaissance buildings by depriving the openings of the liveliness which is derived from the sparkle of a diaper of dark panes. At the same time, however, such mutilation serves to illustrate the dullness of the general design and the lack of inspiration underlying this (Plate 81). It needs to be emphasized that nothing more was intended by the architects of the Renaissance—despite their philosophical pretensions—than to relieve the austerity of a plain façade by applying ornament to it. Regimentation was the keynote. There was little or no attempt to improve proportion, stabilize design, or even to introduce interest other than was automatically achieved merely through the breaking up of plain surfaces.

Many enthusiasts, lacking in knowledge of the practical problems which are the everyday lot of the architect, have laboured to ascribe to the Renaissance designers all kinds of esoteric—even astrological—inspiration until these worthy folk have now become architectural divinities. The plain truth is that they were neither experienced nor inspired and doubtless had quite enough to do to turn out a workable elevation. We do them no injury by recalling the novelty of the Renaissance elevational movement and the absence of hereditary building craftsmanship in the country of its origin. While admiring the products of brush and chisel we should nevertheless endeavour to place architectural creations in a proper perspective.

The new fashion spread with surprising rapidity. Normally it is not easy to introduce innovations into such an ancient craft as that of building, but it was ornamentation rather than actual architecture which was involved in the revolution. Thus the *palazzi* to which the newly-discovered Orders were being applied did not change their plans, nor did any of the new æsthetic devices in the least affect the architectural principles upon which the buildings of the age were being planned. One of the reasons for the spread of the style was the publication by the Italian architect Vignola of a printed book upon the Orders; yet notwithstanding his illustrations of standard examples minutely set out in detailed measurement his western colleagues produced but half-hearted travesties of his examples.

The Renaissance had no effect at all upon the buildings themselves. The form of the French château, for example, had been steadily developing throughout the centuries 'according to plan' and continued to do so without any interference at all from the Italians. When in 1519 Pierre Nepveu set out the greatest of them all, Chambord (Plate 67), the little pilasters culled from Vignola—invited by Francis I to visit France—served quite well to punctuate the elevations and embellish the subsidiary features without in the least altering the inherent nature of the mighty structure. It was still a French château and bore no resemblance to a Roman building or even an Italian *palazzo*. Indeed it was quite the reverse, for western European domestic planning had advanced far beyond the primitive semi-fortified *kasr* type of house; by the middle of the 16th century it was the Italians who were building country villas with an open forecourt on the French pattern.

Thus it was principally owing to the interest provided by a new element in architectural *ornament* that the western architects accepted the Renaissance movement. The two items which they accepted as innovations were, firstly, the ædicular treatment of openings and, secondly, the use of the Orders for punctuation. The former device had an instant appeal not only in France but also in the Low Countries, Germany, and Spain, each of which employed it in characteristic fashion to emphasize its most prominent architectural features. Thus in the two former countries ædicular treatment was enthusiastically applied to the great gables with which the towering Gothic roofs were becoming surrounded; the devoted architects of Spain turned the new device to full use for the further enrichment of the glorious portals of their mighty churches.

The success of the Order utilized as punctuation was less marked. The device was after all a very artificial one and the constant repetition which it involved could produce results far more irritating than attractive. One of the difficulties was the wide intercolumniation of the early examples: a factor soon shown by Vignola and others to be out of step with Classical origins. The use of columns in pairs helped with remedying this defect and also served to add a little interest to break the monotony; it was in this form that the fully-developed device at last began to achieve a certain amount of popularity in Europe (Plate 76).

But still it was obvious that the new elevations fell far short of the dignity displayed by their great prototypes. Something had to be done to achieve the correct intercolumniation and return to the true style of the Classical forms. It is perhaps to Michelangelo that we owe the matured style, for in his reconstruction of the Capitol at Rome in

92. The Flemish Plateresque as established in Germany
(Brunswick)

93. An Early Renaissance town hall in central Europe
(Augsburg)

1546 this inspired architect combined the two stories of his building within a single 'giant order' firmly founded upon the rusticated basement and crowned by a far more imposing cornice than the older single-story Order could have sustained (Plate 80). It is this substitution of a single 'giant order' for the pair of single-story orders which marks the transition to the mature architecture of the later Renaissance which more closely followed Classical forms (Plate 78).

By the middle of the 16th century the Italians and Spaniards, now allied in their exploration of the new style, were both employing full-scale Classical porticoes complete with spreading pediments, the Spaniards in particular seizing upon the idea with avidity as supplying the means of erecting impressive frontispieces at the west ends of their vast churches.

In Italy the era of great churches had passed away. During the republican period a number of cities had built the naves of their cathedrals or civic churches but these still lacked their eastern terminations. The architects of the day were at a loss to know how to complete these buildings in a fashion suitable to the spirit of the new era. Ever since the insidious influence of the archaic 'basilican' church of Rome had succeeded in eliminating the spirit of *hypsosis* which had inspired the Byzantine church-form the architects of Europe had from time to time been evincing a certain nostalgia for the glories of the ancient plan. Thus in 1259 the Siennese set out a hexagonal crossing in the heart of their new cathedral while, rather less than a century later, the genius of prior Alan of Walsingham created the spacious octagon of Ely. The renaissance of the Byzantine plan was assured by the decision of the committee appointed by the city fathers of Florence in 1366 to advise upon the design of the eastern portion of their unfinished cathedral. In the very homeland of Romanism the building was permitted to expand into a spacious octagon; a stern challenge to the long-endured 'basilican' plan.

It is interesting to note that an important contact between western Europe and the Byzantine world was provided by the Frankish settlement in the Peloponnesus where the capital of the 'tyrannarchate', Mistra, had been founded in the middle of the 13th century as a Byzantine city under Frankish lordship. During the 14th century the city was embellished with a number of churches set out upon the normal Byzantine plan and having elevations of typical Byzantine design. It is interesting to note that there is a strong resemblance between the design of these churches and that of the apsidal appendages to the great Florentine octagon.

The problem was how to roof this vast area nearly 140 feet in diameter. In 1420 Brunelleschi supplied the answer, covering it with a great vault set between eight ribs and rising into the air in such fashion as had never before been seen in architectural experience (Plate 76). From this stupendous Florentine vault sprang the great company of domes which characterizes the Renaissance skyline, culminating in that of St Peter's itself. This mighty dome, no wider in fact than Brunelleschi's masterpiece, is framed by sixteen massive ribs; it was designed about 1558 (Plate 77).

St Peter's is one of the outstanding architectural achievements of the world. A sudden, almost unheralded, return to the principles of true monumental architecture it was at the same time its very last expression. On four gigantic piers of masonry stands its towering dome, the last and mightiest of the children of the Byzantines; out of the surrounding aisle three huge apses swell the limits of the plan to a cruciform outline. But the great Byzantine building had to suffer the fate of so many of its predecessors and submit to the indignity of having the inevitable Roman appendage tacked on to its western side, thus ruining the whole composition and making the plan meaningless.

The dome of St Peter's was designed at a period during which Roman architects were becoming more and more intrigued with the architectural possibilities of smaller buildings, especially the circular temples of their preceptors. Thus the drum of the great dome is treated with a colonnaded effect in imitation of these earlier compositions, while crowning its summit is a 'lantern' which is in fact the circular temple in its ædicular form.

It will be observed that the dome of St Peter's is not a true dome, but the exterior exposure of a Gothic vaulting bay having a double web, one on both upper and outer faces of the vaulting rib. A dome of this magnitude was however never again attempted, so the Renaissance architects thenceforth adopted the ordinary Byzantine form of domed construction. The ribbed vault had already disappeared from

Italy with the great republican churches; the groined vault, unsuited to the horizontal lines of the new style, was retained only for use in open-sided loggias. The barrel-vaulted ceiling became the standard covering to the Renaissance church; a large vault covering the main span and lesser ones, at a lower level, ceiling the lateral bays between the abutments. These vaults, which were rib-less and composed of a web only, had their masonry lightened by a system of 'coffering' by which the centre of each slab was hollowed out to form a sunken panel. Renaissance domes were also constructed on a similar system of light ceiling slabs; as technique improved the internal domes became lower in elevation until, as 'saucer' domes, they could be employed merely as ceilings without any external exposure.

It will be observed that the Renaissance dome was in essence no novelty but merely a variation upon the principal theme of Byzantine ecclesiastical architecture. The Italian architects had changed the outward appearance, but structurally there had been little advance during a thousand years. During the long centuries, however, the western architects had been gradually discovering many of the structural principles known to the great builders of the past. The noble aspirations of the Gothic builders had led them to perform feats undreamed of by the Byzantines, but these great achievements had been spectacular rather than practical; what was wanted was not an airy network of flying buttresses but a sound abutment system which could be constructed without the necessity of resorting to such extravagances.

The complicated form of the High Gothic could have played no part in the new architectural style with its insistence upon smooth surfaces of walling upon which to experiment with elevational devices. To do this it was necessary to eliminate all external excrescences by concealing the whole of the abutment system behind the main walls of the structure as in Byzantine times. Such building methods had already been introduced into the Frankish lands as early as the beginning of the 12th century; the cathedral at Angoulême is an illustration. Nearly two centuries later we find a Gothic essay in absorbed abutment successfully achieved at Albi; here, however, the bays are of the narrow Gothic type instead of the spacious sweeps which characterize the Byzantinesque composition of Angoulême.

Brunelleschi, generally regarded—from his exquisite taste in classical detail—as the Father of the Italian Renaissance, made no effort to apply the new style to the church-form of his day but reverted to the primitive 'basilican' type of building as providing an easier subject. It was left to Alberti, the first real Renaissance architect, to examine the structural principles underlying the architecture of the Romans whose detail was being so assiduously copied. He it was who realized

Fig. 12. Deep arches, echoing those of the last of the Roman basilicas, carry the vault of the Renaissance church

that the building representing their ultimate achievement was the great basilica of Constantine at Rome, a structure which with its vast span and three spacious bays was in fact an example of the very technique which the republican architects of Italy had succeeded in developing in the naves of their churches. In 1472 Alberti began the nave of St Andrea at Mantua on the same plan but substituting for the groined main vault a simple barrel-vault springing above the crowns of the lateral vaults flying between the abutments. This building of Alberti's set the fashion for all subsequent ecclesiastical planning (Fig. 12).

Notwithstanding such achievements as are represented by the construction of new domed eastern ends to Gothic churches and the outstanding wonder of St Peter's itself it is clear that the early Renaissance architect had been so absorbed in the erection of palaces as to have lost the art of church-planning. Under the influence of the dome and the resultant temporary emancipation from the mediæval axial plan a number of small centrally-planned buildings were erected but these, charming though their æsthetic appeal, are but minor structures of little monumental distinction. It was a sympathetic cooperation between the Renaissance architects of Italy and the long-established ecclesiastical building tradition of Spain which, by the middle of the 16th century, had produced the standard plan of the Renaissance church as exemplified by Il Gesu in Rome and the Palladian churches of Venice.

Spain, being a Mediterranean country, succumbed easily to the Italian Renaissance movement, successfully absorbing its novelties without however losing anything of the vital national style of the Peninsula. France, after experimenting unhappily with a variety of Italian and Spanish motifs, eventually produced under the genius Mansard the very lovely style of the mid-17th century with its perfect combination of Renaissance detail applied to the traditional Gothic building-mass (Plate 95). Germany and the Low Countries became involved in a morass of ill-digested Spanish detail culled from every conceivable source and applied to buildings which gradually adopted Renaissance principles in that they disciplined their elevations yet continued to display enormous Gothic gables incapable of submitting to punctuation by story Orders without the most fantastic results (Plate 92).

The one feature which seems to have been assimilated without any difficulty by all European nations was the semi-circular arch with a plain flat soffit, either set upon square piers or, in the case of lighter arcades, from Roman Doric columns. Such features only appear, however, as the result of applying Renaissance principles of design to a Gothic arcade; thus we do not find a complete Classical feature such as a colonnaded portico, or even a giant order, appearing in western Europe until at least the second half of the 17th century. One feature of Renaissance architecture, the dome, achieves early popularity in its smaller counterpart the cupola; little domed temples displaying rings of miniature Classical columns take the place of Gothic turrets on the early Renaissance skyline.

It is impossible to watch the spread of the Renaissance movement through western Europe without appreciating that it was essentially an æsthetic revolution, not an architectural one.

Even in the case of churches no noticeable change is discernible in the normal development of planning arrangements; in domestic architecture the abandoning of the *piano nobile* and the bringing down to ground level of the principal apartments is due to social improvements and is if anything in defiance of the principles still maintained by the Italians. Nor is there any attempt to adjust constructional methods to fit the new fashion; the Mediterranean countries already employed low-pitched roofs but western Europe showed no sign of abandoning the traditional Gothic form in order to follow suit.

It is in detail that the Renaissance demonstrates its gradual hold upon the elevational design of buildings. In openings especially we see exhibited the interest being taken by architects in ædicular motifs. By the middle of the millennium the square-headed window had become universal in western domestic architecture; its mullions and transoms made no difference to the shape of the opening itself which was thus easily employed as a subject for ædicular treatment. Wider openings such as doorways were covered by flattened arches of four- or three-centred type, easily confined within a rectangular frame. Once the æsthetic principle of framing an opening had been appreciated it soon became clear that any such could readily be fitted into the lines of a planned elevational treatment, the simplest of which was the standard Renaissance one of punctuation by means of Orders. From this discovery it was easy to accept the complete system with its semi-circular arches in place of the traditional Gothic ones; an important innovation in the construction of these 'Roman arcades' being that their arches spring from plain square piers instead of Gothic pillars and are constructed with flat soffits freed from their primitive rings of recessed orders, a factor which, even when incorporated with an Order, adds yet another note of austerity to Renaissance architecture.

It has to be recognized that the Italian Renaissance was a 'drawing-board' architecture—calculated, unemotional, and lacking the vitality of a style which has been infused with the spirit of the craftsman and the artist. But that its architects plied their T-squares with enthusiasm is shown by the manner in which they explored yet another factor in architecture, neglected since the spacious days of the Romans—the setting of buildings one against another. Michelangelo's Capitol at Rome, begun in 1546, illustrates the rediscovery of the art of monumental planning. Henceforth buildings were not to be sited just where most convenient but were to be grouped in such a fashion that the whole formed a properly-conceived architectural composition.

This preoccupation with the setting of buildings led to the reintroduction of monumental planning features hitherto neglected by western architects. Not only were the sites for buildings levelled before construction began but the site work might even be continued well beyond the essential area in order that the building might have an æsthetic as well as a structural foundation. The provision of a terrace before a building might lead to the addition of others in their turn leading the eye towards the central feature of the composition; the introduction of monumental stairways, in the Spanish fashion, joining these resulted in the addition of yet another important factor in monumental planning. Protection for persons walking upon these features was achieved by the introduction of the curious dwarf colonnades with their distorted 'balusters', known as balustrades, later to be raised above the great cornices for the benefit of persons taking the air upon the flat Renaissance roofs.

Much of this site work must have been developed after study of the remains of similar architectural achievements dating from the days of the ancient Romans. Amongst the most important of monumental —that is to say unnecessary—planning features is the flower-garden; the Renaissance architects reintroduced this lovely conception into the western world. Waterworks connected with the irrigation of gardens were also brought into use as architectural features; such were pools, canals, and those gay fountains upon the embellishment of which the rising generation of Italian sculptors, deprived of the privilege, traditional to their 'Gothic-trained' western brethren, of displaying their craft upon the architecture of buildings, allowed their exuberance to overflow with the waters so joyously dispensed.

Yet over all this gaiety a shadow already hung. A black cloud—as yet no larger than a man's hand—it would relentlessly expand until in the end so much helpless beauty would pass away under its pall.

It was the smoke of cannon. The white arm of the Middle Ages was white no more—the hand of the engineer was stained not with the clean earth of the mine-gallery but the foul soot of gunpowder. The day of the proud castle was over; from military architecture all the stateliness had departed—withered into nothingness at the summons of iron cannon.

The mediæval castle was obsolete for two reasons. The first was that its height and lack of stability against horizontal thrusts made it both a target and an easy victim to cannon; thus only a low structure could hope to withstand the assaults of the future. Moreover its plan provided for no platforms upon which the cannon of its defenders could be mounted and whence they could be fired without exposing the cannoneers to the shot of the besiegers. Defensive architecture had thus to be completely revolutionized so that the masonry took the form of low walls of immense thickness to withstand the battering of hostile shot and at the same time provide firm platforms upon which to mount the cannon of the garrison. Low parapets of immense thickness, pierced by widely splayed embrasures, protected the gun-crews.

Such structures as these could not be combined with ordinary domestic planning; thus we now find domestic and military architecture finally divorced and the castle giving place to the 'fort'. One of the earliest examples of this novel type of structure is that built at Ostia in 1483; a quatrefoil of low massive bastions surrounding an only slightly higher central keep, the whole almost buried within a wide dry ditch or moat in order to increase the effective height of the walls against escalade. Half a century later forts similar to this were being built by our own Henry VIII along the Channel coasts of England.

The gun-bastion became the principal feature of Renaissance military architecture. At first the projections were set out on a circular plan, as had been the case with the angle towers of mediæval castles. But the serious disadvantage of these low-built fortifications was that even the provision of a moat still left them exceedingly vulnerable to escalade, especially at the most salient part of a bastion where it was almost impossible to bring an adequate enfilading fire to bear.

It was at this stage that the architects of the Renaissance began to place their drawing boards at the service of the military engineer.

94. By about 1600 the courtyard of the mediæval great house had been opened up by the removal of the fourth side

(Hatfield)

95. The château of Maisons Lafitte near Paris

Working out the possible lines along which enfilading fire could be brought to bear upon each part of the curtain they had the circular bastion altered in plan to a pentagonal form, thus reducing the actual face of the salient to nothing and exposing the long flanks of the bastion to the protective fire of the garrison. In this fashion they developed the earlier quatrefoil into the formidable 'star-fort' around which the sieges of future centuries were to sway in smoke-haunted struggles (Plate 82).

But it was not so much the isolated fort that interested the Italians of the Renaissance as the walls of their cities. Round Verona in 1534 the architect Sanmichele set out a new system of fortifications: his massive curtains display the new arrow-head bastions and are pierced by fine gateways in the austere style of his era instead of the tall twin-towered structures which had for so long been welcoming the traveller to the cities of Europe. The isolated fortress, a relic of feudal times, was now becoming an anachronism, though Vignola in 1547 did indeed construct a fine castle at Caprarola, making it pentagonal on plan with a circular cortile and surrounding it with true Renaissance fortifications thrusting their bastions into the countryside in the imperative fashion so beloved by the military architect of every age.

Chapter XVI

CHRISTIAN SPAIN

South of the barrier of the Pyrenees lay the powerful country which had during vital centuries played the dual part of bulwark against the infidel and link through which the rising cultural forces of western Europe had been drawing experience from the glorious, if waning, civilization of Islam. As the power of the Moslem shrank before slowly advancing feudal armies the victors had extended their rule to the Mediterranean to make it their highway; in the end they crossed the ocean itself to conquer yet another world and bring thence great riches serving to swell still further the pride and magnificence of Christian Spain.

The Peninsula was still the land of churches. Already sown with thousands of religious buildings, each advance of the Christians saw the establishment upon it of further symbols of the spiritual might of Rome. As each Moslem city fell its great mosque was replaced by a cathedral. The close of the 15th century saw the final victory; a quarter of a century later the Spaniards began a vast new cathedral in newly-won Granada. It is in essence a Gothic church, its eastern termination the finest ever conceived; a development from the French chevet it improves upon this by extending the sweep of the aisles westwards to provide an imposing circular corona roofed with a dome. Westwards again stretches the spacious five-aisled body of the church in the heart of which, in the time-honoured fashion of the Spanish great church, is set the screen-enclosed choir of the canons.

Yet Gothic in conception though this church undoubtedly is, its detail is almost entirely Classical in form. Since the latter part of the 15th century the ever-ingenious Spanish architects had taken to varying the designs of the pillars surrounding their *patios* by every conceivable means, employing Gothic, Moslem and Classical forms in their determination to display the vitality of Spanish art. Innumerable interpretations—some of them undoubtedly of Islamic origin—of the Classical cornice also appear in Spanish architecture of the 15th century. Thus it was with little difficulty that the architects of the early 16th century accepted the approved forms advertised by Vignola and the other Renaissance architects. Yet even then the Spaniards showed their ingenuity by utilizing the Orders after their own independent fashion, as is exemplified by the interior of Granada cathedral, the interior of which displays enormously lofty piers having half-columns of the Corinthian Order attached to each face and the angles filled with slender pilasters. The remarkable compound pier thus contrived is neatly fluted and crowned by a complete entablature following in plan that of the complicated pier below. In this fashion, before 1530, the Renaissance style is seen to be established in Spain (Plate 69).

Unlike what we have seen in the western European countries, it seems to have been the Classical column which first took the fancy of the Spaniards. It may well be that no other Christian nation possessed the knowledge of how to turn large monolithic columns; the Moslems had employed forests of them in their great mosques and it had been the *mudejares* or conquered Moslems who had contributed many of the national characteristics of Spanish architecture. So well before the middle of the millennium we find one of the most fundamental of the factors contributing to the Renaissance movement already well established in the Peninsula.

But the feature which eventually appealed most to the Spanish taste was the ædicular treatment of openings. The Moslems were the carvers of the Middle Ages *par excellence;* their enchanting non-representational ornamentation, executed in almost any conceivable material, bestows on Spanish architecture a degree of richness unsurpassed by any other historical style. During the latter part of the 15th century, architectural carving became so profuse that it could be employed to give texture to a surface; those who complain of the over-exuberance of Spanish detail should not peer too deeply into this but try instead to appreciate the difference between carving applied for this purpose—as it generally was in Moslem architecture—and carving employed to emphasize a feature such as a capital or a pinnacle.

Their great skill as carvers enabled the Spaniards to seize upon the principle of the ædicule as applied to the ornamentation of openings and put it to far better use than the Italian copyists had succeeded in doing. Thus in place of a prim little composition comprising a pair of standardized colonnettes and a pedimented entablature the Spaniards turned the full breadth of their craftsmanship upon their window-cases, turning them into features of surpassing loveliness, the crowning glory being the wrought-iron *reja* grille which introduced yet another subsidiary art into the architecture of the façade (Plate 87).

Spain was indeed a long way ahead of the other Christian nations in the splendour of its culture. The spirit of the Renaissance movement as it entered the cortile of the republican palazzo found it insignificant beside the spacious patio of the princely alcazar: nor were the austere Italian arcades a match for the gay compositions handed down by the Moslems and enriched not only by them but also by legions of Gothic craftsmen who had played no part in Italian architectural history. Externally, however, the Spanish buildings presented much the same fortress-like aspect as those of Italy. But there is one subtle difference which played an important part in the development of Spanish elevational architecture in that the wide spacing of external windows served to discourage the architects from attempting to incorporate these within the restricted pattern of the Gothic bay design. Thus instead of introducing a fussy artificial system of punctuation—such as the application of storied Orders, for example—which would have destroyed the dignity of the unbroken cliff-face of masonry, the Spanish architects indulged in their passion for carved ornament by emphasizing each separate opening and giving it its due importance as an architectural feature. A marked tendency appears for the effect to be expanded until it eventually includes windows above and below each other in the same decorative scheme; this resulted in the fashion of developing the ædicular principle so that features situated one above the other were included in one vertical treatment. This happy device served to emphasize the underlying principle of Spanish elevational design which is that vertical punctuation is achieved by utilizing the openings themselves; an important advance beyond the primitive device of the fictitious bay-unit indicated by artificial punctuation devices such as pilasters.

The Spanish architects had long subscribed to the Gothic practice of concentrating the full power of their elevational abilities upon the west fronts of their churches; nothing was spared to enrich the towering frontispieces of the shrines of Christian Spain. When it came to the embellishment of the entrance of secular buildings full use was made of the new developments in ædicular architecture by building up over the doorway a series of features such as windows and heraldic achievements, enclosing the whole within a common frame of pseudo-Classical motifs—everything, of course, richly carved—and thus producing a frontispiece which could compete to some extent with that of the great church (Plates 58 and 87). These compositions spread throughout Europe, introducing an entirely new feature into its architecture; during the 16th century they make their way into this country where they are well-known to us from their appearance in the buildings of Elizabethan and Jacobean days (Plate 94).

Without doubt the most entrancing feature of Spanish domestic architecture is the high-perched gallery which passes across the front of the alcazar above its main cornice (Plate 87). The practical origin of these may be traced to the upper-story loggias of the Moslem houses. Aesthetically, however, they derive from the arcaded parapets which from earliest times had been provided to mask the rise of the vaulted roofs of the pre-Gothic churches. Exactly the same features may be seen in the Lombardic buildings and were copied with fine effect by the Rhenish architects of the 12th century. Yet the Italians could find no use for these charming features in their perfected designs, presumably because they were unable to trace their origin directly to Rome.

It is unfortunate that the high gallery never left the Peninsula to grace the architecture of Europe. But one invention of the Spanish architects of the middle of the millennium found ready acceptance everywhere and is today a feature in every house. The mediæval grand stair which led to the *piano nobile* had been, if a permanent structure of stone, entirely enclosed within walls on both sides; in the case of a turning stair the inner wall was in the form of a stone newel either solid or pierced with openings. It was left to the Spaniards to invent the 'spandrel wall' which supports the end of the stair-treads and carries the raking balustrade; at first employed upon one side of the stair it was later used on both, thus paving the way for the beautiful 'stairways of honour' of the High Renaissance and, more particularly, the Baroque. The first of these impressive features was the 'Golden Stairway' placed in Burgos Cathedral in 1519; its architect was Spain's greatest, Diego de Siloe, designer of Granada Cathedral.

Much has been made of the architectural achievements of the Italian Renaissance. But upon analysis it will be discovered that the Italians were, after all, quite recent initiates into the mysteries of their art. Having no real architectural history behind them they had no fund upon which to draw inspiration; nor could their imagination be adequately fed except upon the long-dead bones of an archaic style. Patiently they measured and copied, industriously they plied their T-squares, but not all the matching of column with column, the balancing of Order upon Order, could relieve their elevations from a dullness unrelieved by any spark of real imagination, any flash of spectacular daring.

In Spain the architectural tradition was glorious and unbroken. Roman architect, Gothic engineer, and Moslem carver had forged it, and wealth undreamed-of was now in the hands of prince and churchman to foster it as of old. The result was not mere architecture, it was artistry of the very highest order. Within a year of each other were designed the Farnese palace at Rome (Plate 81) and the university at Alcala de Henares (Plate 87); the beauty and dignity of the latter building far outshines the dullness of its Roman contemporary. Well it is for the history of architecture that circumstances enabled Spanish craftsmanship to maintain its virility long enough for it to be able to overcome in some measure the unimaginative austerity introduced at the end of the 16th century under the ægis of the Italian Renaissance.

But the new fashion had to be tried out and by the dawn of this century it had appeared in full fig in the patios of Spain. Externally, however, the Spaniards were loth to exhibit its innovations; too revolutionary for the façade of the alcazar it was yet far too austere for ecclesiastical purposes. It was due to the inventiveness of the craftsmen that it eventually became adapted as an ædicular architecture for use in connection with the details of religious structures; the elaborate style resulting from this adaptation is known as the Plateresque. This fascinating form of architectural treatment quickly caught the Spanish fancy to provide a multitude of decorative motifs for the embellishment of features such as frontispieces, but it cannot be said that it really achieved the dignity of an architectural style.

Throughout the Middle Ages elevational treatment had been chiefly confined to the west fronts of churches. During the 15th century the Spaniards had been fond of huge cavernous arches echoing the section of the church within; an idea possibly borrowed from the portals of the Moslem mosques. But as the 16th century dawned the architects embarked upon a series of vast façades spreading across the street-fronts of their wide churches. The twin towers of mediæval days were resurrected for employment as terminal features supporting with their sterner mass the elaborate frontispieces they flanked. As the century wore on and royal taste tended to turn more and more towards the Italian style of architecture the Orders began to play a more serious part in Spanish elevational design; after the middle of the century the somewhat unimaginative architect Herrera introduced the contemporary Italian style of frontispiece with its imitation portico formed by applying giant Orders to the wall-face. For a time this became the standard Spanish frontispiece, but Spanish genius gradually triumphed over sophistry and the church-fronts were brightened up until eventually they burst joyously into the delightful whimsies of the Baroque.

The return of the tower as a vital factor in ecclesiastical architecture was followed by its development as a Renaissance feature which soon found its way to the angles of the alcazar as well. Ecclesiastical architects even tried to monumentalize the plans of their great churches in order to fit them into vast four-towered rectangles on alcazar lines. Not one of these vast projects was in fact completed, but the El Pilar cathedral at Saragossa indicates something of the intention. The 16th-century Spanish tower was generally a sturdy feature devoid of embellishment except in its belfry stage where wide arched openings provided opportunities for ædicular treatment. As the structure was too light to support one of the usual solid Spanish roofs the tower was usually finished with a pyramidal timber construction like a stumpy spire. Towards the end of the century this was often replaced by an octagonal upper story of ædicular form and supporting a light dome from this source sprang the Renaissance steeple with its attempts to replace in Classical form the soaring spire of the Gothic era (Plate 101).

The primary feature of Spanish ecclesiastical architecture was of course the dome. Domes were no novelty to the builders of the magnificent cimborios of mediæval Spain, still less to their fellow-countrymen the Moslems. The Spanish dome continued to follow the octagonal plan of the cimborio instead of adopting the circular form employed by the contemporary Italian architects but adjusted the ornament of the drum to the style of the latter. The Spanish dome achieved great popularity and spread throughout the Mediterranean area and, of course, to the New World; yet despite the greater simplicity of its construction it failed to make any headway in Europe generally so that it is the circular Italian dome which forms the basis of its Renaissance church designs.

The acceptance of the dome as the presiding feature of the Renaissance church-form necessitated the modification of the standard church-plan of Gothic Europe to allow for a compromise between the traditional 'basilican' type preferred by the Roman Church and the Byzantine centralized structure which had now fully established itself within the very capital city of Catholicism. It was inevitable that the ecclesiastical architects of the day should revert to the solution already discovered when the problem had on two previous occasions arisen. The first of these was the period during which the Byzantine church-plan was being rationalized by the Armenian architects of the 6th century; the second resulted in the importation into Europe of Byzantine churches discovered in the Holy Land by 12th-century Crusaders.

The Spanish architects of the mid-16th century translated their Crusader churches into terms of Renaissance architecture, evolving a neat cruciform plan featuring a dome supported upon four crossing piers and flanked by shallow transepts; eastwards they provided a short presbytery ending in an apse and westwards a compactly-planned nave of no excessive length. The whole system of space and abutment is neatly contrived, as in its prototypes, within a rectangular containing wall; thus from the vast sprawling conglomerations of the great days of the Church we return once more to compactness surmounted by a sturdy dome.

96. An English country house of the eighteenth century
(Moor Park)

97. Curved roofs are a feature of the central European Baroque
(Ellingen)

It is sometimes forgotten that the principal political accompaniment of the Renaissance was the Reformation movement which strove to undermine the power of the Church. Thus one might have imagined that the new style lacked missionaries of the type familiar during the Middle Ages when the orders of monks and friars took turns at carrying the seeds of architectural enterprise throughout Europe. But Catholic Spain produced the Jesuits and they it was who infused a new spirit into the ecclesiastical architecture of the western world. In their church in Rome built by Vignola in 1568 we see the typical Renaissance church-form complete with its well-ordered Classical frontispiece but already exhibiting the lateral scrolls which indicate Spanish influence and mark the beginnings of the gay waywardness of the Baroque.

It was the Franciscans who first introduced into the New World the ecclesiastical architecture of Spain. During the course of the 16th century the missionary friars began a series of monasteries incorporating imposing but simply-planned churches in which we see the principles developed throughout the Gothic era reduced to their fundamentals. Each is a building of broad span set out in three or four wide bays; the height is expanded to its monumental proportion and the vaulted roof is supported on massive isolated piers joined by vast areas of walling set so that the supports project externally as if they were buttresses. Gradually the church-form of New Spain expanded until it achieved the standard eastern termination with its dome; first one and then a pair of sturdy towers were added to flank the frontispiece upon which most of the available decorative skill was expended. Thenceforth the churches of the New World were to advance in architectural splendour side by side with those of the mother country; no other nation has ever so richly endowed a colony.

The churches of Mexico and the colonies in South America form a series unsurpassed for magnificence in the world. They are for the most part aisle-less, vaulted in great bays punctuated by enormous pier-buttresses which either project externally or are absorbed in order that the spaces between them can be utilized as chapels; the altars in these are orientated north or south in a fashion unknown in mediæval days but normal to Renaissance church plans. Over a crossing set between short transepts is an octagonal Spanish dome rising from a drum and surmounted by a lantern. Ornament is often lavished upon these domes, yet they usually take second place in this respect to the summits of the western towers.

The Spanish bell-tower began as a sturdy structure having an arched opening on each face of the belfry story but little else in the way of embellishment. Ornament became concentrated upon this story and the steepled roof with which it was later capped, the rest of the tower remaining plain in order to provide an æsthetic foundation for the richness above and also to act as a foil to the magnificent frontispieces set between the towers. These three features —the belfries and the frontispiece—became a riot of sculpture, remaining characteristic of Spanish colonial ecclesiastical architecture during the 18th century (Plate 85), at which period the architects of the Old World were trying to employ a more restrained treatment collecting towers and frontispiece into a homogeneous composition which could dispense with the assistance of the sculptor.

In the torrid heat of the tropics the Spaniards were able to make the best use of their knowledge, handed down to them from Africa, of how to use architecture to provide shade; thus into the barbaric American continent they brought the courtyard surrounded with its arcaded loggias. Their knowledge of brickmaking enabled them to build in this material where stone was unprocurable or masons untrained; the use of stucco—yet another material borrowed from the Moslem—enabled the colonists to weave their architecture into delightful forms as fancy suggested. The colonial architecture of central America, a style upon which is founded most of the building art of the southern portion of the continent, is not one which can be entirely omitted from a discussion of historical architecture.

In Spain itself the 16th century saw no diminution in the scale of building projects. The defeat of the Moslem and the unification of the Peninsula under a strong monarchy and an all-powerful Church, coupled with the vast wealth which was now pouring into the country from the New World, produced a feeling of security which conduced towards the building of monuments. The nobles could now abandon their obsolete and uncomfortable castles to taste the luxury of the Islamic type of residence, the alcazar with its shady two-storied *patio* surrounded by fine apartments richly ceiled with elaborate carpentry. For the greater dignity of the exterior they were pleased to retain the four angle pavilions which to some extent recalled the towers of the castles they had for so long inhabited; yet they were careful to join them here and there with the delightful high-perched galleries from which they and their ladies could gaze out over the roofs of the city (Plate 71).

The alcazar is the principal secular building of Spain. The Spaniards maintained their independence of western European ideas and forbore to abandon their patios in favour of the more compact plan which was now established throughout the Frankish countries. Long association with the Moslem had accustomed them to privacy within their homes and thus they could never have submitted to the opening-up of the domestic elevation in accordance with the new fashion; indeed they never really forsook their orientalism in this respect.

The *kasr* was not only the fundamental plan-form in domestic architecture but also in buildings of civic status. During the 17th century, when their urban administration had caught up with that of western Europe, the Spaniards began to build town halls of alcazar type, four-square round a patio and with angles emphasized by pavilions.

The interest of the 16th-century Spanish architects in monumental planning is seen in their conventual buildings, the plans of which completely abandon the mediæval forms introduced in mediæval days and become disciplined to fit into the rectangular enceinte which had become the framework of Spanish Renaissance planning. The cloister became the patio, upon one side of which—usually the south, so as to provide shade from the high building—lay the church with its frontispiece displayed at one end of the principal frontage in the centre of which was the entrance to the monastery. In large buildings such as hospitals or colleges the church was sometimes sited at the rear of the patio and on the axis leading from the main doorway, a perfect example of true monumental planning of which the finest example is the Escorial near Madrid, a vast collection of structures forming at once monastery, college, and palace. The whole elaborate composition is set within a lofty wall of enceinte with angle pavilions as if it were a huge alcazar; despite the grimness of the granite elevations, relieved only by a single rather austere frontispiece, the Escorial stands as the mightiest of European palaces, equalled in scale only by those of the Abbasid caliphs of eight centuries earlier (Plate 88).

Despite the tremendous wealth and power of 16th-century Spain it is not immediately apparent that its architecture played an impressive part in the history of that of western Europe generally. The Peninsula seems always to have been a land apart, chiefly owing to the heterogeneous nature of its population and the consequent differences in the mental processes of the Frank and the Hispano-Moor. Another factor was the fanatical adherence of the Spaniard to a Church which elsewhere was losing much of its ancient popularity and was if anything regarded as a symbol of ancient tyrannies rather than a sponsor of progress. Yet in the mid-16th century rebuilding of the royal palace of the Louvre there is evident a certain tribute to the magnificence of the Spanish court and it is certain that the Spanish type of frontispiece had penetrated to the architecture of western Europe considerably earlier than this.

But it is with the 16th-century political contact between Spain and the Low Countries with their German hinterland that the architecture of Spain at last begins to make its influence felt. At the middle of the century Spanish Gothic motifs had completely invaded the Low Countries and the arcaded patio was making its appearance in some of the civic structures; at the same time the ecclesiastical architecture of Spain was here and there penetrating to the very borders of Austria. Later in the century the great gables lining the street-frontages were beginning to assimilate many of the vagaries of the Spanish frontispiece and the characteristic dormer treatments which provided the principal architectural features of the soaring German roofs were being subjected to a Spanish form of ædicular embellishment.

Most striking of all is the manner in which the great German *Schloss* was being converted into a Spanish alcazar. The high walls of the many-storied ranges of lodgings were being disciplined into a rectangular plan with the usual angle pavilions; the only difference lies in the ranges of windows which appear on the façades and serve to indicate that the *Schloss* has now followed the French example and passed from *château-fort* to *château*. The most imposing of these great German alcazars is Schloss Aschaffenburg begun at the very beginning of the 17th century (Plate 89).

98. A Baroque church of Venice

99. By a mass of ornament the architects of the Baroque masked
the junctions of their many curves (Steinhausen)

The appearance of this type of great house is in reality due to the general effect of the Renaissance movement in bringing order out of mediæval incoherence by taking the late-mediæval German castle, setting it upon a rectangular plan, and giving it properly-designed elevations. On the whole it is safe to say that the Spanish architects played a very small part in the modification of the actual architecture of a country so completely different in all respects from their own. But as regards the ornamentation of the Teutonic buildings it was, as we shall see, a very different matter.

The most prominent feature absent from Spanish architecture is the tall gable. The roofs in the Peninsula are flat in pitch, thus the ends of buildings have to all intents and purposes flat tops. The nearest approach to an architectural gable the Spaniards had encountered was the Classical pediment, an unexciting form of treatment quite unsuited to the gaiety of their æsthetic outlook. The towering gables of the Low Countries seem to have delighted the architects who saw them; during the 16th century the Flemish and Teutonic gables became canvases upon which to experiment with all the tricks known to the Spanish architect and his northern pupils. The application of the storied Orders required by the ordinance of a Plateresque elevation involved the designers in difficulties when the gable itself was reached. By filling up the outer spandrels with various forms of scrollwork (Plate 90) they created the 'Dutch' gable which became the most typical feature of the Low Countries during the 17th century and, transported thence by colonists to the Cape of Good Hope, forms the characteristic feature of the 'Cape Dutch' style of farm house (Plate 91).

In their experiments with gable silhouettes the Spaniards were incidentally laying the foundations of their own colonial style as perfected during the late 17th and early 18th centuries under the designation of 'Colonial Baroque'.

The churches of the regions affected were still Gothic in form and remained so until well into the 17th century. The persistence of the Gothic spirit is well illustrated by the curious timber-framed steeples which from the last quarter of the 16th century onwards represent the attempt to convert the Gothic spire into terms of the Renaissance movement. But it is the west fronts of churches which begin to display the full force of the new style of ornament as under the influence of Spanish architects—many of them probably despatched by the Jesuits upon counter-Reformation campaigns—the frontispieces develop interesting compositions on Plateresque lines. The first quarter of the 17th century was the richest period; some of the dormer gables, both on secular buildings and also, in the German fashion, above the aisles of the churches, show ædicular treatments equal to the best examples of the Peninsula itself.

For the most part however the domestic work is decidedly inferior to that displayed by the churches. It would therefore appear that the former is the result of local copyists. During the 15th, 16th and 17th centuries no country in Europe could muster such a force of carvers as was gathered together in Spain. Their repertoire included items drawn from Classical, Gothic, and—above all—the inexhaustible source provided by non-representational Islamic art. The Dutch and Germans had practically no carvers of this versatility, a situation which detracted considerably from the æsthetic effect of the undulating gables and tentative frontispieces produced by local architects in the new style. Hence the curious reduction of the Spanish motifs to a system of plain strapwork devoid of enrichment and queerly-shaped swellings which seem to mourn the carvers who could never be found to apply their chisels to the waiting stone or fill with statuary the empty niches.

But in faraway lands across the ocean there was a race of strange people whose craftsmen had so recently been covering the temples of their savage gods with horrid hordes of dragons and serpents but now were enthusiastically learning how to enrich the frontispiece of many a great Spanish church (Plate 85).

Chapter XVII

AUSTERITY
AND EXUBERANCE

The period covered by the Renaissance movement of the 16th century represents the transition between the embryo civilization of mediæval Europe and modern times. In architecture the phase is marked by the concentration of an enormously expanded building potential away from ecclesiastical direction and towards the improvement of ordinary living accommodation. The Peninsula excepted, the house-plan of the 17th century had reached a stage at which it closely approximated to the productions of present-day architectural practice while elevational architecture had become an orderly style perfectly suitable for reproduction in the street frontages of modern cities.

The 17th-century great house had attained a size far in excess of anything hitherto seen and was threatening to present its planner with the same problems experienced by the designers of the great Frankish churches of the 11th century. It must be remembered that the early Renaissance house was still, like its mediæval predecessor, a simply-constructed building only one room in thickness and that a large house was still but a collection of such units, albeit now arranged in a far more orderly fashion. Sub-division by permanent partitions had vastly complicated the planning problems, for though spacious staircase wells provided communication between floors there was still no provision for horizontal circulation and each room was entered from those adjoining it.

Such a primitive arrangement had the result of forcing the architects to take great pains with their internal planning, especially in the grouping of apartments in suitable relationship one with another and the segregation of those of lesser importance in ranges separate from the main block itself. The problem was then one of assembling these various ranges to form a great house of imposing aspect.

The Spaniards, securely wedded to their traditional *kasr* plan, employed this for almost all purposes. Their Mediterranean colleagues, however, were now opening up their plans to bring them into line with those of the French châteaux, the finest examples of the great house of the epoch. The Germans had been following the same development as the French but were a century or so behind; it was not until the second half of the 17th century that the great *Schloss* lost the fourth side of its courtyard and fell into line with the rest of western Europe.

The next hundred years became the era of great planning schemes in which ranges of buildings were aligned along three sides of a vast open space, itself planned as a formal lay-out and often incorporated with long vistas. This was the zenith of the great European palaces. Nothing in western Europe can equal the immense scale of such compositions as Versailles, Nymphenburg, or Blenheim; every feature of monumental planning known to architectural history is displayed in their spacious acres. Renaissance architecture has at last approached in breadth of vision something of the magnificence known to Classical Rome and Islam of the Abbasids.

The 17th and 18th centuries saw new features being introduced into town planning. The monumental was not to be confined to the forecourt of the palace; the old-fashioned market places were converted into Renaissance *piazzas,* sometimes even provided with loggias and generally overlooked by the portico or frontispiece of a town hall. The erection of 'terraces' of identical houses set together in long rows and the combination of these with a rectangular open space created the residential square or *place.*

While the country houses were expanding the drift to the cities continued. Fortifications being still as necessary as ever—though towered curtain had given place to rampart and ravelin—overcrowding was still acute, hence the ever-increasing height of urban structures. By the beginning of the 17th century the civic buildings of the wealthier cities were already veritable skyscrapers five or six stories in height below their high-pitched roofs full of attic floors.

The Renaissance movement in Italy had been limited in its scope to palatial and ecclesiastical architecture. Miniature palaces or 'villas' had carried the new style into rural areas but neither the farm nor the ordinary town house had changed in character from the simple building endemic to the region. The Italian town house of the sixteenth century was a two- or three-storied structure of little pretensions and in no way comparing with the towering buildings to be found in the commercial cities of Western Europe.

The Italian palazzo was not imported into these cities. On the other hand during the 17th century we can detect a tendency towards the reduction of the mediæval serrated skyline of the street frontage by the introduction of lower roof-pitches and the masking of these behind a parapet in order to create a more orderly appearance. The introduction of 'terrace' compositions enabled architects to design elevations for these which would compete to some degree with those of the Italian palaces. By the end of the century the parapeted street frontage has become almost universal in the important city street.

Elevational design having become finally regimented, architects seem to have had little option but to attempt to give some interest to the dull 'drawing-board' compositions of the new era by introducing some form of punctuation on the lines suggested by the Italian Renaissance movement. Until the middle of the 17th century the storied Orders were employed, Inigo Jones's design for the royal palace of Whitehall being an example of their use. It was, however, the French architect Mansard who developed this device to create a really attractive domestic style; there can be few more charming country houses in all Europe than this little château of Maisons-Lafitte (Plate 95).

But about the period of this culmination of the Early Renaissance elevational style in the achievements of Mansard the giant Order begins to appear on domestic façades and in the frontispieces of those houses which have no general scheme of elevational punctuation. Thenceforth the storied Orders disappear from the scene, unmourned by reason of the fact that the greater length of the new urban façades enabled horizontal punctuation to be dispensed with. In the case of the very tall buildings which were now appearing, Orders of any kind had perforce to be dispensed with altogether; thus such façades had to rely solely upon the arrangement of their window openings for effect.

Unfortunately no western architect—except in Spain—had reached the stage at which he dared to abandon the habit of dividing an elevation into vertical bays of equal width; thus an era of unmitigated dullness began to cast its shadow upon the city streets of western Europe as the 17th century drew to its close.

The great house, however, continued to flourish. One of the results of the withdrawal of its lateral wings towards the central range had been to create a pair of terminal features to this which, at first resembling the angle pavilions of the château, eventually effaced themselves still further to become as it were a pair of secondary frontispieces balancing that framing the entrance itself. Thus was inaugurated a new elevational ordinance: the long façade punctuated by an imposing central 'pavilion' and terminated by a pair of vertical features echoing this in a lesser degree. Variations of this 'three-pavilion' façade played a large part in the domestic architecture of the later 17th century (Plate 97).

It had been an eventful century. Its great architectural contribution had been the frontispiece, a feature which could still produce an exciting splash in the stagnant pool of a Renaissance elevation. On the one hand was the staid Classical portico with its sophisticated Order surmounted by an equally archaic and—to western Europe—strangely exotic pediment. On the other side of the picture was a more promising development: the Flemish Plateresque frontispiece derived from the impact of the art of Spain upon the Gothic gable. Notwithstanding some Spanish pressure, Italy had remained faithful to tradition and even for a spell converted the more virile Spaniards of Philip II to the dreariness of the Herreriano style—from which, however, they soon emerged into the violence of the Churrigueresque. But western Europe devised a compromise, applying Classical pediments to Gothic gables and effecting an adjustment by introducing all the devices learnt from the brilliant Spanish architects who had left such a mark upon the Low Countries. The culmination of the frontispiece is seen in the façades of the churches; by the end of the 17th century those of western Europe had achieved a dignity quite unmarred by the dullness which would certainly have resulted from a slavish adherence to purely Classical motifs. Less skilful domestic architects, however, addicted to copy-books and lacking imagination and intelligent encouragement, produced far duller frontispieces than their ecclesiastical contemporaries.

The domestic architecture of the 17th century was a serious matter. Its exponents had enough to cope with in the complications of planning without having to devise new æsthetic effects in addition. Accommodational requirements were expanding at a tremendous rate and it was as much as they could do to keep up the more and more onerous demands of their new clients. As the 16th century raced to its close in a wave of politico-commercial activity a generation or two of architects witnessed the rapid metamorphosis of a mediæval society into a modernistic era of which they had no experience upon which to draw.

One has only to look upon a vast civic building such as the town hall at Augsburg (Plate 93) to appreciate the architectural problems of the dawn of the 17th century. In scale this structure could hold its own against a modern commercial building. Portions of it are seven stories in height below the eaves of its lofty roof. Yet its plan is quite primitive being simply a pattern of rooms set out in tiers without any thought of convenience of access other than is supplied by the central hall on either side of which they are placed.

The new problem was one of circulation. The Islamic architects had solved this by the simple process of setting their building ranges in a hollow square with loggias surrounding the internal court, a practice which had been copied by the Spaniards and the mediæval Italians. Except for monastic cloisters, this method of circulation was unknown to western European architectural practice.

At the beginning of the 17th century the civic architects of the Low Countries and Germany had taken to building their city halls on something of the same principle but with the inner courts replaced by large covered halls, often communicating with the main staircase, from which many of the subsidiary rooms could be approached. This introduced an entirely new type of structure into western Europe: in place of the long range of apartments we now find a square block with four façades instead of two long ones and two gable ends. The monumental feature of the town hall was still its lofty campanile; this was now often transferred to a central position above the hall which now occupied the heart of the structure. During the 17th century we find the same type of plan employed in domestic architecture, the tall central tower being echoed by a cupola or a small dome which acts as a lantern to light the enclosed central hall or staircase well.

One of the noticeable factors met with in studying the large compact secular buildings of the 17th century is the interest that European architects were now taking in the third dimension. First only the plan had been considered, the elevation having been left to look after itself. Then came the late-mediæval interest in elevational design: how to correlate this with the floor plans of a multi-story building. We now see the whole structure being designed as a *mass*; one which could be viewed from all angles without appearing awkwardly composed.

Such buildings could only be roofed with hips; thus a death-blow was struck at the mediæval gable, which became relegated to ædicular architecture to serve only as the crowning feature of a frontispiece or some other subsidiary feature. The abandoning of gables helped the spread of the Renaissance elevation by allowing the main cornice to pass all round the building without interference. While Germany and, more particularly, the Low Countries, clung to their lively gabled skylines as long as they could, the French developed the hipped roof, often making it in two pitches—the so-called 'mansard' roof—in order to give more space for attics. A favourite device of the French roof-builders was to bulge the faces outwards, especially over square pavilions where it gave the impression of a four-sided dome (see also Plate 97).

So, in a feverish boom of planning great buildings and experimenting—perhaps not so successfully—with the new elevational devices supplied by the Renaissance enthusiasts western Europe embarked upon the task of founding a modern building technique. The ancient lands of Spain and Italy were meanwhile continuing along lines independent of the Frankish countries. At the same time they were drawing closer together between themselves, possibly under the influence of the Roman Church which had lost so much of its prestige in the countries affected by the Reformation.

A notable feature of the beginning of the 17th century is the colonization of south-eastern Germany by the Italians. Renaissance architects begin to extend their influence across the Alpine passes into

Austria, a land still under the spell of mediævalism. Italian Renaissance churches, such as Salzburg cathedral, begin to appear in Austria and soon it becomes clear that the Italian style is about to establish itself there without the violent modifications introduced by western experimenters. Yet Italian ecclesiastical architecture seems to have exhausted itself upon the completion of the great church in Rome; elsewhere its buildings are on the whole designed in a minor key. Wherever funds permitted—as, for example, in still-wealthy Venice—every effort was made to crown the building with a great dome (Plate 98); comparatively few though they be, the Italian domes are on the whole finer than the crowning domes of Old and New Spain. The Italians seem to have had no energy left over to expend upon a west front; this was where the Spanish churches so far outshone those of Italy. Fortunately the latter part of the 16th century saw the architects of both countries in close touch with each other; thus the new church style of Austria—in close political contact with Spain—was able to include the Spanish twin-towered façade as a striking factor in the otherwise Italianesque design.

In the rest of western Europe the ordinary Italian form of church, with everything subordinated to the dome, became the fashion. Some of the domes of Paris—notably that of the Invalides—are equal to the best of the Italian examples. The Italianesque cathedral of St Paul, London, has another fine dome; in addition the building is provided with a considerable façade displaying an original interpretation of the twin-towered Spanish frontispiece translated into a somewhat austere Classic, as if in recognition of the fact that it belongs to a church of the Reformed Faith.

By the beginning of the 17th century Protestantism had become sufficiently well established for it to have begun to develop its own church-plan. The aim of its architects being to abolish as far as possible the old emphasis upon orientation towards the altar, chancels and presbyteries were omitted altogether, leaving only the nave in which to accommodate large congregations gathered to hear a preacher. The result was a firm tendency to abandon the old axial plan in favour of centralization of structure. The first buildings—which were mainly in the Low Countries—were of no great magnificence; it was as if the ecclesiastical architects were following a deliberate policy of austerity pointed at the wild extravagance of their Spanish Catholic colleagues. Thus the Protestant church begins to assume the same squarish mass one finds in contemporary secular buildings, the resemblance being heightened by the incorporation of a bell-tower crowned by a soaring steeple which forms almost the only notable feature of the design.

It cannot be denied that the Reformation dealt the deathblow to ecclesiastical architecture in western Europe. For this, however, it can be forgiven in that it diverted the building potential of the region to the improvement of living accommodation of all classes of the community. Yet something departed from architecture when the great churches were built no more. It was left to the Spaniards to continue to patronize the ecclesiastical architect, still feverishly plying his craft in regions hitherto undreamed-of, urged to greater and greater efforts by still-powerful monastic orders chief of which was the Society of Jesus specially founded as a force to fight the heresies of the Reformation.

It may have been this influence which encouraged the close co-operation between Spanish and Italian architects which is a notable feature of the late 16th century. The Spaniards injected the vitality of their own style into that of the Italian, still in the main a primitive copyist architecture unsuited to the temperament of its practitioners. Both were agreed as to the desirability of the dome; the Spaniards were, however, unable to give it the prominence of the Italian examples without either building gigantic domes or else destroying the scale of their far larger buildings. At the beginning of the 17th century both countries were experimenting with domes rising above an oval; an innovation which allowed for a compromise between the axial plan and a centralized structure dominated by a dome. Hitherto no architect had ever departed from a straight line on plan except for a line which was a segment of a circle; the oval was something quite new in architecture, something ultra-sophisticated marking indeed the first stage of that æsthetic revolution known as the Baroque.

The Italian architects were only too glad to brighten up their designs with the new licence offered by the Baroque planning features; the oval appears in their plans towards the end of the 16th century. But the most striking feature is the appearance of curved walling, introduced for no structural reasons but purely as an æsthetic device, upon the external elevations of buildings. Not only were such walls convex on plan, but might also be concave; examples can even be seen where the wall was planned as a double curve (Plate 100). It is this sinuous planning line which is characteristic of Baroque planning, not to be confused with the elevational curves found in the Flemish Plateresque frontispiece.

By the end of the 17th century the spirit of the Italian Renaissance had worn itself out. The day of the feudal palazzo upon the elevation of which the style had been born was long past. Even the churches had failed to attain the magnitude of their mediæval predecessors while the private house—now the most important building of all in a world carried upon the shoulders of the merchant and trader—had never been absorbed into Italian architecture at all. The 18th century saw the great palaces already beginning to look forlorn amongst the shabby houses which seemed to have failed to attain the promise of past years. Rome was once again becoming a museum.

Meanwhile the Italian architects, more interested in sculpture now that there was no building of adequate scale upon which they could practise, were contenting themselves with interior decorating, designing pretty little oval chapels and exercising their facile chisels upon fountains and other trivial *objets* affording them every facility for the introduction of fashionable eccentricities.

During the last two centuries the principal feature of the palace interior had been its grand stair; this was now always designed to rise about an open well. During the 16th century, experiments in monumental site planning had led to the development of wide external stairways arranged symmetrically about an axis with each flight duplicated so that a double stairway resulted. The introduction of the Baroque oval into these plans enabled the ascent to appear more gracious through the elimination of right-angled turns while still retaining the axial principle in the layout; these Baroque stairways form an important contribution to the palatial architecture of the late 17th and early 18th century.

The architectural aspect of the Baroque is best illustrated by the buildings of those lands which were colonized by the more vigorous architects of Spain and Italy. It will be found that a new style of building generally finds most favour in a country which is in process of development and has as yet acquired no long-established tradition of its own. Thus it was central Europe which opened its arms to the Baroque.

Fig. 13. The Baroque façades of Poland are as lively as may be found anywhere in Europe

By the close of the 17th century the Baroque had taken a firm hold of Austria and Bohemia (Plate 100); at the dawn of the 18th it had taken hold of Poland also (Fig. 13), thus striking a swath across Europe to provide a link between the puzzled Renaissance of Germany and the primitive architecture of semi-Byzantinized Russia.

Less than a century saw a hitherto backward region burst into an architectural style of great magnificence as the High Baroque inspired a splendid series of buildings, ecclesiastical and secular, surrounded by elaborately-planned settings—the culmination not only of the Renaissance movement but of the whole history of European architecture.

The Central-European Baroque may best be described as Spanish architecture tempered by the restraining influence of less imaginative but more scholarly Italian architects. Its domes are on the whole Italian but the twin-towered façades of the churches are clearly Spanish in origin. Few architectural sculptors were available, thus there was little chance of the frontispieces breaking out into the violence of the Ultra-Baroque 'Chirrugueresque' of contemporary Spanish examples. The Italian architects carefully set out their sinuous plans and gathered towers and frontispieces into neat compositions punctuated with the inevitable Orders. Only when it came to steeples and gables did they have to admit of the inadequacy of their style and allow a little licence with scrollwork, strange finials, and bulbous caps, relics of the 'Flemish Plateresque' elevations of earlier days.

It may be argued that the curving of what should normally be the straight lines of a plan may not in truth be a legitimate device for introducing interest in a façade but rather an eccentricity savouring of exhibitionism. The use of the oval, however, which by suggesting an axis serves to stabilize the design without detracting from the sense of *hypsosis,* produced the most delightful results if used in moderation. A multiplication of ovals, as in the Vierzehnheiligen near Bamburg, resulted in chaos; in this weird church the architect tried to squeeze his plan into the lines of an ordinary cruciform building while its interior confusion has been deftly camouflaged with bursts of that wild ornament so inseparable from the later Baroque of central Europe. (See also Plate 99).

The Spanish origin of the Baroque is further illustrated by the foundation in south-eastern Germany of huge monasteries planned four-square after the fashion of their prototypes in the Peninsula. These fortress-like monasteries spread throughout most of Catholic Europe, rivalling the château and the *Schloss* in the extent of their imposing elevations and surpassing both in the magnificence of dome and twin-towered frontispiece which characterizes the monastic church itself.

The Baroque, primarily an ecclesiastical style, set the seal upon the architecture of Europe during the 18th century. Although the main lines of secular plans remained unaffected, portions of these were continually breaking out into sinuous curves for no reason other than was provided by the campaign against Protestant austerity. In elevations the bowed or concave front appears as a vital feature in ædicular architecture. The standard half-round arch of the Renaissance tends to become replaced by the less formal three-centred Spanish type of head. As was to be expected with a 'sculptor's architecture', the 'broken' pediment with its gap for a bust or some other purely decorative object became popular. As the regional force of sculptors and painters expanded these were turned loose upon buildings in order that they might apply still further decorative schemes to what was already overloaded architecture; an orgy of unrestrained and undirected craftsmanship which eventually provoked the inevitable reaction and resulted in the return to the austerity of the Classical style which marked the close of the 18th century.

But the Baroque left an ineradicable stamp upon the buildings of western Europe. French domestic architecture is still redolent of it; their colonists carried it to the Levant, Egypt, and the sunset lands of Islam. England had neither the wealth nor the architectural potential to play any conspicuous part in the movement; its chief offspring in this country is probably the bow window of Regency days.

But the most astonishing result of the Baroque invasion of Austria was its effect on the architecture of Russia. This vast barbaric country, Byzantinized only in so far as its ancient cities were concerned, had been so ruined by the Mongol invasion of the mid-13th century which had wrecked the civilization of the Abbasids that its development had been arrested and it had taken no part in any of the architectural experiments of the past five centuries. The national building technique differed from that of the rest of Europe in that it employed axe-wrought fir logs set horizontally in what is known as 'blockwork'. It was not possible to construct high-pitched roofs suitable for shedding the snows which played such a vital part in its climate, but the flattish log roofs of more important structures were provided with a curious construction, known as a 'cask' roof, which was rather like an over-developed pointed barrel-vault set upon the roof instead of beneath it. These outer-cask roofs helped to shed the snow and at the same time kept it from lying upon the inner roof which formed the ceiling of the building itself (Plate 104).

The section of these roofs may be compared with the bulbous domes which as early as the 13th century were being employed upon Russian churches. In this connection it may be remembered that the domes of Abbasid Persia, which like Russia has a rigorous climate, were also bulbous; it may be conjectured that their shape may be due to the same cause as the Russian examples. The bulbous caps upon 17th-century steeples in north-western Europe, retained by the Baroque architects of the next century and developed by them to form fantastic features, must presumably have been derived from Russian examples seen by traders in Baltic ports.

Entirely free as it was from the influence of the Catholic Church, the Russian church-plan remained at all times true to the centralized form introduced by the Byzantines. The late-mediæval village church was an octagon of blockwork the roof of which rose high above it in the form of an octagonal pyramid of the same type of construction (Plate 102). Humble in scale though they be, these provincial tent-churches in no way fall short of that ideal of *hypsosis* inseparable from the creations of Byzantine-trained architects. Even the central lantern of the western churches could not inspire the feeling of mystery which hovers within the towering interior of the Russian tent-churches. (See also Plate 103.)

The difficulty encountered in designing structures of this sort is how they can be enlarged; in blockwork especially it is impossible to cut tall openings through the walling. The solution was partly achieved by duplication of the octagons with their towering tents so that the building became a cluster of cells each of which formed a chapel. The result, though barbaric in the extreme, produced an exterior aspect striking in the extreme as the huge tents clustered in ever-increasing numbers; by the middle of the 16th century even large brick churches were being erected to this design. Perhaps the most remarkable of all is the church of St Basil at Moscow built by Ivan the Terrible in 1555; around its central tent are eight others, fitted like the cells of a honeycomb, with the four ordinal tents sub-ordinated in scale to the other four and the whole overshadowed by the central feature—an example of *hypsosis* terrible in the barbarism of its ornament (Plate 105).

So popular were these striking buildings that in 1650 the Orthodox Church felt it necessary to issue an edict that in future churches were to follow traditional Byzantine lines: that is to say, the cubical type of building containing a central space covered by a lantern dome supported upon four piers and surrounded by a galleried aisle. The interior expanded into the usual cruciform shape while four lesser domes rose above the angles between the arms of the cross—hence these buildings were known as 'five-dome churches'. The cultural centre of Russia seems to have been Vladimir; by the end of the 12th century its churches had begun to show that curious variation on normal Byzantine practice which is characteristic of Russian ecclesi-astical architecture. This is the exposure of the wall-arches of cross-vaulting on the external face of the wall instead of masking them behind a parapet; from the sort of rounded gable resulting from this treatment was later developed the remarkable Russian systems of exposed squinches (Plate 105).

The recovery of the country after its devastation by the Mongols centred round the new capital of Moscow which during the 14th and 15th centuries was provided with a number of new churches of orthodox design. But architecture generally made little progress until the 17th century when ancient Kiev became the centre for a new revival in church-building and another school of architecture, also on orthodox lines, became established in the region of the newer city of Yaroslav in the Moscow region.

At the period when the Baroque style was entering Austria, Peter the Great was czar of Russia. Seized with the current building mania he decided to abandon the Byzantine brick-building, which had for centuries supplied the principal Russian monumental architecture, in favour of the sophisticated masonry style of the rest of Europe. In order to consolidate this conversion he gave orders that all Russian building was in future to be executed in timber while in St Peters-burg itself—the city which he was founding as one able to compete with other European capitals—he experimented with his new projects.

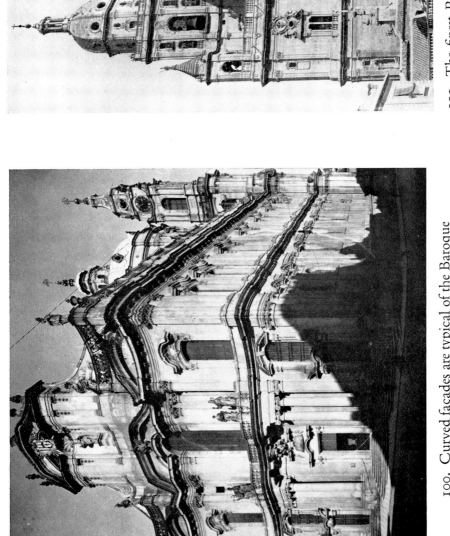

101. The finest Renaissance bell-towers are those of Spain (Murcia)

100. Curved façades are typical of the Baroque (Prague)

103. The style of brick building derived from the tent-

102. A Russian 'tent-church' built in blockwork

Instead of entirely extinguishing Russian architecture this edict had an amazing result. The timber church with its tall blockwork roof not only came into its own but developed into a truly remarkable edifice. The architects of the 18th century set out their wooden structures upon the same lines as the Byzantine buildings and even on a comparable scale. Under their brilliant direction the new timber churches soared to incredible heights. In place of the Byzantine lantern dome a vast tower crowned by a hollow 'tent' spire soared into the air while the short arms of the cross became covered with a series of cask-roofs mounted one upon the other. The summit of the spire began to assume the appearance of a western steeple while Baroque detail made its appearance upon every hand. While to western eyes the result must necessarily appear barbaric it is impossible not to admire the vigour with which humble builders developed the use of a despised material to produce, at the shortest notice, churches of such undeniably monumental appeal (Plate 104).

Russian domes are never large, having been developed from the late-Byzantine type perched upon a high drum. Persian influence is indicated not only by the bulbous shape but by the use of the squinch in preference to the pendentive; during the 17th century a form of 'honeycomb' vaulting was devised comprising ranges of squinches mounting in decreasing rings. Russo-Byzantine churches often expose the wall-arches of aisle vaulting externally and apply an arcade echoing the internal arrangement (Plate 33); after the end of the mediæval period the large squinches of the main vault were similarly exposed. Under the influence of the Italian Renaissance external arches were provided with moulded cornices so that the exterior of the building became covered with a number of segmental pediments crowning the walls and climbing the sides of the 'tent' (Plate 47).

The Byzantine bell-tower was introduced to Russia as a timber construction; during the 17th century it became a huge erection of brickwork often surpassing in scale its brethren throughout the world. Never attached to the church itself until the Baroque boom of the next century even then it was not absorbed into the design but remained in splendid aloofness as a monumental structure entirely overshadowing the building at the foot. The Russian bell-towers of the 18th century are the largest of their kind in the world and possess a grace and charm never attained by those of the rest of Europe.

Russian architecture, in conjunction with so much that is interesting and instructive, has hitherto been completely ignored by the historian, presumably for the reason that the Russians never adhered to Classical, Gothic, or Italian Renaissance standards of taste. Yet no building style since the Byzantine so determinedly responded to the summons of *hypsosis*. Not all the barbarism displayed in their external ornament can prevent the Russian churches from displaying the true spirit of architectural aspiration which lifts their clustered roofs soaring towards the sky.

It will be seen that the keynote of 18th-century European architecture was undoubtedly exuberance. But—if Spain itself be excepted —it was mainly in the newer regions of the east, where modern architecture was as yet in its infancy, that the Baroque made such tremendous headway. In older countries such as France, England, or western Germany, there was still a very conservative element which mistrusted the extravagances creeping into the Renaissance elevation. Indeed by the end of the 18th century the tendency was towards a reform of the Classical style by purging it of all Renaissance elements and attempting to get back to original sources. Architecture had become more than a profession; it was now a subject of research and criticism by scholars.

The rise of England as the centre of a vast colonial empire had placed this country in a position from which it could direct the cultural as well as the political development of large areas of the world. Even the loss of the North American colonies made no difference to their dependence upon England for guidance in such matters as architecture. As has been noted, this country took practically no part in the Baroque movement but was content to develop an austere but essentially practical style—the Georgian. Its buildings were compact, their elevations orderly and only allowed simple Classical porticoes as frontispieces; churches were equally unimposing but dignified by bell-towers surmounted by steeples devoid of any exhibitionism.

The publication of architectural copy-books and their circulation in America soon resulted in the introduction of the Georgian style as the foundation stone of American architecture (Plate 106). In the absence of an established building potential the earliest structures were of carpentry, ingeniously framed together and covered with boarding painted white to give a general impression of stonework. The columns of porticoes being formed of fir trees instead of being built up in masonry, the porticoes of the American 'Colonial' style present a far more graceful appearance than their English prototypes. In order to protect the wooden walls of the buildings from the elements they were often surrounded with storied verandahs (Plate 107); these sub-tropical appendages are also met with in the Regency buildings of British India.

The introduction of soft pine in place of the hard oak hitherto used for building raised the problem of how to protect external woodwork from the weather; hence the introduction of white paint was primarily a protective device. (Coloured paint was not employed architecturally until comparatively recent times; it is a matter for consideration as to whether it can ever be employed legitimately on the exterior elevations of buildings).

Another decorative material employed externally with considerable effect during the 18th century was wrought iron. The balcony, a Byzantine feature which crept into Renaissance architecture from Islam and was gladly accepted by European architects, was an excellent situation in which to display wrought iron; internally it became popular for the balustrading of staircases. Originally used for decorative purposes connected with ecclesiastical screenwork, wrought iron spread to the palisades and gateways of the great houses; the 18th-century mansion still displayed its grand entrance feature, now removed to the boundaries of its surrounding park and often accompanied by a pair of 'lodges' for the accommodation of the gatekeepers.

In this fashion the architecture of the European Renaissance spread throughout the world. During the progress of the last two centuries a number of new types of building had made their appearance. The new learning had brought many an ancient university into prominence and enriched it from time to time with groups of educational and residential structures. Libraries were not only founded in connection with these but were also to be found in the palaces of the period. Charitable institutions, mostly of ecclesiastical origin, still played a large part in European economy; the hospitals of the 16th century were no less commodious than those of modern times.

A type of building resurrected from Classical days by the architects of the Renaissance had been the theatre. Towards the end of the 16th century this had reappeared in its Roman form, a semicircle of tiered seating facing a lofty scena wall beyond which lay the great stage, the whole covered by a wide roof. Many an amateur architect of the Renaissance—Inigo Jones, for example—could utilize the stage of a theatre for experiments with elevational projects (Plate 83). No one had to live in his pasteboard palaces, nor was it very difficult to make these stand up. Thus Commoditie and Firmeness could be set aside in order that the designer's whole interest could be concentrated upon Delight. The oval-conscious Baroque architects of the 18th century exploited the potentialities of the theatre plan and also evolved ingenious structural compositions as they added tiers of galleries such as were appearing in the Protestant meeting-houses of the period. The nature of the theatre gave the Baroque architects every opportunity for indulging in riotous schemes of interior decoration; their example has been imitated in spirit by their successors up to the present day.

By the 18th century the day of the poor man was already in sight. During the Middle Ages he had existed as best he could. No one built him a house and he had no means to do so for himself. He was the slave of the landowner, whether the latter were embattled nobleman or merely country squire. One of the results of the Reformation was the emergence, in the place of the dispossessed ecclesiastic, of the small farmer; many such were able to build themselves humble houses attended by a few primitive farm structures. In the farm-houses of the 17th century we begin to see the emergence of a vernacular style of architecture which was to cover the countryside of Europe with unsophisticated versions of the neighbouring great house. But it was not until the latter part of the 18th century that anyone began to consider it necessary to build cottages for labourers.

104. A fine example of the elaborate timber churches of Russia
(Kishi)

105. The 'Russian Baroque' utilises every type of feature discoverable in the national architecture (Moscow)

Chapter XVIII

THE INDUSTRIAL ERA

We have now followed in outline the progress of architectural development in western Europe through its period of incubation preceding the zenith of the mediæval era during the 14th and 15th centuries and touched upon the nature of the cultural revolution which followed this. By about the year 1700 the Renaissance had completed its work of obliterating the architecture of mediæval Europe and replacing this with one approaching that of modern times. The glamour of elevation-designing, except where the Baroque enthusiasts were busily displaying their novelties in south-east Germany, was beginning to fade. The streets of western European cities were gradually being lined with multi-storied buildings displaying interminable façades of regimented rectangles and ruling cold straight lines against the sky.

Although the Europe of the 18th century had left the mediæval epoch far behind, its social structure still resembled that of the Middle Ages in that it was primarily an agricultural one. Its vitality was being augmented by an ever-expanding transport network extending throughout the world, but it was the countryside with its great estates which maintained the cities with food and the materials of trade. Attendant upon the former were now the rural farmhouses, while in the back streets of the towns were workshops containing primitive devices worked for the most part by simple man-power. The transport of goods was by water or—far more laboriously—by the horse-drawn cart.

Building construction was much as it had always been: the wall of masonry or brickwork supported the timber floor and the rafters of a roof the pitch of which varied according to the requirements of the material with which it was covered or the traditional taste of some particular region.

After the orgies of the 18th century its close saw elevational architecture settling down to a purely copyist style which not only reproduced features of Classical buildings stone-perfect but even transplanted copies of complete structures such as temples to western Europe and proudly employed them for the varied purposes of the day. Continental architects, unwilling to carry austerity too far, favoured the Corinthian style; England, less ebullient, was content to employ the sturdier Doric.

The close of the century witnessed the birth of a new era marked by the increasing employment of steam for driving machinery. The new source of power enabled far larger machines to be operated without diminishing the number or variety established in any one factory. The result was a considerable expansion in industrial building which introduced the factory as a new class of structure destined to play an important part in the architecture of the future. Early factories were simply large workshops: halls of no great height but as capacious as possible so as to hold the largest number of machines. Roofs were pitched as low as the nature of their covering would permit and supported by trusses scientifically designed and framed together in carpentry.

The times were such that even the owner of a building containing machinery had to pay due attention to the architectural presentation of its external elevations. The late 18th century had been a period during which much study had been devoted to architecture; society expected of all building owners that they would respect the conventions and see to it that elevations conformed to the accepted style of the period.

Fortunately this was one which was not unsuited for application to structures of a severely practical nature. The scholars of the second quarter of the 18th century had been industriously studying Classical sources and publishing illustrated volumes upon the results of their labours. This produced, a generation later, the beginnings of a Classic Revival which could be made to produce elevations suited to almost every kind of structure without the need for resorting to sculptural or other types of detailed ornament. This is particularly true of 'Doric'

England which by the end of the century was displaying façades for every class of building, sometimes complete even to a colonnaded portico. (See also Fig. 14.)

Fig. 14. The Classic Revival is the architecture of British India

Factories were apt to cover a large area of ground—valuable in a manufacturing town—unless they could be made multi-storied; the problem was then to make the upper floors strong enough to carry machinery without obstructing working space below by the insertion of masonry supports. The industrial engineers met this by making columns of cast iron; a column of quite small diameter could carry a considerable weight while taking up very little room.

The introduction of cast iron as a building material suggested further developments in structural engineering. Iron bars had already been used to tie together the side walls of buildings threatened with overturning by the spreading of a weakly-designed roof; they were now being utilized as a legitimate means of tying together a wide roof of low pitch. From this it was not a very difficult step to construct complete roof trusses in iron; by the beginning of the 19th century this innovation had become an accepted feature of industrial architecture and attractively-designed cast-iron roof trusses were taking the place of the older timber ones.

Although England was now established as the leading nation of the world its architectural achievements at this period cannot be described as spectacular; this, however, was no indication of its material prosperity. When the railways came, its restricted area made it suitable for the construction of railway systems the development of which resulted in the diverting of yet more building potential to the construction of engineering works. The country became covered with railway alignments marked by structures never before seen in architectural history. Strong bridges—of iron as well as masonry—spanned the English rivers; the countryside was covered by many-arched viaducts and pierced by deep cuttings lined with massive retaining walls. Nothing comparable with such engineering feats had been seen since the days of the great civilizations of the past; the very earthworks themselves represented enormous effort in the transport of material alone.

Europe joined in the railway boom and architecture found it had a serious rival. The railway station introduced another class of building. The modification of cast-iron framing to enable it to be glazed resulted in the covering-in of larger stations with glass roofs: another impressive innovation which challenged the creations of the architects of more conventional structures and became adapted to a variety of uses.

A change had come over the method of making window-glass. The blown glass of mediæval days fixed with strips of lead was by the 16th century being made in large sheets set between wooden glazing bars: the 19th century saw glass being cast in huge 'plates' which obviated the need for any division of the window and in consequence took much of the old liveliness out of elevations. As it happened plate-glass windows were not unsuited to the prevailing Neo-Classical architecture of the period.

Mid-19th-century affluence was beginning to seek the advertisement of a more opulent style of architecture than the Classic. Railway travel had so opened up Europe that its architects were able to investigate the possibilities of reviving something of the spirit of the ancient buildings of their own countries. Classic discipline had been firmly implanted in them—as much as anything through the mechanization which had completely permeated architecture through the medium of the T-square—but they were able to recover many of the old ornamental devices and introduce them into designs. The buildings of the period were enormous and could stand a good deal of this treatment; the mid-19th century architects made the most of their opportunities and erected façades which were a riot of pomp and opulence.

A period of architectural research was being inaugurated. In England, Georgian taste for scholarly excursions into Classical archæology was intermingled with a romantic nostalgia for our traditional Gothic, a trend which is well illustrated by a number of English buildings of the second half of the 18th century.

The western world was becoming saturated with architecture. A vast amount of building connected with the expansion of the new industrial cities was confronting everyone with architecture no matter which way they turned. The result was a general interest in the craft which brought it to the forefront of criticism directed at it from all sources.

By this time many had become depressed by two of the most prominent factors in the new building art. The first of these was the motive of industrialism, the second was the manner in which this was expressed by Classicism, either in its original or Renaissance form. The result was a tremendous reaction in favour of romanticism as expressed by a return to mediævalism. Thus by the middle of the 19th century the Gothic Revival burst into a spate of activity, all over western Europe, which rivalled the determined austerity of its Classical antagonists and almost threatened to extinguish their efforts entirely.

On the other side of the picture of these mid-19th-century monumental elevations is one of a very different type of building. Attendant upon the busy factories were the homes of the workers. Great numbers of labourers had been drawn from their rustic hovels to be housed in interminable rows of cottages set cheek by jowl and back to back: miserable parodies of the middle-class 'terraces' of a century earlier but doubtless more than adequate for the needs of a workman of the period. In all directions the manufacturing cities expanded into suburbs for the accommodation of many classes of persons forming a part of the industrial machine.

It was during the 19th century that the architectural skyline of the civilized world became transformed as forests of tall chimneys began to rise above its roofs; structures of monumental proportions but in fact purely engineering devices designed to speed the operation of the furnaces at their feet.

The introduction of steam-driven machinery made it necessary to expand the industrial system in order that factories might be erected which could make this machinery; hence the development of 'heavy industry' the products of which could be distributed upon the new railway systems instead of by horse-drawn or waterborne transport.

Heavy industry could not operate upon cast iron alone; steel, hitherto used for tools and weapons, had now to play a far larger part in manufacturing operations. As knowledge of the material improved and steel could be worked in the mass instead of in small pieces, steel beams began to take the place of the far weaker cast-iron variety which had been used at the beginning of the century. The greater reliability of steel and the ease with which it could be cut and drilled made it an important recruit to the growing company of building materials without which it would have been difficult to construct the large structures with their vast apartments which characterize the latter part of the 19th century.

The 18th century had seen the development throughout Europe of the middle-class house or 'villa' which in the next century spread throughout the countryside and gathered at the skirts of the towns. Such houses were usually compactly planned in the economical fashion which builders had learnt from the architectural copybooks and usually exhibited elevational treatments modelled on the popular style of the region and period.

The expansion of domestic architectural practice during the 17th and 18th centuries in order to provide accommodation for the middle classes had resulted in more attention being paid to economy in planning. It was now no longer possible to rely upon centrally-placed halls to provide circulation between the various rooms; thus the internal corridor was by the 18th century in general use. This innovation made for far better planning in all buildings of civic and commercial types as well and enabled the trading concerns of the 19th century to erect blocks of offices which could accommodate considerable numbers of clerical workers.

To improved planning appreciation may also be attributed the gathering together of individual homes into a single block of tenements or flats and the erection of large hotels, these often treated to architectural embellishment in a palatial fashion. Towards the end of the century the simple shop expanded into the multi-storied department store. The whole scale of buildings increased; to keep pace, their elevational treatments became more and more overloaded with 'architecture'.

The effect of the industrial age upon architecture was thus to introduce a new type of structure, the compact block of apartments which replaced the long range of the early days of the Renaissance. It is these building blocks which are the principal structures of the cities of the present day, corresponding to the 'house' factor in the secular architecture of the Middle Ages.

Enlargements of factories and the consequent improvement in roof design by the use of new materials had the effect of reintroducing the 'hall' factor which had lapsed since the end of the mediæval era. The great hall—be it railway station, cinema, stadium, or concert hall—now forms the second of the two chief types of great building met with today. It is in the external presentation of their great roofs that the modern architects are faced with an urgent problem which, at the moment, they appear to be making no attempt to reduce.

The industrial developments of the period—more particularly the railway boom—was playing a great part in the architecture of North America. The Spanish colonies in the south had completely surrendered to the entrancing Proto-Baroque extravagances of their mother country and had become transformed into a land covered with magnificent buildings displaying a rich but already archaic architecture indicative of the lost position of Spain in so far as the modern world was concerned. The United States, however, gladly followed the cultural leadership of the country whose political sovereignty they had set aside.

North American architecture of the 19th century was based on the Classical Revival as exhibited by English buildings but was already overshooting them in matters of scale. By the end of the Georgian period they had assimilated the Italian dome and were raising it above purely Classical buildings with such success that there could have been no doubt as to the future potentialities of their architects. Their principal buildings were the 'capitols', civic palaces erected in the principal cities and accommodating the governments of the individual states. American cities were not behind those of Europe in constructing factories, commercial and public buildings, all presented in monumental fashion but with strictly Classical elevations in a scholarly vein and probably the finest examples of their kind in the world.

By the end of the century the scale of American buildings had increased until they had become the largest structures ever seen. The peculiar situation of New York, tightly constricted upon its peninsula, made it necessary to raise the heights of buildings to a fantastic degree; hence the development of that peculiarly American structure the skyscraper, a building which is in fact simply a tower covering a considerable ground area and raised to a proportionate height.

These remarkable buildings excepted, by the end of the century the architectural efforts of America and Europe were being directed along approximately parallel lines. Planning and building technique had been as it were internationalized; only in elevations could regional and personal tastes provide variations upon the standard types of building. The generally approved monumental style of the period had degenerated into a despairing assortment of architectural features collected from various sources; most of the changes had been rung and there seemed to be no future at all for elevational architecture.

During the second half of the century a number of books had been published upon the buildings of past ages which architectural his-

106. An eighteenth-century middle-class home in America copied from a 'Georgian' prototype in England ('Westover')

107. American 'Colonial' is a style of Classic Revival architecture translated into timber and adjusted to suit the climate

torians—mostly amateurs—had been collecting together and classified under 'historical styles'. These publications gave architects opportunities for assimilating information concerning the elevational details of any particular 'style' and attempting to convert their buildings into examples of this. In almost every case the task they set themselves was impossible of achievement so that they had to content themselves with making certain that all details conformed in every particular with those of the style they had selected. The educational system by which the profession was carried on meant that the articled pupil very often had no alternative but to perpetuate the tastes of his principal.

The schools of architecture which were being founded also made much use of these architectural histories. The Ecole des Beaux Arts, however, tried to detach itself from the movement by teaching the principles of design and encouraging the student to ignore past examples and create original ornament. Unfortunately the theory was taken too literally so that no use was made of the fine designs handed down through the centuries while the 19th-century artist proved himself unable to make good the deficiency at a moment's notice. Moreover the architectural schools had become so obsessed with the elevational side of architecture that they took no account of the fact that the design of the building itself was the first duty of the architect and that its ornamentation was a matter of secondary importance. Lacking any true foundation whatsoever, the 'Art Nouveau' happily proved ephemeral.

The modern architect has other matters to attract his attention than the external presentation of his building. For every monumental structure which appears today there are hundreds of purely practical ones of comparable scale but erected to play a vital part in the bustling economy of the modern world. The 20th-century architect has no time for the comparison of Byzantine detail with Egyptian; he has to produce something which is convenient, quickly erected, and not too expensive. He is searching for new materials and constructional devices—æsthetic details can be left to a specialist with less comprehensive responsibility.

The discovery of the steel beam had been followed by the development of the efficient structural system by which steel beams and stanchions are framed together and the floors and walls filled-in as separate panels. The metal beam had taken the place of the heavy timber girder but still carried wooden floor joists covered with boarding until the invention of the solid floor which resulted from the discovery of concrete.

Concrete is the latest of modern building materials. Derived from mortar, it is simply a mass of this mixed with large pebbles and cast in a mould which is removed after the mortar has 'set'. The ground floors of factories were first formed of concrete laid upon the earth to provide a solid foundation for machinery. It could also be laid upon wooden floors, but a better method was to apply it to metal joists which were less perishable and could satisfactorily be enclosed within the floor itself as reinforcement. From this was developed the scientifically-engineered reinforced-concrete floor which could be employed with advantage in the horizontal panels of the steel-framed structure. From this type of floor it was an easy stage to the flat roof of reinforced concrete, covered with a layer of asphalt to render it waterproof.

The introduction of the steel frame and the flat roof into building design had revolutionized building mass. The building bay is an ancient planning device, but such bays had hitherto been traverse divisions of a long building having a pronounced axis. The new type of planning bay was not a strip but a rectangle which might be entirely enclosed within the structure; bays could be added in any direction and to fill any outline so that the ground-plans of buildings began to expand to cover large areas of ground beneath a single roof. Vertically, each bay was a box enclosed within the members of the steel frame; these boxes could be piled one upon the other to any height and to produce almost any kind of shape. Thus the structure could be separated into any desired component masses by adjusting the steel frame to suit.

Throughout architectural history large buildings have been designed to incorporate several component parts. The 17th-century town hall with its bell-tower is an example. But such designs may have been produced without any true appreciation of the principles of proportion; the architects of the day were possibly unable—even when models were first set up—to visualize exactly how a huge structure would actually appear in three dimensions. In the early days of the Renaissance architect a building was composed of a plan surrounded by four elevations; from the point of view of presentation it was these that counted and not the general mass of the structure seen without its architectural or sculptural ornament.

The problem as to what constitutes good proportion is a vexed one and—although a very great deal will always be written on the subject —it may well be that the whole matter is one of personal taste. It is perhaps unwise to be too glib about it or even to assume that the taste of, say, the 15th century would have been the same as ours today. Or indeed even that the old architect could appreciate any other factors beside scale and ornament. Certainly many of the elevational designs of the magnificent buildings of even the Renaissance would receive low marks in a Royal Institute of British Architects examination on the score that the proportion was disagreeable.

In other days, when planning requirements were simple, most of the architect's skill was expended upon the elevational presentation of his building, especially in the siting of its sculptural ornamentation. As today this constitutes the least important of the architect's duties it has been found possible to assist him by formulating certain elementary principles of design for the most part concerned with the factor of contrast as displayed in mass, form, direction, and proportion.

Soon after the beginning of the 20th century the architectural schools began to appreciate that the scale of modern buildings was now such that it was essential to apply these principles of design both to the structure as a whole and also to the individual masses of which it was composed. A building could no longer be left to develop as it would, thereafter to be equipped with laboriously-conceived elevations in some 'style' or combinations of these. It was the mass which had to be considered and designed; the planning of internal accommodation must be adjusted to suit this and the bay system determined by the stanchions of the steel skeleton round which the mass was framed and which had thus to be carefully designed to this end.

The art of elevation-designing was relegated to the background of architecture. This was not only inevitable but indeed fortunate as it emancipated the architect from the scourge of the historical 'styles' from which most of the known motifs were derived. Above all it freed architecture from the shackles of the 'Orders' which for half a millennium had loaded the practitioner with a burden of responsibility to which every generation has added its devoted quota. The great buildings of the 20th century could not assimilate the Orders any more—nor, indeed, could they in the magnitude of their ever-increasing masses incorporate any of the familiar features of historical architecture.

Modern taste no longer requires the addition of sculptural ornament to architecture. Even the old architectural devices once employed to punctuate elevations are no longer deemed necessary. Aedicular treatment, unsuited to the modern scale, has vanished together with the 'styles' which employed it. The fine building of today is an essay in proportion: firstly in the mass, secondly in the pattern of dark openings contrasted with the solid walling around them. This is true architecture, which owes nothing to the assistance of the decorator—the 'sub-contractor' upon whom the engineer-architect of the past was often so completely dependent for aesthetic effect.

The modern building block, constructed of a steel skeleton with the panels filled-in with various types of material, needs to be covered with a skin of some sort. While monumental structures can be completely cased in masonry or brickwork, many industrial buildings are simply 'rendered' in plaster of some kind. Lime plaster has been employed to cover the walls of buildings, externally as well as internally, for thousands of years; it is, however, not a very permanent covering if continually exposed to the rigours of the European climate. During the 18th century various experiments were made to improve the quality of external renderings and at last a stone was found which would produce an insoluble cement in place of the lime hitherto used. The cement used today is synthetic and to all intents and purposes indestructible; renderings made with it form a universal method of covering the structure of modern industrial buildings.

One of the results of emancipation from the historical styles was the abandoning of the conventional form of opening. Hitherto the width of an opening had been governed by the ability to span its head with a lintel or an arch; steel beams now made it unnecessary so to limit the design. The new 'landscape' window could be expanded laterally until it passed, if required, all round the building to give the maximum light possible to any given story; hence the development of 'stratified' elevations which are nowadays popular with multi-storied factories and even commercial buildings.

In such experiments as these most modern nations co-operated; architecture was no longer regional but international. The search for new materials went on. Throughout the history of architecture builders have been searching for methods of bridging openings. The strength of supports was never a serious problem; the pier of masonry or brickwork could always be depended upon to carry any normal load. The stone lintel had a limited carry; the arch increased the span but threw an eccentric load upon supports which in many cases—as in the crossings of the Frankish churches—shattered or overturned them. Cast-iron and, later, steel beams, broadened still further the spans of openings; there was, however, a definite limit in that the long steel beam was extremely heavy and wasteful of an expensive material.

The failure of a beam takes place firstly by deflection and then by fracture. The deflection introduces two stresses within the beam itself, one of which is compressional and the other tensional. Thus a beam should be designed so as to be compressionally strong at one point and tensionally strong in another; thus it can best resist the action of the two stresses to which it is being subjected. This is the principle of the reinforced concrete beam in which the concrete takes the compressional pressure while the reinforcement of steel bars embedded in it is so placed as to resist the tensional strain.

Reinforced concrete can now be designed to withstand pressure of any magnitude and in any direction no matter how eccentric. Thus the old problem of how to span an opening has taken on a new aspect. There are no longer any openings, and no longer any spans. The modern reinforced-concrete building is not erected by the traditional method of placing objects one upon another in such a fashion that they will not fall off. Today we can produce a cohesive frame, calculated in advance down to the most minute detail: its construction is not a matter of erection but of casting in a mould.

Primitive architecture was concerned with the construction of buildings; civilized architecture with their external presentation. Plastic, functionalistic—to what new heights of architectural splendour will these latest adventures lead us?

POSTSCRIPT

'Commoditie, Firmeness, and Delight' . . . three hundred years ago they constituted the conditions by which an aspiring architect was to be directed. How do they stand today?

'Commoditie' . . . as always this is the architect's first concern. Accumulated experience has now taught us how many square feet of floor space a man needs in which to live in adequate comfort or occupy himself efficiently in any other task. The provision of accommodation is thus a matter of assembling a multiplicity of units each of which is itself planned in accordance with an established formula. A percentage must of course be added for circulation horizontally and between stories, the heights of these being calculated as the minimum necessary to provide adequate ventilation and space for plumbing and electrical services. Economy in circulation influences both the area of each floor and the number of stories. Thus a rectangular prism having its three dimensions calculated by such methods will provide the most efficient form of building for any specified purpose.

'Firmeness' . . . throughout the course of architectural history the architect has had to invent his own constructional devices—therein lies the secret of much of the architecture of the past. But the dragons are all dead now. Skilled engineers can supply the knowledge by means of which almost any architectural conception can be converted into reality.

'Delight' . . . in the days of Sir Henry Wotton every building was treated as a work of art. The architect was a novelty, a dilettante consorting with the world of fashion and eager to contribute to its conceits. Walls, ceilings—floors even—not only served their structural purpose but were also considered as canvases upon which to display decorative schemes in curves, carving, and colour. Those were the old days. Nowadays we know that a building is a machine, speedily constructed and efficient in operation—a machine in which to live, or, in order to live, to work.

STIRLING COUNTY LIBRARY

GLOSSARY

abacus: uppermost member of a capital.

ædicule: structural composition employed on a reduced scale for ornamental purposes.

aisle: longitudinal division of a building, especially those flanking the main structure.

alcazar: Spanish palace, modelled on large Arab house (*al kasr*).

ambulatory: aisle passing behind the high altar of a great church.

andron: reception room of Hellenic house.

anta: pilaster forming respond at end of colonnade.

apse: semicircular or polygonal end to a building.

apsidiole: small apse, generally serving as chapel.

arcade: range of arches.

architrave: lintel; lowermost member of entablature; surround to window or door opening.

arcuated: architectural style employing the arch.

aron: cult niche in synagogue containing sacred scrolls.

atrium: entrance feature; outer court of Roman house; forecourt of early temple or church.

axial plan: church having central tower but no transept.

baluster: short shaft, generally bul-bous, used in Byzantine windows and Renaissance parapets.

barrel-vault: simple vault like that of tunnel.

basilica: Hellenistic and Roman structure provided for public gatherings; early church of simple form with nave and aisles but no central feature.

bastion: solid tower provided to carry military engines.

bay: transverse subdivision of a building, hence unit of measurement.

bell: tall concave echinus.

bifora: two-light window with central shaft.

blockwork: building with logs laid horizontally.

boss: feature covering junction of vaulting ribs.

brace: diagonal timber employed as tensional member.

buttress: masonry provided to resist overturning thrust.

calidarium: steam room of Roman bath building.

capital: feature provided at top of column to carry lintel.

cavetto: concave moulding.

cella: principal apartment of Roman temple.

centering: temporary wooden framework upon which to turn arch.

chamber: room on upper floor, especially bedroom.

chancel: eastern portion of parish church containing altar.

chevet: elaborate eastern termination of a great church.

choir: part of great church containing stalls of monks or canons.

cimborio: central lantern of octagonal form.

clerestory: central portion of aisled building raised above its aisle roofs to provide sites for windows.

cloister: square yard enclosed by principal monastic (claustral) buildings; walk surrounding this.

coffer: sunk panel in ceiling or vault.

colonnade: range of columns.

column: circular support, either turned out of single stone (monolithic) or built in drums.

conch: vault of apse, a quarter of a sphere.

corbel: stone bracket.

corbelled: stone courses arranged as a series of corbels, especially as in a primitive form of vault.

cornice: projecting band appearing at wall-top; uppermost member of entablature.

cortile: courtyard of Italian house.

course: single layer of stones in walling.

cove: concave cornice.

crenellation: military parapet provided with crenels or apertures through which to shoot.

crossing: central area in cruciform building, especially church.

cross-vault: barrel-vaults intersecting at right angles.

cruciform: building planned with four arms meeting at central area or crossing.

cubiform: capital formed by cutting off the angles of a cushion capital.

cupola: small dome.

curtain: wall of fortification extending between towers or bastions.

cushion: Byzantine form of Doric capital with echinus square on plan.

distylar: porch with two columns supporting lintel.

dog-leg: stair passing from floor to floor in two straight flights set side by side.

dolmen: megalithic tomb-chamber with large capstone supported upon orthostats.

dormer: window set in pitched roof.

dosseret: capital placed above another.

drum: stone forming part of column.

duplex: arcade in which columns alternate with piers.

echinus: lowermost member of capital, supporting abacus.

elevation: vertical aspect of building.

enceinte: wall surrounding group of buildings.

entablature: horizontal feature passing above Classical colonnade, comprising architrave, frieze, and cornice.

entasis: deliberate bowing of a wall or column in order to counteract optical illusion of concavity.

exæron: central area of Hellenistic basilica.

exedra: large semicircular planning feature, generally external and not roofed.

fan-vault: late development of mediæval vaulting system in which ceiling appears as series of open fans.

flying buttress: arch carrying thrust onto buttress isolated from wall requiring abutment.

foliated: soffit of arch subdivided into series of smaller arches as ornamental device.

forebuilding: tower provided to cover first-floor entrance; porch-tower.

four-poster: Byzantine building having central feature supported upon four pillars or posts.

freestone: building stone capable of being worked by masons.

frigidarium: swimming bath in Roman bath building.

frieze: medial feature of entablature; horizontal band, often ornamented.

gable: end wall of building covered with pitched roof.

groin: intersection of two portions of cross-vault.

hall: large communal apartment in mediæval house.

haunch: sides of arch between springing and apex.

hip: intersection of two pitched roofs at external angle of building.

hypostyle: apartment having ceiling supported by numerous closely-spaced columns.

hypsosis: term suggested as convenient to indicate the motive which inspires the architects of monumental buildings to pile these around a lofty central feature; the dominating mass rising above a structure thus inspired.

iwan: cave-like reception-room of Moslem house having one end open to the air.

jetty: projecting ends of floor-joists carrying timber framing of upper story.

joist: beam carrying floor-boards.

kasr: Moslem great house with internal court.

khan: caravanserai; large courtyard surrounded by arcaded loggias for sheltering travellers.

lantern: central feature of Byzantine or Gothic church raised above surrounding roofs to provide sites for windows lighting crossing below.

light: subdivision of window.

lintel: stone or timber beam bridging opening in wall or colonnade.

lodge: small building adjoining larger structure and having lean-to roof; mason's workshop.

loggia: open porch fronted with colonnade or arcade.

machicolation: military parapet brought out in front of wall-face on corbels.

makad: first-floor loggia in Moslem house.

mandara: reception room of Moslem house.

mansard: roof having two different pitches, a flatter above a steeper.

maqsura: sanctuary of mosque.

masonry: walling built of dressed stones set to display two faces and filled with a rubble core.

mastaba: wide stone bench outside Egyptian house; early Egyptian sepulchral monument of similar form.

medressa: Moslem school.

megalithic: building with very large stones set on end and interlocking one with another.

megaron: principal apartment of a house of the Aegean era.

metope: square panel between two triglyphs of a Doric frieze.

mihrab: Moslem prayer-niche.

Minoan: architecture of ancient Crete.

Moghreb: 'sunset-land', western Islam (hence Morocco).

mullion: vertical stone bar separating lights of window.

Mudejar: Moslem under Spanish domination.

naos: principal apartment in Classical temple, called by Romans 'cella'.

narthex: loggia passing across façade of Byzantine church and sometimes returned along its flanks.

nave: principal arm of church, accommodating laity.

newel: masonry nucleus or shaft around which a stair revolves.

nymphæum: Hellenistic wall fountain and public washing-place.

oecus: Hellenic house; principal apartment in this; principal living-room in Roman house.

ogee: sinuous curve struck from two centres.

Order: ordinance of Classical architecture.

order: one of a number of arch-rings set with their faces projecting one before the other.

oriel: bay window of first-floor apartment carried upon corbelling instead of rising from ground level.

orthostat: large stone set upon end.

parabemata: sacristies flanking the presbytery of Byzantine church.

parapet: low wall provided to protect persons walking upon roof or wall-top, also employed as decorative feature.

pastos: colonnaded loggia fronting principal apartments in Hellenic house.

patio: Spanish courtyard.

pavilion: tower with tent-like roof forming part of early-Renaissance great house; vertical feature recalling this in later façades.

pediment: Classical form of gable with low-pitched roof.

pendentive: masonry in form of spherical triangle provided to carry base of dome down upon square plan.

peribolos: large enclosure surrounded by colonnades.

periptal: building entirely surrounded by colonnades.

peristyle: courtyard surrounded by colonnades.

piano nobile: first floor of a domestic building containing principal apartments.

pier: masonry support.

pilaster: column attached to wall.

pillar: supporting member, less massive than pier.

pinnacle: weighting member set upon buttress; ornamental feature derived from this.

pitch: angle of slope of roof.

plate: timber at feet of rafters and carrying these upon wall-top.

plinth: base of a building; thickening of walling at this point; architectural feature emphasizing this.

porch: small building provided to protect an entrance.

portico: large porch incorporating colonnades or arcades.

presbytery: portion of great church extending between choir and sanctuary; eastern arm of great church.

pronaos: ante-chamber of naos.

propylæa: monumental entrance feature of Hellenistic architecture.

proscenium: stage of Hellenic theatre.

prostyle: free-standing colonnaded portico open at both ends.

pseudo-cruciform: church with transepts but no central feature.

purlin: longitudinal roof-timber helping to stiffen rafters.

pulvin: wide capital set above another to help carry heavy walling without damaging the former.

qibla: direction of Mecca.

quadripartite: ribbed cross-vault.

quoin: angle-stone.

rabat: Moslem fortified monastery.

rafter: roof-timber.

relieving arch: one constructed in walling above arch or lintel to relieve pressure upon this.

respond: support at one end of arcade.

ridge: meeting-line of rafters of pitched roof.

roll-moulding: simple moulding of half-round section.

rubble: rough unwrought stone.

rustication: masonry with face undressed; joints incised to accentuate them and prevent fracture of edges of stone in the event of movement of building.

salon: post-mediæval successor of great hall.

scena: long building passing behind stage of Hellenic theatre.

shaft: portion of column between base and capital; slender support or decorative feature imitating this.

six-poster: four-poster church having two additional supports to carry lateral galleries.

soffit: underside of arch or lintel.

solar (pron. *soller*): upper floor in mediæval building.

span: width of a building, roof, or opening.

spandrel: triangular area in elevation, especially walling above haunch of arch.

spire: tall tapering roof above tower.

springing-line: level above which an arch begins to turn.

squinch: arch bridging across internal angle.

steeple: tall compound structure above tower.

stela: tall Classical tombstone.

stoa: long colonnaded portico of Hellenic days.

string-course: band of ornament employed for horizontal punctuation of elevations.

strut: timber member designed to withstand compressional stress.

tablinum: reception room of Roman house.

temenos: sacred enclosure, usually surrounding temple.

tepidarium: great assembly hall of Roman bath building.

trabeated: style of architecture displaying the lintel in preference to the arch.

tracery: decorative arrangement of stone glazing bars in large mediæval window.

transept: lateral arm of church, generally flanking crossing.

triclinium: dining-room of Roman house.

triconch: a feature comprising three apses, one fronting and two flanking, a sanctuary or some such important apartment.

triforium: access passage to clerestory windows of great church; (*not* gallery above aisle).

triglyph: vertical component of Doric frieze alternating with metope.

trilithon: megalithic feature comprising pair of orthostats supporting lintel.

trimmer: beam provided to carry end of another deprived of its support from wall or pillar.

tumbling: brickwork laid obliquely in gable or coping.

tumulus: sepulchral mound.

turret: small tower, generally set upon a building and not itself rising from the ground.

tympanum: semicircular area between lintel and soffit of relieving arch over.

vault: arched stone ceiling.

volute: spiral feature forming principal motif of Ionic capital and also seen in reduced form at angles of Corinthian capital.

voussoir: arch stone.

web: stone filling between ribs of vaulting.

ziggurat: Sumerian pyramid.

INDEX

[*For definitions, see Glossary, pages 291 to 296*]

INDEX

INDEX

Corinthian capital and column, 71, 82, 84, 165, Pl. 18, 206, 209; at Bosra, 116; Frankish, 163; Gothic, 193; half-columns, 247; porticoed, Pl. 18; post-baroque, 278; pulvin and, 112; rediscovery of, 177, 182; in tepidaria, 94

Corneto rock-tomb, 81

Cornices, 237, Pl. 80; bracketed, 228; classical, 68, 228, 229; Egyptian, 53–4; external arches with, 273, Pl. 47; of S. Croce, 208; Spanish late-mediaeval, 247

Cortile: origins of, 142; and patio, 223, 248; Pl. 84

Cotswold domestic style, 214

Cottages, early labourers', 276

Country house, 15th c., 224–7; *and see* Great House

Courtyards; Byzantine, 128; covered Egyptian, 45, 49; an English example, Pl. 94; Italian arcaded, 222–3; Hittites' avoidance of, 58, 59; in early church planning, 101, 107; mosques and, 132, 137–8, Pls. 36, 37; oval, in megalithic architecture, 55; peristylar, 71; principle of, 128; Roman colonial, Pl. 13; west-European, 200, Fig. 10; zenith of, 223

Courtyard mosque, 137–8, Pls. 36, 37

Cremona, municipal palace at, 175

Crete, *see* Minoan

Cruciform plan: Armenian, 123; Crusader, 173; origins of, 154; Russian, 125; Spanish, 16th c., 252

Crusades, The, 164–79; Anatolia and, 137, 139, 140; brickmaking and, 196; castles and churches of, 169 seqq.; Pls. 25, 26, 30, 40, 46 48, 55, Fig. 8; Syrian sources, 170

Ctesiphon, 109, Pl. 19

Cubiform capitals, 163, 166

Cupola, Renaissance forms of, 241

Curtain-walls, 176–7

Curved timber, Gothic and, 21

Curved walls, baroque, 266–7, Pl. 100

Cushion capitals, 127, 166, 177

Cuxa, Church at, Pl. 48

Dadoes: Assyrian sculptured, 38, 41; orthostatic, 56, 59, 60

Damascus (mosque), 133–4

Decapolis, basilican churches of, 108

Deir-el-Bahari (Thebes), Pl. 3

Delphi, Fig. 3

Dendera (temple), 50

Department stores, 283

Design, principles of, 287

Diana's temple, Ephesus, 70, 72

Diaphragm: principle, 93, Pls. 16, 17; arches, 110; walls, 59

Diocletian: palace of (Spalato), 94; thermae of, 95

Distortions (Parthenon), 69

Distylar porticoes, 47–8; Persian, 144

Dog-leg Stairways, Minoan, 62

Domes: Pls. 23, 28, 29, 77, 98; of American

revival, 284; Armenian, 116, 122, 123; bulbous, 126, 148, 271; development of true, 102; 'four-sided', 264, Pl. 97; as Islamic feature, 147–8; Italian, 265, Pl. 98; Italian Renaissance circular, 252; of London and Paris, 265; Mexican ornamental, 253–4; of *mihrab* bay, 141, Pl. 38; Moslem introduction to, 138; Renaissance, 239; Russian, 273; of St Peter's, Rome, 238–9, Pl. 77; of mosque sanctuaries, 141, 146; Sassanian, 115, 121; Seljuk use of, 139; saucer, 121, 123, 239; Semi-, 119, 178; Spanish ecclesiastical, 252; stages in evolution of, 114, 115; with winged projections, 154, Pl. 23

Domestic developments, 210–30; Byzantine, 174, Pl. 34; Frankish, 162, 174–5; Islamic, 146; seventeenth-century, 262 seqq.; thirteenth-century, 211 seqq.; western mediaeval, 174

Dominicans, 207

Dorian: debt to Aegean, 69; origins, 66

Doric order, 68–9, 129, 241; English post-baroque, 278, 279; temples of, Pls. 9, 14

Dormers, 214: gables, 256, 257, 258; window, origins of, 197

Double-curved walls, 267, Pl. 100

Draught-exclusion, 229

Dub-lah-Makh (Ur), Pl. 2

Dugga, Pl. 18

'Duplex' system, 154, 155, 156, 157, 160

Dura fortifications, 75–6

Durham cathedral, 156, 157

'Dutch' gable, creation of, 257

Early: Egyptian temple, 50–1; Renaissance styles, Pls. 76, 93

Ecole des Beaux Arts, 285

Edfu (temple), 50, 53, 74, Pl. 6; debased Corinthian at, 74

Egypt, 42–54; dominant religion of, 21, 42; empire period, 48–9

Eighteenth-century country-house: American, Pl. 106; English, Pl. 96

El Ahmar (mosque), 140

Elevational architecture, 26, 227–8; civic buildings and, 221; experiments in, 231 seqq.; Gothic, 201, 202 seqq.; interior decoration and 229; Italian 221–2; late mediaeval, 213 Pl. 68; relegation of, 277, 287; Renaissance study of, 219; Roman revival of, 232–3; schools, concentration on, 285; Spanish, 248; theatrical essays in, Pl. 83

El Hakim (mosque), 134

Ellingen, Pl. 97

Elliptical arch, brickwork, Pl. 19

El Pilar cathedral, Saragossa, 251

Ely cathedral, 157, 161, 237, Pl. 42

Enclosed courtyard principle, 25

English architectural influence, 274, 275

Entablatures, 68, 84, 232, Pl. 75

Entasis, Sumerian, 35

Erectheion, 70

INDEX

INDEX

Grille, as façade feature, 248, Pl. 87
Grooved flanking portals, 36, Pl. 2
Gun bastion, 244

Hadrian's tomb, 102
Hagia Sophia, Constantinople, 119, 141, 189, Pls. 28, 29
Haikal, 117
Half-columns, 82
Half-domes, 83, 84
Half-timbering: Minoan, 61; possibilities of, 62–3; Roman provincial, 97
Halicarnassos, 102
Hall-chamber, 212
Hall-churches, 196, 197, Pls. 60, 63, 64
'Hall' factor, in factory building, 283
Hammurabi, 1, 36, 60
Hanging gardens of Babylon, 37
Hanging mats as room walls, 31
Hardwood, and W. European styles, 21, 22, 151
Harem's influence on architecture, 145
Harlech, 203
Harun-er-Raschid, 135
Hassan, Sultan, tomb-chamber of, 140
Hatfield House, Pl. 94
Hathor columns (Dendera), 53
Hatra, 109
Hattusas (Hittite city), 58, 59
Heating as new preoccupation, 230
Heavy industry, building for, 282
Hebrew temples, 58
Height (*see also* Hypsosis), 24, 25, 32–4, 94, 103–4, 184, 187, 203; in Gothic 'vertical,' 203; in urban planning, 260
Heilsberg, 202, Fig. 10
Hellenism, 106–8; after Alexander, 73–85; eclipse of, 85
Hera's temple, 68
Herrera, 251, 262
Herringbone bricklaying, 19, 30
Hersfeld abbey church, 155
Hertogenbosch (church), Pl. 54
High baroque, 269
High galleries, 249, 255, Pls. 71, 87
High Gothic, 188, Pl. 51
Hilani (sanctuary), 58
Hilly sites, Hittites and, 59
Hipped roof: Etruscan, 81; Frankish, 152; 'mansard,' 264
'Historical styles,' 284–5, 287
Hittites, 50, 51, 55 seqq.; Anatolia and, 37, 38, 40, 41, 60; Assyrians' debt to, 41, 57; Byzantine debt to, 58, 59; citadels of, 58; 'great houses' of, 57–8; houses of, as European ancestor, 128; importance of, 58; newel-staircases of, 58; *piano nobile* of, 58; portal of, 60; temples, paucity of, 58; terrace construction of, 59; Troy attacked by, 63
Hollow walls, 19
Honeycomb: dome, Russian, 273; pendentive, 148–9

Hoods over windows, Byzantine, 128
'Hook and band' door-and-window-fastenings, 234
Horizontal circulation, problem of, 259, 263, 283
Horseshoe arch, 135, 147
Hospitals, 16th c., 276
Hotels, in modern sense, 283
Hôtels (nobles' 15th c.), 223–4
Houses: Byzantine type, 128, Fig. 5, Pl. 34; early functions of, 23; Persian, 143; Roman gentleman's, 96; Roman provincial, 97; winged, 144; wooden, 112. *See* Figs. 2, 5 *and 6, also* Pls. 13, 34, 91, 94, 96, 106, 107, *and* Oecus
Hulagu (Mongol conqueror), 138
Hyksos dynasty, 48, 61
Hypaethral halls, 80
Hypostyle: Egyptian origins of, 46; features, at Persepolis, 144; halls, 46, 47, 48, 49, 50, 52, Pl. 4; sanctuaries of mosques, 133 seqq.
Hypsosis (height factor, see Glossary), 153, 154, 158, 271, 272, Pl. 28; Byzantine, 119, 128; Greek, 128; Justinian's, 117; later Byzantine, 104; Moslem disregard of, 141, 142; oval plan and, 269; Roman brick and, 124; Russian, 271–2, 274, Pl. 105

Ibn Tulun mosque, 134
Iconian (Konia) and Islam, 136, 137, 139, 140, *and see* Seljuk
Ictinus, 69
'Ifriqua' (Tunisia), 136
Ile de France, 177, 182; Gothic of, in Rhineland, 187–8
Il Gesu church (Rome), 241
Imhotep, 43, 44, 46, 52
Imperial Roman arch, 95
Indestructible cement, 288
Indo-European cradle of architecture, 30
Industrial era, 277–89
Inner courtyard, late Babylonian, 39–40
Intercolumniation, 94, 236
Internal corridor, and circulation, 283; *see* Horizontal c.
International nature of modern architecture, 289
Intersecting vaults, 89
Invalides, Les, 264
Ionian origins, 66–7, 70, 76
Ionic, 70, 71, 129
Ireland, Roman churches in, 152
Iron as building material, 280
Irrigation, Moslem, 150
Islam, 131–50 contribution of, to Gothic, 205; congregation problem solved by, 132; S. Mediterranean peoples and, 179; waning influence of, 246
Islamic: great house, styled on, 201, Fig. 10; minaret, 129; Sevillian, 211, Pl. 53
Ispahan mosque, 141
Italy: absence of detail in, 209; city walls (Renaissance), 245; impoverishment of, 190;

INDEX

Renaissance architecture in, defects of, 250; republican churches of, 208–9; Spanish fusion with, 241

Ivan the Terrible, 271

Iwan, 65, 96, 109, 110, 134, 136, 137, 138, 139, 140, 141, Pl. 19; origin of, 56; at Omayyid's palace, 145; stone-roofed, 110; in triconch development, 145; of Ukheidr, 145

Jerash, 108–9, Pl. 10
Jerichow, Pl. 40
Jesuits, the, 253, 266
Jewish synagogue, 99, 100, 101
Joinery, invention of, 18, 22
Joists: metal, for concrete floors, 286
Joisted floors, 226, 229, 230; successors of, 286
Jones, Inigo, 261, 276. See Pl. 83
Julius Caesar's memorial basilica (Antioch), 83
Justinian's churches, 116, 117

Kairwan (mosque), 134, Pl. 38
Kalaat Siman, Pl. 25
Kalawun, sultan, mausoleum of, 140
Karnak (Thebes temple), 48, 49, 50, 72, Pl. 4; lotus columns at, 52
Kasr, 142, 200, 201, 204, 225, 255; Italian adoption of, 176; Teutonic Knights and, 215
Kassites, 37
Keep: *see* Fortified house; survival of towers of, 215
Khans, 134, 142
Khorsabad columns, 60
Khufa (pyramid), 44, 46
Kiev, 272
Kiln-dried bricks, 20, 30
Kings: Ahmose I, 38, 63; Akhenaten, 51; Amenhotep III, 51; Mena, 43; Sargon of Akkad, 32; Thothmes III, 52; Zozer, 43, 44; names of, on bricks, 30–1, 37
Kish, Temples of, 38
Kishi church, Pl. 104
Knights Templars, 154
Knossos, 60, Fig. 1
Kolomenskoye, Pl. 103
Kufic lettering as ornament, 149
Kurdistan, 29

La Madeleine church (Verneuil), Pl. 57
'Landscape' window, 288
Landshut, Pl. 63
Lantern towers: English, 173; Lombardic and Ottonian, 158–9, 162; of Saint Peter's, Rome, 238; Spanish, 168; tendency of, to collapse, 180, 181; of Toro, 173, Pl. 46
Laon cathedral, Pl. 50
Lateral spaciousness replacing vertical, 197, 198
Lay-brothers, 171
Lead, as roof cover, 193, 212; strip, for glazing, 280
Leptis (Tripolitania), 83
Lerida cathedral, 188

Liebfraukirche (Trier), 187–8
Light-wells, Minoan, 62
Limburg: abbey church, 155; cathedral, 187
Lime: mortar, 20; plaster, superseded, 288
Lincoln cathedral, 203, Pl. 61
Lintels: early Greek, 68; Egyptian, 54–5; Hittite, 60
Lion Gate: Boghaz Keui, Pl. 7; Mycenae, Pl. 8
Lion tympanum, Mycenae, 66
Living-room, modern, 230
Lodges, of 'great house,' 275
Lodging apartments for travellers, 212–3
Loggias, 62, 67 seqq.; arcaded, S. European, 176 domestic, 112, 151–2, 174–6, 223, 254; Frankish domestic, 162; Frankish ecclesiastical, 152; of Greek temples, 67–8, 72; ground floor, domestic, 162; Islamic, 132, 143, 144, Fig. 6; Italian, civic, 222–3; Italian multi-storied, 223, Pl. 86; Minoan, 62; pillared, 77; as protection against snow, 151–2, 174; roof-top, origin of, 145; Spanish arcaded, colonial, 254; of wooden houses, 112, 151–2, 174
Loggia del Capitano (Vicenza), Pl. 78
Lombardic styles, 157, 161–2, 173, 207; architects of, 160, 162
Lotus-type columns, 52, 53
Louvre, royal palace, 256
Luxor, 49, 51; temple at, 49

Macedonia, 73–5, 76
Machicolations, 206, 216
Magna Graecia, 81, 82, 86
Maisons-Lafitte, château of, Pl. 95
Makad, 144, 145
Mandara, 33
Mansard roof, 261, 264, Pl. 95
Many-gabled domestic style, 214
Maqsura, 141
Marburg, narrow aisles of, 196
Marienberg Marienwerder, 201
Marienkirche (Prenzlau), Pl. 60
Marienwerder, Pl. 59
Masonry, origins of, 19; Armenians and, 122; walls, as engineering device, 184
Masons, Egyptian, 102
Mastabas, 43, 44, 102
Mastara, early domed churches at, 122
Mausoleums, 102
Maxentius, basilica of, 114
Measuring devices, early lack of, 27
Mechanics and architecture, 118–19
Medinet Habu, 53
Mediterranean rock-tombs, 18
Medressa, 139
Megalithic architecture, 41, 55, 56; beginnings of, 55; brick and, 56
Megarons, 59, 64 seqq.; as Byzantine house, 128; disappearance of Aegean, 67, 77; great hall, Aegean, 64–5; as Parthenon's ancestor, 65; with four pillars, 67
Melle, Pl. 26

303

INDEX

Mendicant orders, 194

Mentuhotep's temple, 47, 48, 49

Mercantile influences, 210, 220, 221, 225, 226

Mesopotamia, 29–41

Mettlach abbey church, 154

Mexico, 253, 254

Michelangelo, 236, 237, 243, Pl. 80

Middle classes, 282–3

Middle Kingdom era (Egypt), 47

Middlesburg, Pl. 70

Mihrab, 132–3, 134, 164, 168

Military architecture, 142, 143, 176–7, 191, 215, Pl. 66; Aegean and Hittite compared, 65–6; Byzantine, 130; cannon's advent and, 244, 245; façade treatment in, 203–4; influence of on civil building, 206, Pl. 66; of Moghreb, 135, 136, 137, *and see* Rabat; Rome's bias toward, 98; of Seleucid empire, 75–6

Minarets, 146, 147

Minerva Medica, nymphaeum of, 103, 104

Minoan: culture, 52, 60 seqq.; houses, 66; lack of punctuation, 63; palaces, 63; pillar, 52

Minos palace (Knossos), Fig. 1, 62

Mistra, churches at, 237–8

Moats, 244

Moghreb, 134, 135 seqq.; 146, 147, 148, 149, 223

Mohammedan temple, 51

Mohammed at Medina, 132

Monasteries: Franciscan, 253; German baroque, 269–70; Ptolemaic-Egyptian, 111; Syrian, 111

Monastic: Gothic, 192; Norman, 157; tenth-century Spanish, 255–6; twelfth-century, Pls. 40, 41; western, 155, 156

Mongol invasions, 136, 270, 272

Monotheism, birth of, 99

Monreale, cathedral of, 171

Monumental factor: in civil architecture, 191, Pl. 66; in courtyard plan, 35, 36; first effort toward, 24; Imperial Roman, 101; Moslem disregard of, 146; in palazzi, 220; rediscovery of, 243; Russian, 273, Pl. 104; St Peter's as, 238; Spanish, 255–7

Moor Park, Pl. 96

Morgenster, Pl. 91

Mortar, early use of, 20; Roman increased use of, 88

Mosaic: artists in, 128; floors, early, 98

Moscow, 272, Pl. 105

Moslems, 108 seqq.; city buildings of, 146; impact of, 111, 131, 207, 246–56, 258; Spain and, 246 seqq.

Mosques: Pls. 36 *to* 39; of Amr Ibn el As, Pl. 37; Byzantine influence on, 141, Pl. 39; destruction of, in Spain, 246; early sanctuary of, 133; early Cairene and other, 132–4, Pl. 37; earliest Islamic, 132–3, Pl. 36 (Ibn Talun); of Selim II (Adrianople), Pl. 39

Mould casting of buildings, 289

Mudejares (Moslem craftsmen), 207, 247

Mud: as building material, 19, 20, 33–5, 38, 58, 59, 68; concrete, Babylonian, 179; for bricks,

58, 59, 68; plastered roofs, 31, 33, 35, 38; temple walls of, 68; with matting, 31, 38

Mullions, 205–6, 209, 213; precursors of, 177

'Multifora' arcades, 175

Multi-storied houses, 174–5; Minoan, 61, 62; Syrian, 110; *see* Skyscrapers

Municipal buildings, 14th c. expansion of, 220–1, Pl. 70

Murcia cathedral (Spain), Pl. 101

Mushidabad palace, 279, Fig. 14

Mycenae, Pl. 8

Nannar (moon-god), 34, 35, 37, 38

Naos of temple, 78, 83

Narthex, 107, 108, 110, 170; becoming loggia, 124; at Kiev, 125

Natchez (house at), Pl. 107

Nativity; church of the (Bethlehem), 116, 117, Pl. 24; Constantine's, 105

Natural features, Greek exploitation of, 79

Naves, 110, 190, Fig. 9, Pls. 24, 51, 63; added to 'four-poster' church, 156; Armenian, 172; as axial building, 119; basilican, 207; Constantine's, 106; Corinthian-columned early, 108; Roman, 160; romanesque, 156; vaulted, early, 159

Nazareth cathedral, 169

Nebuchadnezzar, 37

Nepveu, Pierre, 235

Newel staircase, 58

New York skyscrapers, 285

Niche: basilica form, 166; in classical architecture, 83; in form of apse, 83; for statue of the cult, 31, 99; as wall decoration, 84

Nile valley pre-Christian culture, 42 seqq.

Nomad's tent, 63–4

North American 19th c. architecture, 285

Novgorod cathedral, 125

Nymphaeum, 96, 103

Nymphenburg, 200

Octagonal structures, 105, 115, 116, 117, 120, 125, 170; Byzantine, 153, 154; cimborio, 171, 172, 173; Florentine, 237, 238; lantern, 168, 169, 172; pyramid, 271, Pl. 102; Russian blockwork, 271; with squinched arches, 148; with turrets, 162

Odeon, 79

Oecus, 71–2, 96

Office blocks, modern, 283

Old Kingdom (Egypt), temple plan of, 45–6

Olympia: temple of Hera at, 68

Olympiad, the first, 67

Olympian gods, eclipse of, 90

Omayyid palace

Openings and spanning, modern, 289

Ordered arch, 122, 178, 179, Fig. 8, Pl. 31; sculptured and, 178–9

Orders, classical, 112, 235 seqq.; in early synagogue, 100; in Italian Renaissance, 250; in later Spanish, 251; in post-trabeated styles, 94;

INDEX

INDEX

Temples: barrel-vaulted, 90; classical, 67, 83, *and see* named temples; earliest, 24; Egyptian pyramidal, 45–6; enclosed courtyards of, 25; Greek, 67; pylon-pyramid, 52; rectangular, 39–40; sepulchral, Middle-Kingdom, 47–8; wholesale destruction of classical, 112. *See* Pls. 2, 4, 5, 6, 12, 14, 18, 36 *to* 39, Fig. 4, for temples and mosques.

Temple of:
  Amun (Karnak), Pl. 4
  Horus (Edfa), Pl. 6
  Isis (Philae), Pl. 5
  Jupiter (Damascus), 105
  Jupiter, Juno and Minerva (Dugga), Pl. 18
  Mars Ultor, 83
  Poseidon, Pl. 14
  Venus, 84, 90, Fig. 4
Tenements, Roman, 97, Pl. 20
Tent-churches, 271, 272, Pls. 47, 102, 103
Terrace cultivation, and early building, 29
Terraced houses, 243, 260, 282
Terra-cotta; Etruscan ornamental, 86–7; tiles, 83
Tepe Gawra excavations, 56, 57, 58
Tepidarium, 91, 92, 93
Teutonic brick-built castles, 196, Pl. 59
Teutonic Knights, 196
Texture-carving, 247–8
Thalish cathedral, 123
Theatres, 83, 94, Pls. 11, 15; baroque, 276; Greek, 79, Pl. 11; pasteboard architecture in, Pl. 83; *and see* Jones; Pergamon, Pl. 11; 16th c., 276
Thebes: cliff-tombs at, 44; site-planning at, Pl. 3
Thermae, 91 seqq.; of Gallienus, 102; as planning complex, 95; social significance of, 91
Theseion (Athens), Pl. 9
Third-dimension, new awareness of, 264
Tholos, 101, 102, 115
Three-aisled tent design (Doric temples), 67
Three-centred arch, 211, 270
Three-pavilion façade, 262, Pl. 97
Timber-built architecture, 21, 22, 97, 151, 153, 186, 275; churches of, in Russia, 273, 274, Pl. 104; cloisters, Islamic, 146; Frankish, 151 seqq., Pl. 43; introduction of, 18, 20 seqq.; Gothic, 189–90, 191–2, Pl. 56; houses, west-European, 174, 224, 227; later-mediaeval, 224–5; wall-frames, 22
Tiryns, architectural remains at, 65–6
Titus's baths, 91
Toledo, 86, Pl. 71
Tomb, types of, 101–2, 139, 140: Augustan, 102; domed Seljuk, 139–40; of Hadrian, 102. *See* Bodily preservation
Torcello cathedral, 165
Toro, Pl. 46
Tournai (church), 157, 158, 162
Tower of refuge, 25
Towered gateways, Etruscan, 86
'Towering' church, 182, Pl. 51. *And see* Gothic
Towers: 'dead-ground,' 191, Pl. 55; on fortified walls, Byzantine, 129; as Gothic features, 191;

late mediaeval, castle, Pls. 66, 67; military arch., 13th c., 191; of municipal buildings, 220. *See* Fortified buildings for Tower-houses; with alcazar, 251; *see also* Twin towers
Town halls, Spanish 17th c., 255; *see* Municipal buildings
Town planning, 79, 260, 281 seqq.
Trabeated styles: Egyptian, 54; and the Orders, 120, 127
Tracery, 199, 206, 209, 233; of bifora head, 186; of oak roof, 200
Trajan, 109; basilica apse of, 183
Transept, western-church, 155, 156
Transport changes, and architecture, 277, 282
Transverse abutment, Gothic, 184
Treasury of Atreus (mausoleum), 101
Triangular bricks (Roman), 88
Tribune of Makad, 144, 145
Triclinum, (dining-hall), 96
Triconch, 116, 120; chevet, 173
Trier cathedral, 153, Pl. 21
Trifora, 177
Triforium, 158, Pl. 42
Triglyphs, Greek temple, 68
Triple walls, Byzantine, 129
Triumphal arch, *see* the Frontispiece
Troglodyte towns, 18
Troy, 63
True-arch, Etruscan, 86
'Tumbling,' 206
Turrets, 161, 192, 215, 224; Frankish, 161, in Gothic, 192
Tuscan Order, 82
Twelfth-century, as century of landmarks, 136
Twin-towered structures, source of, 162; Roman gates, 98, Pl. 21; Spanish revivals, 251; façades, 265, 269; gatehouses and gates, 59, 75–6, 203, 216–17
Typical buildings, succession of, 127–8
Tyre, cathedral at, 103

Ukheidr palace (Abbasid), 135, 145
Um el Jemal (Jordan house), 111, Pl. 34
University of Alcala de Henares, 250, Pl. 87
Ur, 32, 35, 36, Pls. 1, 2

Valley of the Kings (Thebes), 48
Vaulted: Burgundian ceiling, 170; halls, 93; iwan, 141; undercroft (Hittite), 59
Vaulting: Frankish, 159; of ambulatory, 165
Vaults: Florentine Renaissance, 238; mediaeval cloistral, 205; Moslem introduction to, 138; Parthian, 109–10, 111; quadripartite, 160; ribbed, 238–9; Roman, 89
Venetia, Venice, 207, 231, 232, 233, 265, Pls. 73, 74, 98; palaces of, Pl. 73, 74; Palladian churches of, 241
Verandahs, 46, Pl. 5; American colonial, 275, Pl. 107; Byzantine, 128
Verneuil, Pl. 57
Versailles, château de, 260

308

INDEX

STIF

S